CW00347267

WE NEVER WIN AT HOME
AND WE NEVER WIN AWAY...

DON PRICE

First published in 2018

EMPIRE PUBLICATIONS
1 Newton Street, Manchester M1 1HW
© Don Price 2018

ISBN: 978-1-909360-59-7

CONTENTS

About The Author v

Preface vii

Introduction.. 1

1 - The Way It Was 3

2 - A Bit Of Nostalgia... 13

3 - We're Not Really Here.. 26

4 - Once A Blue.. 33

5 - City In The Faroes... 46

6 - Around The Grounds.. 53

7 - King Of The Kippax 68

8 - Tales From Paddy's Coach 76

9 - Vienna Final 1970.. 81

10 - My First Away Game.. 85

11 - City V Arsenal 97

12 - The Trials Of A Female Football Fan 101

13 - The Football Widow.. 109

14 - My First City Game 118

15 - From A Foreign Fan Back Then 122

16 - Why I Became A Blue 143

17 - Back In The Day 148

18 - Typical City.. 158

19 - Football Fanzines... 173

20 - Safe Standing 181

21 - Middleton Blues... 192

22 - Moonchester Just For One Day 206
23 - Over Land And Sea 210
24 - England 217
25 - Favourite Players 224
MCFC - A Quick History 230
Epilogue 232

This book is dedicated to our first granddaughter Ayla

ABOUT THE AUTHOR

Don Price has been a Manchester City fan all his life, following the blues from the early 60's onwards. He joined the Royal Navy in 1969 and served for 8 years. He went on to work for the NHS for 30 years until he was made redundant. He then trained as a driving instructor (which is a book in itself!). Don is the author of the very funny and best-selling book ''A Football Fan's story - The Royal Navy, Manchester City And Me''. Don is married to his wife Catherine, they have two sons Steven and Sean and a granddaughter Ayla.

CONTRIBUTORS

Many thanks to all the people who have contributed to this book. Whilst three of the lads have written books themselves and have contributed to City fanzines, other contributors haven't written so much as a letter for donkey's years. Many thought they didn't have the skills or talent to write what they have; I encouraged them by saying 'just write it as you would talk to somebody in a pub or the front room of your house about the given subject'. I wanted the rawness and emotion of ordinary fans to shine through and I think that objective has been achieved admirably. In no particular order the following is a list of the contributors.

Dave Tracey from Wythenshawe

Mark McCarthy from Milton Keynes
Jane Riley from New Moston
Dante Friend from Sale Moor
Ian McMahon from Manchester
Loz South from Salford
Phill Gatenby from Tampa Bay, Florida via Moston
Eric Jonker from The Hague, The Netherlands
Sean Riley from Failsworth
Dave Wallace from Leigh
Keogh from Middleton
Alan Oakes from Winsford
Catherine from Manchester via Glasgow
Ray Gill ex-Royal Navy
David Walker www.readbutneverred.com

PREFACE

While much has been written about various football clubs and hundreds of players and ex-players have written books about themselves, apart from the so called hooligan books there has not been much written about ordinary football fans and the culture surrounding those fans.

What makes a football fan tick?

At the start of the twentieth century that would have been easy to answer as there wasn't much else for working class people to do except drink beer and watch football. Nowadays the answer is a bit more complicated as there are a lot more things people can do in their leisure time plus people seem to have many more commitments and hobbies. Fans go to the games and support their team for many reasons; there is a culture among football fans that is unique, it doesn't matter if you are a fan of a mega rich club like City, Arsenal, Chelsea, Spurs or whether you support a team from the lower leagues like Bury, Crewe, Rochdale or Blackpool, the passion you have for the team is exactly the same. Fans of all clubs have the same highs and the same buzz when the team does well and have the same lows and bitter disappointments when their teams lose a game.

Fans from all walks of life make all sorts of sacrifices to get to a match, most fans have missed a birthday celebration, wedding anniversary or phoned in sick just to make sure they can follow their team. The fans involved in this book are not unique in any way or different from other football fans up and down the country or around the world, all fans can share their stories, their heartache, sadness, joy and happiness as all football fans that go to the games will identify with what has been written in this book as they will have all been there, done that and worn the t-shirt.

As the famous Manchester City fanzine King of the Kippax

says 'this book is by the fans, for the fans and most importantly it is about the fans'.

So please relax sit back put your feet up get a brew or a can of lager and join us on our journey as we take you through the world of the ordinary football fan. I will get my ramblings out of the way first then the fans I have mentioned will take over. We are sure you will all identify with the book's contents and hope you enjoy reading the book as much as we enjoyed writing it.

ACKNOWLEDGEMENTS

Many thanks to Empire Publications, especially Ash who gave me loads of great help and advice. I must have done his head in at times with all my questions and mithering but he took it all in good spirit with a smile on his face, also to my long suffering wife Catherine who had to make sense of my ramblings and turn my words into something that made sense for this book

Needless to say the book would not have been possible without the magnificent effort from all the people that contributed. I have no doubt I did their heads in as well as I pushed them to get their chapters in for deadline day, then I asked most of them to add something extra.

A special mention for Ric from Bluemoon, Ian from Bluewatch and Dave and Sue from King of the Kippax. Plus a big mention to Phill & Dante who gave me loads of help advice and encouragement

INTRODUCTION

THE STORY BEHIND THE BOOK TITLE

We Never Win at Home and
We Never Win Away
We Lost last Week and We Lost Today
We don't give a Fuck coz were All Pissed Up
M.C.F.C OK.

IT MIGHT SEEM A LITTLE CRAZY and a bit bizarre for fans supporting a team who are currently playing their best football ever and who are breaking all sorts of records and rarely getting beat, to sing a song that seems to celebrate failure but it hasn't always been that way. Unlike some other clubs that have achieved success, we are not about to rewrite our history and pretend everything in the garden has always been rosy because as you will read in this book, it most certainly hasn't. However, as a set of fans we have a proud history of being loyal and whilst our loyalty has been tried and tested on many occasions, our support has never wavered.

We lost in the FA Cup to Shrewsbury in 1979 and Halifax in 1980. Bury FC did us at Maine Road barely 20 years ago and the same fate happened to us at York the following season. If you think things couldn't get any worse, well they certainly did as Middlesbrough beat us 8-1 at their ground in 2008. At one stage it was pretty normal to be on the wrong end of a 4 or 5 nil score-line, especially away from home, and this was when City fans showed their mettle. We could have spat our dummies out and sulked. We could have saved a few quid and stopped going to games, especially away from home, but oh no, we were better than that. Fans from some other clubs might call it a day when their team is up against the ropes but we hung in there and this is where our gallows humour kicked in and that's why the above song was sung back in the day and the reason it is sung today is to remind ourselves how far we have come.

For donkey's years we didn't have a sniff of a chance of winning a trophy but that little problem didn't stop us from turning up week after week to follow City. Our neighbours over at the 'Theatre of Nightmares' took great delight in our inability to win a trophy and with the backing of the hierarchy at The Swamp had a banner made highlighting how many years it had been since we last won a trophy.

What United fans would like to erase from their memories and wipe from the history books is the fact that from the 1910-1911 season when they won the league until the 1947-1948 season when they won the FA Cup they went a total of 37 years without winning a trophy, albeit there were two world wars during this period. Oh is that too far back? Sorry, how about not winning the league then, they went 26 years from 1966-1967 to 1992-1993 without winning it – another little statistic they would love to wipe from the record books.

The difference with us though is we won't pretend any different and don't deny our past. We have had some very lean times but as supporters we had an unbreakable bond and that's what the song is all about. We could have either been as miserable as sin and down in the dumps while supporting the Blues or we could stand proud, carry on supporting City win lose or draw, have a laugh and sing some cracking songs and deep down have the belief that one day we would come good.

Now we have come good we won't pretend the hard knocks didn't hurt us, because they did, we won't pretend the digs we got from other supporters didn't get under our skin, because they did, but we took it all on the chin and the rewards are now here for all to see as another song says "We're City 'Till We Die" – you never know, that might be a title of a future book!

1 – THE WAY IT WAS

SINCE THE FORMATION OF THE Premier League in 1992 the game of football in England has never been so popular. Billions of pounds have been poured into the game enabling state of the art stadiums to be built, the world's best players are enticed to play in England and more people than ever are watching the game, whether live at the ground or, if they cannot get tickets, they can watch the game in the pub or put their feet up at home and watch it on TV. Fans around the world congregate in bars at all times of the day so not to miss a game.

One of my early memories of going to Maine Road was seeing people cycling to the ground and many of the terraced houses nearby charged the cyclists for looking after their bike while they went in to watch the game. When more and more people started to use cars to go to the matches, the young entrepreneurs who lived nearby were out in force to 'mind' people's cars. On a match day, as fans got out of their cars, young lads ran up shouting the immortal words 'mind your car mister' it seemed harmless enough giving them a couple of bob but woe betide if you didn't cough up as after many a game the back windows of some of the cars would be smashed and nice shiny cars keyed by the youngsters because people had not paid up.

These youngsters were very well organised and fought to protect their own territory as there was much money to be made on a match day. Nowadays, at the Etihad, if you want to park near the ground you have little choice but to pay anything up to £10 to park.

While over the years the game of football itself has changed considerably, so the fans have also adapted to the changes. No longer are grounds dingy, horrible and at times unsafe places where thousands of pre-dominantly male fans are crammed into grounds unfit for human habitation. It was quite normal to stand in the open air when it was raining cats and dogs and you were lucky if the roof you were sheltering under didn't have a leak in it!

In the 1930's more football clubs were building new stands and were upgrading seating areas with roofs where people could sit and watch the game in a degree of comfort. Some grounds also installed roofs in some other areas of the ground where the fans stood so at least some supporters were getting shelter from the elements.

Back in the day football was watched almost exclusively by adult males on a Saturday afternoon as football was cheap. It was seen as a great way to relax after working all week down the pits, in the local steel works or a factory. The facilities at most grounds were very basic with little in terms of places to eat and drink. Toilet facilities were grim and the health and safety of fans was not a priority to those who were in charge whose policy seemed to be 'pack 'em in'.

Over the years the game has been transformed. The grounds, facilities and fans 'match day experience' have changed considerably. No longer can the average fan just turn at the ground and pay cash to get in, nowadays if they are not season ticket holders or fortunate enough to be invited to the hospitality lounges then they need to have a membership card and book a ticket in advance. For away games it is even more complicated; unless you have loyalty points or are entitled to a ticket through the corporate hospitality scheme, it is very likely most fans will be lucky if they ever get to many away games, unless they have good contacts.

Gone are the days when fans just turned up at the train station, jumped onto the Football Special and paid to get in at an away end. When I first started going in the 1960's many fans entered the ground with a wooden rattle which they waved above their heads and it made a right bleeding loud noise – fuck me, if you took one of them into the ground nowadays you would be arrested and charged with possession of an offensive weapon!

Over the years grounds have either been upgraded to a very high standard or been demolished and rebuilt with state of the art facilities installed. More and more women, children and whole families attend the matches on a regular basis. No longer are games just on a Saturday at 3 o'clock but are on almost every day of the week and at almost any time. Fans have reluctantly responded to the changes sometimes at a massive inconvenience to themselves.

In the late 60's and through the 70's and 80's football hooliganism was a constant threat to the average fan, with almost every club in the land having a hooligan element. For many years the clubs and police were overwhelmed as fights broke out on a weekly basis in most cities and towns on the way to and from the games. Sometimes when supporters happened to arrive at the same service station or train station even though they weren't playing each other. The violence put lots of people off travelling to games and few women and children attended matches.

It was many years until the police, clubs and government, backed by modern technology and increased resources, got their act together and the situation came under some sort of control. Nowadays, the vast majority of games are peaceful and violence free, although there are occasions at some grounds when trouble has kicked off, especially when the away fans have somehow managed to get tickets for the home section.

At the Etihad there have been many complaints by the City fans that at European games, common sense and strict segregation has gone out of the window and opposing fans have ended up in the same sections as City supporters. When City played Celtic in the 2016-2017 season many fans were upset, disappointed and frightened as many away fans were in parts of the ground that were not allocated to them and Blues were concerned that there could have been a major outbreak of violence.

Also in that season a handful of Liverpool fans got tickets which were allocated for United fans at Old Trafford, and near the end of the game Liverpool fans unfurled a banner and started to sing songs. Fighting swiftly broke out - all the Liverpool fans and several United fans who were involved in the violence were sent to prison for up to ten months each.

If people are determined to cause trouble in the ground they will do so but thankfully nowadays incidents like that are few and far between. Trouble still breaks out from time to time in city centres, pubs and on the way to and from grounds but nothing on the scale it was in the 60's, 70's and 80's.

In October 2017, after City had demolished Stoke City 7-2 at the Etihad, it was reported that a group of about fifteen so called United fans tried to storm the Crown and Anchor pub in the northern quarter of the city because they thought a small group of City fans were in there having a quiet drink. In a bizarre coincidence the BBC had been filming a documentary about football violence outside the pub during the day. The landlady, who was also attacked by the mob, had spoken to the documentary crew earlier as she was not happy that they were filming outside her pub as she had been a licensee there for 14 years without any trouble from any football fans. The United fans smashed three windows and one of the door staff had his arm broken while stopping the hooligans from getting into the pub. The police were called but by the time they arrived the thugs had scarpered although someone videoed the attack and put it on YouTube so I would imagine some of the yobs would have been identified and picked up by the police. It just shows what cowards and bullies they were, about fifteen of them attacking two doormen and the landlady, dead hard or what? Yeah right.

In Oct 2017 a Napoli fan was sentenced to five months as he was part of a gang who attacked a group of City fans and a young Blue was badly injured in the incident. The attack did not last long and the police were quickly on the scene to bring the situation under control but it was still a terrifying situation to be in for innocent fans who were caught up in it. City fans were also attacked in the return leg in Italy and a waiter had his nose broken when he tried to protect City fans. In another incident on the way to the ground it was reported City fans were confronted by knife wielding thugs who forced Blues to hand over a flag. To me I wouldn't call these thugs or hooligans but out and out bullies as they just prey on people who have no way of defending themselves.

Generally speaking, going to a game or taking the family to a football match is usually a safe day out and also a great experience, but can also be a bit of an expensive one compared to ten to fifteen years ago, especially if you have a big family and go on a regular basis. Having said that the standard of football is so much better, many of the players are world class and for City fans the Etihad is a top class stadium so while it may be dearer to go to the games now, to most City fans it is a price worth paying to watch a top class team managed by one of the best managers in the world. I was talking to an Arsenal fan who couldn't believe how cheap tickets for the Etihad are compared to the Emirates and other grounds in London, so I suppose everything has to be put into perspective and it's just a great time to be a City fan.

City nowadays are one of the best teams in England and are challenging to be one of the best in Europe. For thirty-five years City didn't win any trophies, were relegated several times and even ended up in the old Third Division. City fans being City fans, they never let the fact that our team was shit get in the way of having a good time and show their support for the club. While in the old 3rd division the amazing fans packed Maine Road for every home game with the loyalty shining through. Thousands of City fans turned out for every away game as well, much to the delight of the home team as most clubs saw their attendances increase dramatically when City were in town.

One Boxing Day game away at Stoke City saw thousands of City fans attending the match in fancy dress, it was a great day out but needless to say we lost the game but the City fans still went home with a smile on their faces. City fans also started the inflatable craze that swept the country. Some fans started going to Maine Road with large inflatable bananas soon after, as if an epidemic had taken place, thousands of blues started taking not only bananas but inflatable swimming pools, inflatable Frankenstein's, inflatable Dinosaurs, you name it; if it could be inflated City fans would take it to the ground. It didn't take long until fans from other clubs (but not United, – no sense of humour!) started taking inflatables as well, it was funny as fuck to see Bury fans with inflatable black puddings and Grimsby fans going to the game with inflatable Haddocks.

Our team might have been shit but nothing would stop us going to the game with a smile on our faces and having a laugh over a few pints. I think the inflatable craze had a lot to do with helping to cut out violence at the grounds as no respectable hooligan would have any street cred if they had attacked someone carrying an inflatable banana or a black pudding. As quickly as the craze started, after a couple of seasons it just fizzled out and pink panthers were no longer seen at Stoke City's ground or inflatable hammers at Upton Park.

While hooligans in the UK nowadays hardly ever have pitched battles in the football grounds, the same cannot be said for our counterparts in Europe. When fans from the UK watch their teams abroad, warnings are often given out on where to go and British fans are regularly attacked and sometimes it's the police doing the attacking. In 2017 at a pre-season friendly at Burnley the game had to be abandoned as Hannover fans were having pitched battles with home fans, club stewards and the police. Many families, instead of enjoying a nice day out watching the game, had to flee to safety as riot police were called in to regain control. For safety reasons the referee consulted with the police, club stewards, both managers and Burnley's head of security and the players did not come back out after half time and the game was abandoned. While that sort of violence was a common occurrence in the 70's and 80's, it came as a big surprise to most people that so many fans would make the journey from Hannover to Burnley not to watch the game but just to fight with anyone and everyone. If that violence had taken place in a European competition both clubs would have been put on a charge but as it was a friendly little or no action was taken.

Most landlords near football grounds love it on match days as the pubs get packed and their takings go up. Having a drink before the game gets fans in good spirits and in a good mood in anticipation for the game. I always enjoy having a drink after a game as well, as you can have a good chat about the game and it's great listening to different people's take on it as everyone has a different opinion of how great or how shit someone played. Football fans are the same the world over and I also enjoy talking to fans of the opposing team as you usually can have a good bit of banter. I like it better though if we have won the game when chatting to the different fans. It's not only the fans who enjoy a drink and a laugh after a game. I remember Joe Royle when he was City's manager going mad as so many players let their hair down by having a few drinks, he even threatened not to let a couple of players on the team photo as he was fed up with their antics. Joe relented in the end and the players concerned were eventually allowed in the team photo.

Many stories have been written about players who have liked to party and enjoy a drink. Players often turned up for training the worse for wear and had to be sent home, it wasn't unknown for players to turn up on a match day under the weather. After games players used to go in the players' lounge for a few beers and then out on the town to carry on the session. Players coming to England from abroad just could not get their heads round the fact that so many great players drank so much as it was alien to their culture; players from abroad were more used to having a quiet glass of wine than having ten pints after the game. Many players have been arrested and some even jailed for their behaviour under the influence of alcohol, while it is not as widespread now especially in the Premiership as the playing standard is so high and most managers won't stand for any nonsense but from time to time high profile footballers still hit the headlines for all the wrong reasons.

In September 2017 ex-England and Manchester United and now Everton player Wayne Rooney was arrested for being about three times over the drink drive limit whilst driving a female companion home. He received a driving ban plus he had to do unpaid community service. A whole host of well-known footballers have in the past have had to receive treatment for their drink problems and one young City player who seemed to have the world at his feet 'retired' from the game in his early 20's because allegedly the demon booze had taken a grip on him.

For many football fans, drinking, and to a lesser extent music and drugs, have been part and parcel of some football fans' match day experience. Going to away games meant taking cans, crates or bottles onto the coach, mini bus, car or train and fans would meet up in a pub near the ground and carry on drinking, singing and having a good time. Laws have changed over the years and it is no longer allowed to have a drink watching the game inside the football stadium, although fans are allowed to have a drink on the concourse. While it is illegal in England, our European friends can drink to their heart's content and at most grounds in Europe it is much easier getting served at the bars. Many people in the private boxes and corporate hospitality lounges in England find a way around the rules.

As the law stands you cannot have a drink in view of the playing area. Rugby fans, Cricket fans or fans going to pop concerts can have as much as they want to drink, it is also illegal to have alcohol on a coach going to a football ground and for some high profile games they even stop you taking alcohol on the trains and the stewards on the train are not allowed to sell alcohol to any of the passengers so the only drinks you can have are non-alcoholic. It seems a bit draconian to me...

While fans have moved on from the dark days of the 70s and 80s, those in power haven't and still don't trust football fans to have a quiet drink whilst watching the game. One thing Manchester City fans still miss is the great choice of pubs we had in Moss Side. There were a couple of dozen within walking distance of the ground and on match days most were packed and full of great characters. The first pub near the ground I remember going in was The Parkside on Lloyd Street South where, as a fifteen year old, I was hidden at the back and there I was thinking I was cool as fuck drinking a pint of Chester's Mild. The bouncers always did a collection for a 'charity' but how much was donated and to which charity was anyone's guess. The building is still there now but has been turned into 'luxury' apartments. One of my favourite pubs was the Clarence on Wilmslow Road. Middlesbrough fans smashed it up one match day but the brave lads from Boro did it when all the City lads were in the ground and there was no one there to defend it. The best time I ever had in there was September 1989 when we played United, the place was jam packed with City fans and everyone was singing and dancing on the tables, I don't think I have ever seen as many fans in there as I did that day and certainly not as drunk as they were on that occasion.

The game itself was held up for a while and the players were taken off the pitch as there was fighting in the North Stand and a large group of United fans had somehow got tickets for the City end. I remember a City fan getting arrested for throwing a meat and potato pie in a United fan's face. I felt sorry for the City fan but I thought it was funny as fuck and nearly pissed myself laughing. It did not take long for the United fans to beat a hasty retreat as once it kicked off they could not get out fast enough and the delay did not stop us humiliating them on the pitch as well as we went on to win 5-1. City fans were partying well into the night while United fans went home for an early bath. The last time I passed the Clarence it had turned into an Indian restaurant. Still on Wilmslow Road was The Huntsman, it was a bit small but served a great pint. In 2012 the landlord was jailed for six years after stamping on a regular's head after beating him senseless for not drinking up quickly enough after last orders. Unfortunately the customer later died of his injuries and in 2015 the landlord was brought back to court and after being convicted of murder he was sentenced to a minimum of fourteen years. The pub then closed and it remains to be seen if it reopens, I wouldn't be surprised if it gets knocked down.

The Albert just off Wilmslow Road was always a popular pub for not only the football fans but for students and locals alike. In the 1970's the then landlord used to buy our group a pint either every Christmas or New Year, there were plenty of pubs on Claremont Road. The Sherwood was one of the most popular and many City fans used to gather outside and give any away fans walking past a load of stick, last I heard it was boarded up and no doubt sooner or later it will be turned into flats. The Lord Lyon has already been knocked down and the Beehive has recently closed and is boarded up.

The Claremont never seemed to have any refurbishment, painting or cleaning done to it but on match days it was always busy and it was great chatting with the locals as there were some great people that went in the pub. More favourites with the fans and locals alike were the Ducie Arms, The Denmark, The Whitworth, The Welcome and Hardy's Well, all were belting pubs on match days. A couple of other popular ones were The Osborne and The Gardeners and they were on Victory Street, The Salutation pub in Higher Chatham Street in Hulme was where a lot of City lads would meet after the game before making their way into Manchester. Sadly, quite a few of the pubs mentioned are no longer with us as many have made way for new businesses and apartments.

Once City left Maine Road it was always going to be an uphill struggle for many to survive, also with the smoking ban and cheap booze from the supermarkets it was only a matter of time before some of the pubs went under. All of them will have cherished memories for City fans. Apologies if I have missed your favourite boozer out, it's just a pity that there is not more of a selection of similar pubs within walking distance from the Etihad.

2 - A BIT OF NOSTALGIA

EVER SINCE IT WAS BUILT in 1923 to replace the old ground at Hyde Road, Maine Road was a passionate place for City fans. In its heyday it could hold upwards of 80.000 fans and the official capacity is reported to have been 85,000 with City's highest recorded crowd being 84,569 on March 3rd 1934 against Stoke City in the FA Cup and for many City fans, especially the older generation, Maine Road will always be seen as the club's spiritual home.

As well as City games being played there, after the war it was rented out to United so they could play there as their ground had been bombed by the Luftwaffe. It's also been used for other stuff including England Internationals, Rugby League Finals, FA Cup semi-finals and a League Cup final replay. In the 1970's at Maine Road I remember going to watch the England under 21's playing there and Peter Barnes the former Manchester City player was in the team.

Loads of pop concerts over the years were held there including Oasis of which Noel and Liam Gallagher are both fanatical City fans. For one game against Portsmouth the Gallagher brothers were invited onto the pitch to be introduced to the fans. Liam was swaggering about near the away fans and I thought he was going to cause a riot, in the end it was all taken in good spirits so all's well that ends well. We all enjoyed the game which ended up 2-2 then went into the city centre for a few drinks.

THE MAIN STAND

The Main Stand had a roof on top when it was built, it was the only part of the ground that was covered. Over the years the roof was replaced and in the 1980's there were plans to have executive boxes built underneath the roof, but those plans were quietly shelved. When the Main Stand was first built it could hold up to 10,000 people and due to improvements and reconstruction the final capacity had been reduced to just under 8,500 fans. Besides the fans being in the Main Stand, if you went in the front entrance you might be lucky enough to bump into players or ex-players as the players changing room and the players' lounge was situated in the Main Stand. There was also an area where the referee and linesman could get changed and relax. The press box was also situated at the top of the stand and the chairman and directors had their own lounge and seating area. On match day several fans would hover outside the main entrance both before and after the game in the hope of getting some autographs. While it might have been purpose built and state of the art when it was first built, in its later years it was quite run down and not really fit for purpose, especially if it is compared to the new ground.

THE PLATT LANE STAND

This area was behind the goals just to the right of the main stand it was originally a standing area with room for around 20,000 fans and in the 1930's a roof was fitted to give some shelter to the fans from the Manchester weather. In the early 1960's seating was installed but when I say seating it was just rows of wooden benches installed, but the good thing about it you could just go in and sit where you wanted and around 9,000 fans could sit there comfortably. It was later given over completely to away fans, United fans vacating well before the 5-1 game finished1

In 1992 the Platt Lane end was demolished and rebuilt with corporate hospitality boxes installed, although it was officially called the Umbro Stand fans still called it the Platt Lane end. Again capacity was reduced and this time around 4,500 fans could sit and watch the game in a much better degree of comfort and a section for families was incorporated into the stand. To be honest though, the way it was being talked up and the amount of money spent on the project most fans thought it should have been a much more impressive stand, but like most things at City this was just something else which did not go according to plan. By the time Maine Road had played its final game, I had been sat in the family stand for many years and I, like hundreds of other fans, bought the seats we had sat in – I still have them today.

THE SCOREBOARD END

The Scoreboard end part of the ground was directly opposite the Platt Lane end and was originally a standing area and away fans would also use that end from time to time and the poor sods didn't get a roof until the 1970's when it was demolished and a new stand was built and reopened in 1971. It only remained as a standing area for one season as in 1972 seats were fitted leaving the Kippax as the only part of the ground where fans could still stand. The original capacity was put at around 18,000 but after installing the seats it was reduced to around 8,500, it then became known as the North Stand. Before I go any further I just wish to mention about the term 'official capacity' and why I have not been precise with how many people were in each area. While some people, especially statisticians, will swear by these figures, I believe that the official capacity at any ground and at any part of a ground should, in my humble opinion, be taken with a huge pinch of salt. Let's face it, there is no one counting people in and out as the turnstiles should have recorded the amount of people entering but I am not sure how reliable those recordings would be as fans had ingenious ways of getting into the grounds for nothing and even in the seating areas it was not unusual to see fans standing at the back of the stand or to see fans doubled up on a seat. Quite a lot of City fans never believed the official attendances as at some games the figure would be given at say 45,000 when everyone attending new it was obviously much more. There were a lot of conspiracy theories banded about why the official attendances seemed on occasions to be on the low side but I will leave that for you to figure out. After the seating of the Kippax, the capacity was greatly reduced once again.

There were various ideas and plans about how to increase

capacity in future but the damage was done when we didn't make the most of the opportunities we had when redeveloping the Platt Lane (Umbro) stand and of course the Kippax. As the Kippax was being developed Franny had one eye on what was going on over in East Manchester where a brand new stadium was being built in preparation for the Commonwealth games which was to be held in Manchester. Give Franny his due, he was at the front of the queue advocating that City should be in consideration for the tenancy of the stadium once the games had finished. Eventually temporary seating was installed between the North Stand and the Kippax and it was nicknamed the Gene Kelly Stand by the City fans as they soon had to get used to "singing in the rain". To be honest it was a bleeding eye sore and it looked quite dangerous, especially if it was windy. Because all the different parts of the ground had been either upgraded or rebuilt at different times, usually with financial restrictions, none of the different stands matched and the whole ground had a disjointed feel to it. I was at a game with ex-City player Bobby McDonald once and he went a step further and called the Gene Kelly stand 'a fucking monstrosity' – I don't think anyone could argue with him.

THE KIPPAX

Unlike most grounds where the popular end was behind the goals, like the Kop at Liverpool, the Shed at Chelsea or the North Bank when Arsenal were at Highbury, the Kippax ran the length of the pitch opposite the Main Stand. In its prime, 30,000 if not more fans were crammed in, and at times it resembled a mass movement of bodies swaying from side to side and the noise could be quite electrifying and awe inspiring to the City players but terrifying to some of the players from the opposition. When Maine Road was first built there was no roof but after the roof was fitted on the Kippax the noise level just grew with the improved acoustics. The Kippax was named after the street it backed on to which was not surprisingly called Kippax Street, so there was nothing scientific or ground-breaking about its name (I thought I would share this bit of useless information with you all just in case on the odd chance someone out there did not know the origins and they would probably not sleep at night trying to figure it out!). To gain entry to the Kippax, depending which way you were coming from, many people had to walk through an area lovingly known by locals and fans alike as 'dog shit alley' which was a series of passageways which backed on to the houses which, as the name suggests, there was dog muck everywhere as the locals did not have pooper scoopers in them days – you never know if Dragons Den was on telly back in the day someone might have made a fortune.

During the day it was bad enough walking through that area, but in the evening it was even worse as you did not have a clue what you were stepping into but as you got nearer to the ground the unmistakable whiff of fried onions from the burger vans let you know you would soon be at the ground and on the plus side the smell of the fried onions masked the smell of the dog shit, which was no bad thing. Many away fans, to their horror and dismay, not only had the dog shit to worry about but the possibility of being ambushed in the passageways, as some times City fans lay in wait for away fans to make their way to the ground. It must have been a very frightening experience for them because I remember as a youngster I used to shit myself walking through them especially at a night game, more so if I was on my own. In the 60's and 70's it was very cheap to watch football and apart from the Derby and some cup games you could just queue up and pay on the day at the turnstiles. Many fans used to 'jib in' which is a northern term for not paying to get into the ground and they used to double up with the person in front of them which more often than not was a total stranger. At one time there was no segregation in the Kippax as the away fans usually went in the scoreboard end behind the goals. Violence between City fans and the away fans became more prevalent in the late 60's and right through the 70's and 80's. Away fans were often attacked as they left the ground – quite often, rightly or wrongly in revenge for City fans being attacked on their travels. Most right minded people now-a-days would be appalled at such things happening at a football match and would think it stupid, dangerous and right out of order and I could not disagree with them but back in those days it was seemed as normal behaviour.

I remember in the early 70's playing the rags at Maine Road, because by then the scoreboard end had been transformed into the North Stand and City fans occupied that part of the ground. United fans were given a section of the Kippax to watch the game from, I don't know which bright spark thought that would be a good idea but to make it even worse the fans were only separated by a length of rope running from the top to the bottom of the Kippax. I kid you not! It didn't need Sherlock Holmes to work out that it wouldn't be long before both sets of fans participated in a bit of pre-match fisticuffs, it was absolutely bonkers; no-one could believe that the 'powers that be' could not come up with a better way of keeping both sets of fans apart. What on earth were they thinking? Oh well, it was only one of numerous barmy decisions made by the people that ran the football club at that time.

Many people made life-long friends from standing on the Kippax as people always had their own area where they would stand for each game. Even though it's long gone and it has been many years since I last stood there, a load of us from Prestwich used to stand 30 steps down and just to the right of the half way line, so over the years we got to meet loads of people from different areas of Manchester who all had their favourite spots from which to watch the game. Lads from Blackley, Middleton and Wythenshawe also stood near us so if you went to the game on your own there was always someone you could have a chat with. The only downside was once you were in the Kippax and if it was jam packed, it was hard to get out so if people wanted a piss it was usually done in an empty drinks container and poured on the floor but if you were unlucky the back of your legs might cop for it!

Tommy Booth and Peter Barnes have said many times how they loved running out onto the pitch before the game started to hear the roar of the Kippax in full voice. Peter once told me if he was having a quiet game he would be told in no uncertain terms to "pull his socks up" or words to that effect. There have been some absolutely brilliant atmospheres on the Kippax over the years and while all fans will have their own cherished memories, two stand out for me; one is when we played Middlesbrough in the semi-final of the League Cup. We were a goal down from the first leg but unusually for me I was very confident that we could overcome the deficit and get the victory that would take us to Wembley for the Final. We ended up winning 4-0 on the night and the noise was something to be savoured. I think it was the occasion as much as anything else as we knew if we won we would be Wembley bound. We had been beaten at Wembley a couple of years earlier so we wanted to make up for that defeat and go back and win the trophy.

The best and most emotional atmosphere I have ever witnessed was on Boxing Day 1977 - we were playing Newcastle United and at half time the score was 0-0 - enter the King alias Colin Bell. Colin had been seriously injured in a game against United a couple of years previously and had endured a long hard road back to fitness. Paul Power was injured so on came Colin to an unbelievable reception. Everyone in the ground was on their feet clapping their appreciation and singing at the top of their voices, it was absolutely electrifying, deafening and emotional all at once. Grown men were in tears. He inspired the whole team and we soon cruised to an easy 4-0 victory. Out of all the games I have been to, that one will always bring back happy memories. I realise there have been many brilliant moments witnessed including games against United, Liverpool, Leeds and all the great cup and European games but the two I mentioned ticked all the boxes for me.

While there have been so many positive occasions, there are two negatives that stand out. First of all the 'powers that be' decided the best way to treat football fans was to fence them in and in line with other clubs in England, a fence was erected the length of the Kippax to stop fans getting on the pitch. As Jackie Charlton once said, "if you treat football fans like animals don't be surprised if they start to act like animals." The second is when we played Spurs in the quarter final of the FA Cup in1993. I honestly believed we would win the game and win the semi-final then go on to win the FA Cup at Wembley. So much for my prediction as we went on to get beat 4-2. I was watching the game in the family stand with my eldest lad Steven and when we went 1-0 up I thought happy days and we were already thinking who we would get in the semi-final. I should have known better as before too long we were 4-1 down. I was still thinking 'how the hell did we lose this' when Terry Phelan scored a cracking goal to make it 4-2 but it was too little too late; when our second went in there was only a couple of minutes left and it sparked a pitch invasion from the City fans with loads piling onto the pitch from the Platt Lane end and from the Kippax to attack the Spurs fans. Police with horses had to come on the pitch to restore order and the game was held up for a few minutes. It just goes to show how people's emotions can change in a short space of time and the things that people do in the heat of the moment when the red mist comes down.

In 1994 the Kippax as we knew it was demolished to make way for a 10,000 all-seater stand which was fitted with private boxes and luxury lounges where those who had a few spare bob could watch the game in style. I was lucky enough to be invited in both a private box and also in one of the lounges and it was certainly a great way to watch the game. I tell you that is the way to watch football - no more getting squashed and swaying in the old Kippax wondering if you were going to get crushed or if someone was going to piss up the back of your legs. However the Kippax has gone but is never forgotten.

In May 2003 Maine Road hosted its last game against Southampton and yeah it won't come as a great surprise to anyone to discover we got beat. It was an emotional day for all City fans as it was truly the end of an era, people had made life-long friendships there and my mate Karl from Blackley got married to Sharon in one of the lounges in the Kippax. Happy days.

THE ETIHAD (THE CITY OF MANCHESTER STADIUM)

While we now have an up to date and extremely modern football stadium with fabulous facilities, it is important not to forget how we ended up playing football in East Manchester. It has been widely documented that Franny Lee wanted a new stadium for City, but it was under the Chairmanship of David Bernstein, who was City's Chairman at the time the stadium was being built for the Commonwealth Games, who had the vision and confidence that City could take over the stadium once the games had finished. As much as Maine Road was cherished by so many Blues who were reluctant to leave, looking back the decision to move proved to be the right one given where the club is right now.

Far too many times in the past, at various events around the world, millions and millions of pounds have been poured into building new stadiums only for them to be abandoned and fall into disrepair once the events for which they were built had finished. The fiasco at the Olympic Stadium in London and West Ham's experience of moving into it proves that London should have followed Manchester's lead in knowing what was going to become of the venue after the games, before it had even begun to be constructed. The Commonwealth Games is in most people's opinion regarded as a stepping stone in Manchester's recent history as money was poured into many areas of Manchester and it helped to regenerate many parts of the city.

I remember Manchester City club officials conducting a series of road shows about how the new stadium would look once the Blues moved in. The Prestwich and Whitefield branch of the Supporters Club invited the public relations team from the Commonwealth Games and also City club officials to one of the meetings so we could find out first hand more about the games and for the City officials to explain the plans for our new stadium once they had finished. Two things I remember about the meeting. Firstly everybody in attendance thought the meeting was extremely informative and both sets of parties presented their case well and we were all impressed and confident that the games would be a huge success and also that the stadium would turn into a very good football ground. The second thing is that the official mascot was called Kit the Cat so it turned up to dish out goody bags to the youngsters and to prance about and entertain the kids just like our very own Moonchester and Moonbeam do. Like all guests at the Prestwich and Whitefield meetings, we asked Kit if she wanted a drink or two - what a stupid question! Could she bleeding drink! I asked Paul Kerry, who was dishing out the drinks to the guests, what she was drinking (I will refer to her as a she as it was a lady in the costume) Paul's reply was 'anything and everything and lots of it'. Oh well, she kept the kids entertained and everyone went home happy and that was the main thing. I bet Kit the Cat had a hangover the next morning though.

The Commonwealth Games Stadium, as it was originally known, had a capacity of 38,000 seats for the games, City first played there in the 2003-2004 season after investing money to convert the stadium into a football ground. During this development extra seats were fitted allowing the capacity to reach 48,000, since then more development has taken place and the capacity is now around 55,000 with plans to increase it to 61,000 when the 'powers to be' think the time is right. If it wasn't for the much publicised takeover in 2008, I doubt very much we would have had the finances to increase the capacity. The name was changed to the City of Manchester Stadium or COMS for short.

In 2008 the stadium hosted the UEFA Cup Final between Zenit St Petersburg and Glasgow Rangers. The Rangers fans rewarded our hospitality by running riot in Manchester city centre and did their best to wreck the place; windows were smashed and innocent people got hurt and many Rangers fans were arrested. The stadium has also hosted England games.

The ground is very easy to get to, there is now a Metrolink outside the ground, loads of buses stop nearby and there are plenty of parking spaces. When the weather is nice it is a pleasant stroll to and from Piccadilly. Loads of money continues to be invested in the stadium with many seats, private boxes and hospitality lounges getting a good make over and there is the newly formed Tunnel club which is extremely exclusive and while it is a bit pricey for us mere mortals, if you get the chance to get in there it will be well worth going as I've heard some great reports about it.

Some of the season ticket prices at the Etihad, hang on a

minute! Commonwealth Stadium? Eastlands? City of Manchester Stadium? COMS? Etihad? The stadium has had more name changes than Royal Mail. Well it is definitely called the Etihad now, so you can sack the others off, the reason it is called the Etihad is because the airline invested a shed load of money for a ten year sponsorship deal so fair play to them. Where was I? Oh that's it I was on about season tickets wasn't I? Some season ticket prices at the ground are very cheap and credit to the club for keeping them low. If people can afford them and they go to the games regularly it can be a very good investment to buy a season ticket compared to purchasing a ticket on a match by match basis. The owners have invested heavily in not only the ground, facilities and top class players but across the road from the ground are some of the best training facilities in the world with the modern version of everything including three gyms, a hydro-therapy area, medical facilities and a mini stadium where the juniors and Manchester City Women's team play. There are also sixteen first class training pitches on which players of all age groups and both sexes train, as well of course the first team players. There is also a hotel on the complex and even a bridge has even been built to connect the training ground to the stadium. Blooming heck, all that must have cost a few bob! I have seen photographs of the complex and it is mind blowing in terms of what is provided for the players. The 'powers that be' will be hoping we can both develop players for the first team and also for the players not making the grade at City the hope then is they have a decent career when we flog them on to make a few quid - here's to the future.

One thing I will have to do soon is go on one of the official club tours. I have done one at Maine Road, Barcelona and also at Ajax's ground the Amsterdam Arena. The Etihad tour is definitely on my 'to do' list, I have heard it is very interesting and great value for money.

While we are on the subject of football stadiums, one thing that City, as well as all other clubs are seriously taking on board is the threat of a terrorist attack at a football stadium in the United Kingdom. Some experts reckon it could happen because of the worldwide popularity of the sport and that football grounds are "soft targets". Although there has been no specific intelligence about potential attacks in the UK, terrorists have carried out such attacks elsewhere and we all have to be on our guard. Back in the 1970s, even at the height of the IRA terror campaign on mainland Britain, no-one ever thought that a football ground would be subjected to an attack by terrorists. Nowadays the threat is only too real and fans routinely have their bags searched and fans themselves get frisked with many getting scanned with a 'wand'. While all this is for the fans protection, many have questioned these procedures and the way the searches are carried out as some clubs are more thorough than others. While fans are urged to get to the ground early, many can't because of work and family commitments. There have also been complaints that searches are not always consistent and often haphazard. No one wants to make light of a serious situation but what is a security guard at the ground supposed to do if he or she actually searches someone who has a suicide vest on? Or finds a bomb in a bag? A suicide bomber would probably detonate it there and then. These guards probably have not had much training or experience to deal with these situations and I hope they never have to. It is one thing security guards searching for offensive weapons or alcoholic drinks but it is a whole different ball game searching for bombs or guns. The guards are not issued with pepper spray, tazers or even a truncheon with which to defend themselves. Only in the UK would we expect unarmed guards to apprehend a potential terrorist and to disarm and detain them. I just hope the situation never arises.

Many people have pointed out that a terrorist doesn't even have to get into the ground but could, God forbid, detonate a bomb on the metro link on the way to or from the Etihad or simply launch an attack on people queuing to get in. On both counts there would be an appalling death toll and horrific injuries just like the attack at the Manchester Arena where music fans of all ages were targeted. The truth is there are no simple answers and no fool proof way of stopping a determined terrorist as the bastards will always opt for a soft target.

In December 2016 a twin bomb attack outside Besiktas Football Stadium in Istanbul, Turkey killed at least 38 people including 30 policemen and dozens more were injured. In November 2015 there were three bomb blasts around the Stade de France in Paris when France were playing Germany in an International friendly and again there were many casualties and if it hadn't been for tight security, casualty figures would have been far worse.

Sport is no stranger to acts of terrorism; in 1972 at the Munich Olympic games, nine Israeli athletes were killed by the Palestinian Black September Organisation which was just one of many atrocities that the organisation carried out.

Counter terror police believe the world wide appeal of the Premier League means the United Kingdom could be a target. The warning comes after recent terror attacks in Europe and the United Kingdom. Police have already held anti-terrorist workshops at Wembley and Old Trafford with football club officials. The workshops were designed to address any terrorist threat at stadiums. It does not give you great confidence though when you remember it was not too long ago that a fake bomb was found in the toilet at Manchester United's football ground leading to the postponement of United's game with Bournemouth. The fake bomb was left behind by mistake by a security consultant who had been carrying out a training exercise, but he forgot to take the fake bomb with him when the exercise was over, unfortunately in this day and age this is a wicked world we live in, let's hope and pray that the police and security personnel can prevent an atrocity taking place in and around our football stadiums.

3 – WE'RE NOT REALLY HERE

WE'VE BEEN SINGING this song for twenty odd years to the tune of 'We're On Our Way To Heaven, We Shall Not Be Moved' which, by the way, was a belting song by The Seekers in the 1960's. City fans have been singing the 'Invisible Man' song up and down the country and in the last few years in Europe as well. The song has created a mini industry with fans producing invisible man pin badges, t-shirts, flags, banners, a book and in 2017 an opera by City fans called 'We're Not Really Here' was performed at the Contact Theatre in Manchester.

So what is the origin of this iconic, some say cringe worthy, song and why has it stood the test of time? Before I delve into the origins of it, please bear with me while I deal with the myths, assumptions, inaccuracies and Chinese whispers about the song. About ten years ago someone on the Bluemoon forum asked the same question wanting to know the history of the song, he thought it was inspired by City fans who trashed the Metropole hotel in Cork while on a preseason tour of Ireland, apparently City fans started singing it to police officers who were sent to deal with the situation in the belief there was no proof as to which individuals were responsible for trashing the hotel. I can state categorically that the hotel was not trashed by City fans or by anyone else for that matter. Bill Black from Levenshulme and myself organised two coach loads of City fans to go on that trip and to stay in that hotel for two nights, other fans were also staying at the hotel and at no time was there any damage done to the hotel and the police were never called. The City fans were singing, being noisy and having a great time but were rather loud and the manager came to see me and Bill and asked us if it was alright if he could shut the bar early in the hope things would quieten down a bit but added that everyone could still get drinks from room service, so loads just went to their rooms ordered drinks and brought them back down to the bar to re-join the party. When the manager realised that his plan hadn't worked as anticipated he just re-opened the bar and everyone carried on partying into the early hours. I had a good chat and a laugh with the manager – he thought we were a great set of fans and he even bought me a drink. The manager and staff were brilliant and so were all the City fans that stayed there. So that story clearly was nonsense.

Someone called 'Bluesmith' said there was a story going round that the song originated from the 1980's when the away fans were banned from Kenilworth Road, Luton Town's ground. Another Bluemoon member called 'Avoid Confusion' thought it was made up when the tabloid papers claimed City had poor attendances during their games yet he reckons more fans were going to watch City than United fans going to the swamp so the City fans had made it up for a laugh!

Another poster, 'Blueallover', is adamant that it actually originated from a Millwall away game during the darker days of football when City fans were banned from attending the match. He then states, 'A few hundred City fans managed to make it into the Millwall stand and started singing the song which he said was absolutely hilarious.'

You would have to ask how a few hundred City fans managed to avoid the stewards, the police, not to mention thousands of angry Millwall fans to then gather in their main stand and start singing and then to get out in one piece without getting battered or arrested...

'Blue MO' was convinced it started on an away trip when a coach load of Blues got lost but he never mentioned where the City fans were from, where they got lost or what game they were going to. He then went on to say they passed through some place where there was a street map saying 'You are here' and some of the lads took a shine to this little map so after stocking up with beer they took the map and after driving off started singing 'We're Not Really Here'.

In pubs and in fanzines and over the internet many fans keep coming up with their own weird and wonderful versions of how it came about. John Mac reckoned everyone was wrong and it was from when City played in the Isle of Man Tournament. What amused me, and I admit to having a little chuckle while reading these stories, was that many people argued passionately where the origin of the song started and not one person said they were at Luton, Millwall or the Isle of Man or anywhere else where it was supposed to have originated but that is 'what they had heard'.

Well, I have never been one to piss on anyone's chips but a few of my mates have always said 'why don't you put the record straight about the original song'. To be honest I never gave it a thought as it never bothered me. Dante, who is one of the contributors to this book, contacted me and suggested that, as this book is about the history and culture of City fans it would be an appropriate time to finally put the record straight. So with one arm twisted up my back here we go…

First of all, it started as a pub song not a football song and was not started at a game. However, it did turn out to be a sentimental song to us in Prestwich when it was first sung. It was not as nostalgic as people would have you believe and the origins had nothing to do with either football or Manchester City or even its fans. Here we go then…

In the early nineties a group of us from Prestwich went on a stag do to Amsterdam (what went on in Amsterdam stays in Amsterdam!) and while we were there we got word that a great mate of ours who, for one reason or another had not come with us, had committed suicide. Unsurprisingly it knocked the stuffing out of us and to be honest we were glad to be going home the next day as it was impossible to enjoy ourselves knowing something as tragic as that had happened to one of our mates.

The weekend after we got back we all met up in the Forester's pub in Prestwich, on one hand to carry on the stag do, and also to have a drink to our mate. Now at this point I just want to make clear, the people in the pub consisted of a mixed bag of ordinary people; some were football fans, some were cricket fans, some were rugby fans some didn't give a shit about football or any sport and wives and girlfriends were also with us. Half way through the afternoon one of the lads Phill (RIP) called everyone to silence and we assumed he wanted to make a speech but instead he stood on a chair and came out with these iconic words.

If you drink, you will die,
If you don't drink you will die,
So it's better to be drunk than be sober when you die,
Just like the fan of the invisible man,
We're not really here.

Now I never knew what inspired Phill to come out with those words but to us that were there they seemed the right thing to say and the right time to say them, as the song was in memory of our mate. Looking back now it was an emotional experience.

The pub was packed and everyone joined in with the singing. As it happens, the lad who died although it does not matter, was not a City fan and neither was Phill. The only reason I mention that they were not City fans is to emphasize the fact that the song had absolutely nothing to do with football and absolutely nothing to do with Manchester City as the lad who died wasn't a City fan and Phill would have sang the song anyway. Somewhere in my pile of junk at home there is a video tape of us in the pub singing it and I will have to dig it out sometime.

As if to underline my point, the stag do/wake was not even during the football season and the song was sung by both City and United fans and by people who didn't give a shit about football. So how did it become an iconic song sung by City fans for over 20 years?

In 1994 the Prestwich and Whitefield (P&W) branch of the City Supporters Club was formed and by 1995 it was taking off big time and at the end of each meeting we used to get on the microphone and blast out different songs, and one evening after having a chat about our mate who passed away we got on the microphone and decided to sing a full version of the song in his memory. As the song caught on everyone in the room (about 300 people) stood up and started singing it and everyone was clapping and cheering and we sang it over and over. It went down so well we started singing it at the end of most branch meetings.

In 1996 I organised a couple of coaches to go to Ireland on a pre-season friendly to watch City play both Athlone and Cork, there was not much else to do on the coach except drink and sing songs (cocaine was not cheap in them days!) and, as loads of our branch members were on the coaches, it wasn't long until the 'if you drink you will die song' was blasted out, and it was also sung many times in the pubs of Athlone. The next game was in Cork and the song was sung quite often on the drive from Athlone to Cork and also in the places where we stopped en route. While we were in Cork we were invited to a branch get together by the Cork branch of the Manchester City Supporters Club. It wasn't long before we took to the stage and started singing our song. For the next couple of seasons the song started to take off but unless the P & W lot were there to sing it in the pubs, the first verse was sacked and so was born 'The Invisible Man Song'.

I am sorry if this disappoints people who thought it had some other nostalgic reason connected with the club but I cannot rewrite history. To be honest, though, I think it only really took off because we were relegated and playing in the lower divisions, as in truth it had more meaning singing it at the likes of Grimsby, Lincoln and Swindon than it would at Arsenal, Liverpool or Chelsea.

The first time I can remember ever hearing it at an away game was in 1996 in Lincoln and I thought 'how the fuck has this happened?' because it was usually us lot that started it off in the pub at a meeting or on a coach but at that game to be honest we were a bit too pissed to stand up, never mind start singing songs.

My mate 'Little Oz' (who was a DJ at our branch meetings as well as at Mary D's) told me once I should patent the song as a brand, I didn't have a fucking clue what he was on about but to be honest I should have taken more notice.

Another website called mancityfans.net also had a debate about the origins of the song, again there were many different explanations and it still amuses me that many fans give a similar version of what I have just said, some on there were convinced they knew the real reason. One fan is convinced it was because the late Peter Swales used to fiddle the attendance figures at Maine Road (allegedly) and the crowd used to sing 'We're not really here'

What does President Trump say about fake news?

One lad on Bluemoon called 'There Is A Light' who was on the right track posted the following,

"It's definitely not Millwall, there was definitely nowhere enough City at Millwall to be singing anything, as I remember at the time there were a few Blues that went but kept their heads down and maintained a very low profile, there were no crowds of City at that match. I also read the Luton Town version of events but I've heard that version was denied by a few City lads who know the score. I have heard many times though that the song actually originated from a pub song in respect of a lad from Prestwich who died on a trip abroad. (The lad actually did not travel but had stayed in Prestwich) because of this they sang: 'If you drink you will die, if you don't drink you will die, so it's better to be to be drunk than be sober when you die, just like the fans of the invisible man, we're not really here'. This was picked up by others and it was sung on the Irish tour then the song just stuck, it also took on a new meaning when we were playing Macclesfield etc. – ie. this is not really happening, we're not really here."

Yes mate, you are nearly spot on and in Richard Edghill's autobiography 'Once a Blue Always a Blue', a similar version was given in his book. There is also a mention in Wikipedia about how the song came about. Gary James, who has written tons of stuff about Manchester City's history, even mentioned during some of his research about City songs and chants that he could not find any record of the song being sung before 1996.

I can understand why it has turned into an iconic song as it was adapted and accepted while going to the lower divisions. City fans couldn't believe they were there plus it is a catchy little chant. I just hope this has cleared up few myths and fantasies regarding the origin of the song, as the people who were in the Foresters that day will never forget where and why it was started. I have purposely not mentioned the lad's name because of the tragic circumstances of his death. I don't think it would be appropriate to do so.

4 - ONCE A BLUE ALWAYS A BLUE

IT DOESN'T REALLY MATTER at what age you start supporting City but once you start it is usually impossible to stop. With the internet, 24 hour TV channels and mobile phones it is easy to keep abreast of what is happening at the club on a daily basis no matter where in the world you are and with all the fantastic attractive free flowing football City are playing, it is little wonder that we are attracting new fans on a regular basis and playing to a packed Etihad stadium every home game.

When I joined the Royal Navy in 1969 things were very different... these new fangled gadgets would have been laughed at as creations of science fiction. Consequently, it was very difficult for me to get much information about City, especially in the first twelve months when I was at the training establishment HMS Ganges which was based in Shotley Gate near Harwich, not far from Ipswich. I had to rely on my mum sending me the Football Pink which was a sports paper printed in Manchester (many of us oldies still miss the 'Pink') whose downfall would be the aforementioned internet and 24 hour rolling sports news channels. My brother used to send me the match programmes as well. When we were serving at sea it took a lot longer to get any news about football and we had to wait for the air drops from the Royal Air Force. One thing we always looked forward to was the football results on a Saturday which would be piped over the ship's Tannoy system and there was always plenty of banter and piss-taking over the results. None of the ships I served on had more than one or two City fans on board but even in those days there were many United fans from all over the country, although I don't remember any coming from Manchester - nothing new there then...

There was one United fan from Worksop who had a tattoo on his buttock saying 'Manchester City fans kiss my arse' What a prick! His party piece was to drop his trollies to show his tattoo off when he had few too many to drink, I felt like filling him in on a couple of occasions but I kept my cool.

When the ships were in the UK it still used to be a logistical nightmare to get to a match depending where the ship was moored or where I was based and where the game was being played, and whether I was on duty or having any money was another consideration but if I was skint I just used to hitch it anyway.

I remember when I was on HMS Achilles, a type 21 Frigate, we had been on operations for eight weeks patrolling the Mediterranean and taking part in exercises off the coast of Italy, Malta and Gibraltar. We were due back into Plymouth on the Friday morning as I was going to Manchester for the weekend and I had planned to watch City v Arsenal at Maine Road. Happy days! As per tradition in the Navy, everyone who was not on duty was having a good drink on the Thursday night in anticipation of the sailors returning to our own Naval base; most of the sailors were also looking forward to meeting wives, girlfriends and family that they had not seen for about two months but in my case I was anticipating going to Manchester to meet my mates, have a few good drinks with them, then go on to Maine Road to watch City. I hadn't been in my bunk long when the alarm sounded and we were summoned to emergency stations where we were informed that a cargo carrier which had tons of bananas on board had caught fire off the coast of Scotland and HMS Achilles had to steam up there at full speed to help in the rescue operation. Half the duty fire crew on our ship were either still pissed or hung over when we approached the stricken vessel, some of the lads were landed on the cargo ship by helicopter and it took many hours to get the ship under control and we had to escort the ship into a dock in Scotland so repairs could be carried out. Luckily nobody was killed and nobody was seriously injured in the operation but our good deed scuppered my chance of watching City that weekend.

When I was serving on HMS Devonshire, which was a guided missile destroyer, we were docked in Portsmouth and as City were playing Sunderland at the weekend one of the chefs, Woody –

a Sunderland fan, asked me if I fancied going to the game and staying at his parent's house over the weekend? 'Do Bears shit in the woods?' was my reply. Fucking right I wanted to go, it was a right trek from Portsmouth to Sunderland back then (it's probably not much better nowadays) but that was a great weekend. I was made very welcome by the Sunderland fans, until that is we won 2-0.

While on the ship I was mates with another City fan called Gilly and once, when we were based in Scotland, we were due to sail in the early hours of the morning after we had played Middlesbrough in the League Cup semi-final at Maine Road. Gilly is going to tell you shortly what happened. I met up with Gilly a few months ago for a drink in Liverpool along with a few other ex–crew mates from HMS Devonshire for old times' sake, as you do.

When I told him I was going to write a book about the history and culture of Manchester City fans he told me to make sure I gave him a mention, he then emailed me with the following…

Ray Gill Royal Navy Stoker, HMS Devonshire in the 1970's

LEAGUE CUP SEMI FINAL - MANCHESTER CITY V MIDDLESBROUGH
21ST JANUARY 1976

One day I was on the HMS Devonshire docked in Rosyth, Scotland, the crew were getting the ship ready to set sail the next morning on an overseas deployment to the then USSR thus being the first Royal Navy ship to visit Odessa in the Ukraine for about 25 years. The trip was part of a good will tour and a ship from the USSR at the same time was going to visit Portsmouth. Both the Devonshire and the USSR ship would be hosting dignitaries from the respective countries and hundreds of people would be taken on a tour of the ships, that's why we had to get everything cleaned to a very, very high standard.

While all the preparations were taking place some bright spark (Don Price, the author of this book) came up with the idea of hiring a car and driving down to Manchester to watch City play in the League Cup Semi-Final at Maine Road.

There were a few problems with his master plan; neither myself or Don could drive and it was a 500 mile plus round trip. What's more, the weather was shit and the game would not finish until about 10 o'clock at night but these minor details unfortunately didn't deter Don as once he has a bee in his bonnet, there is no stopping him. Don managed to talk the only other City fan out of a 500 strong crew, a lad called Shonkey Crossley (can't remember his real name) to hire a car and drive us to the game; to help with the car hire and petrol expenses Don also talked Nobby Clarke, the only Boro fan on board, to come with us.

The duty officer got wind of our little master plan and we were summoned to see him. He explained that in no uncertain terms that what we were doing was barmy and ill thought through and that it would be touch and go if we got back to the ship before it sailed, he explained in serious detail how much shit we would be in if we were one second late. To put it mildly he was not happy but as we were all off duty there was sweet fuck all he could do about it and there was nothing that he could say that was going to deter Don – that was for sure.

As we set off I started wondering if we were doing the right thing but as Don started to open the cans of beer as soon as we left the dockyard all thoughts of being put on a charge and a possible visit to the cells or any other form of punishment was soon a distant memory. We made good time to Manchester and then went for a drink in the Salisbury Pub next to Oxford Road train station where we met a lot of Don's mates and what a motley crew some of them were but they were all great lads – Shonkey's brother also turned up and we had a few good drinks before we set off for the match.

Although we were 1-0 down from the first leg I didn't think we would be in any danger of booking our trip to Wembley, some were worried that City would balls things up and let us down big time but there was no chance of that happening; we blitzed them from the start and hammered them 4-0 securing our place at Wembley where we went on to beat Newcastle United 2-1 to win the League Cup.

Don in his wisdom thought it would be a good idea to go in the pub for a couple of pints so that the traffic could clear and who were we to disagree? So full of joy and plenty of booze we set off back to Bonny Scotland. The closer we were getting to Scotland the worse the weather was getting and I started to worry a little that we may not get back in time plus the fact we kept having to stop so Don could have a piss. Just as we were crossing the border the snow was coming down big time and as the car was going round a bend we hit a patch of ice; my life and Royal Navy career flashed before my eyes and I honestly thought we were goners. We skidded all over the place for what seemed like ages and ended up on a grass verge. Luckily we were all okay and miraculously there was no damage to the car. Don, who was half asleep at the time, decided it was time for another can of beer! We eventually made it to Rosyth where we dumped the hire car and made it back on board with an hour to spare, a proper trip.

At 06.00 Don should have been in the galley to help cook the crew's breakfast but there was no fucking chance of that happening – he went straight to his bunk. I met up with Don a few years ago in a pub in Liverpool and he has not changed, he still likes a drink. I keep having a chuckle to myself about that trip as it was one I shall never forget.

Another time I won't forget was when I was on a long weekend leave from the ship and went to stay with a mate of mine Rattler Morgan in his home town of Liverpool. We spent most of the time sampling the local ales and then we went to watch Liverpool play at Anfield. After the game we had a few more drinks and had a good bit of banter once the Scousers knew I was a City fan.

On the Sunday night Rattler had a surprise lined up for me (no it wasn't a stripper) we went to a pub in the Waterloo area of Liverpool called The Alex and I got the shock of my bleeding life when I walked in and who was serving behind the bar but none other than Tony Coleman, our left winger from the glory days. He had won the League and FA Cup with City. I was like a blubbering wreck when I ordered my beer, we then had a great chat and a few more beers together, I felt a bit sad for him when he told me he had given his medals away but he told me some great stories about his time at City and which players he liked and disliked. Tony had a brief spell at Sheffield Wednesday but they were relegated the night they played us at Hillsborough, Tony scored against us that night but we went on to win 2-1 without even trying very hard and it so happens that I was at that game. Tony said the City players later told him that they wanted the Owls to stay up but they were so shit they couldn't muster a win. What a great down to earth guy he is and to think not long after winning the Football League and the FA Cup he was working as a barman in a back street pub in Liverpool. Last I heard of him he was living and working in Australia. Talking to him summed up the way football and the way footballers used to be, for me it was a great weekend with great memories I was so chuffed Rattler took me to The Alex.

I am still a season ticket holder now and it is so much easier getting to the games since I left the Royal Navy; I still meet up with Don from time to time and we have a good chat about the old days- once a Blue always a Blue!

Cheers for that Gilly. I'm sure it won't be long till we meet up again for a beer or two but next time, please make sure you don't knock a table full of drinks over like you did the last time we met, I'm glad I wasn't sat at your table, oh and try and remember to get the correct train home, it makes life a lot easier!

Following City for so many years you get to know so many different fans and many of them are great characters just like they are at other football clubs. I remember going to Blackburn one Boxing Day to watch City play, it was freezing cold but a male City fan was wandering about in stockings and suspenders - oh well, each to their own! Live and let live, that's what I say.

One lad at Maine Road used to take a dead chicken to the game and used to wave it above his head in the Platt Lane / Umbro Stand, don't ask me what that was all about? Apparently he was a chef at a top hotel in town. The club stewards had to have a word with him and he was stopped from bringing his chicken to the game again for health and safety reasons, as bits flew off into the crowd! The next home game, he then received a roar of laughter from the crowd when he pulled out a rubber chicken and swung it around!

In contrast to waving a dead chicken about, one of the most famous City fans was Helen Turner, who used to have a big heavy bell that could be heard all round the ground when she rang it. Quite often the crowd would start singing 'Helen, Helen ring your bell', if the team needed lifting. She would immediately do as requested. I honestly don't know how she kept ringing it, as it was very heavy as I had a go at ringing it once. At one game in the early 1980's at Coventry City's Highfield Road, Helen was ringing her bell in the seated area when the brave police came in and took the bell off her. Those of us on the away terraces were booing like crazy at that decision – but roaring with laughter minutes later when Helen produced a tiny bell out of her bag and started ringing it. Then up went the roar ''Helen is a big fat football hooligan!''. Helen famously made it onto the pitch at Wembley in 1976 and joined in the lap of honour with the team after the League Cup win. She also was a steward on Coach A on the supporters' club coaches for many a year, keeping the older lads in check and making sure we weren't bringing beer on board but also keeping a motherly eye on the younger Blues too. Sadly, Helen passed away a few years ago, but as with the wooden rattles there would be no way that bells would be allowed in the ground nowadays.

Pete Green is another fan everyone recognises but few know who he is. In the late 70's and into the 80's, Blues called him 'Mad Pete' because he had to be mad going to every away ground dressed like he did, as a walking souvenir shop. Two brothers, Jim and Steve Ferris, went to a game at White Hart Lane in the late 70's and were walking towards the away end, trying to be blend in and not attract attention. They knew they were being followed by a small mob that was getting bigger by the minute. One whispered to the other, suggesting that as they turned the next corner, they should just leg it to the turnstiles. It was only when one of them took a quick glance behind them, just before they turned the corner, that they noticed Pete walking five feet behind them. The pair instead carried straight on and as Pete turned left towards the ground, the mob followed him!

At that time Pete lived in Accrington and went to every game despite being on the dole. Football was affordable to the unemployed back then. Then he got a job at Heathrow airport and moved down south. Pete was never afraid to 'dress up' as he did at any ground and will tell you he never encountered any trouble. And if he did, his steel toe cap boots would take care of him! He always had a bottle of Scotch in his City bag and I remember one time at Highbury in the early 90's, when he was stood right at the front of the away terrace and took his bottle out in front of a bewildered steward and took a swig from the bottle. Pete was told to leave the bottle in his bag for the remainder of the game.

Today, in his seventies, he is retired and lives in the Milton Keynes area and still comes up for home games and is affectionately known by Blues as 'Pete The Badge' as his jacket still remains covered in old City badges collected from over the decades. A true individual character and a fantastic Blue.

Over the years there have been many, many City fans that have earned the title of legendary Status – especially the fans that organise supporters clubs and coaches for away games, including the ones who raise money for various charities and good causes. They do it in their own time without reward and from experience I can tell you at times it can be a right pain in the arse!

Well my mate Eddie Richard Sparrow ticks all these boxes. Not only is he involved with the Bluebells supporters club he also runs a Facebook page 'MCFC Memorial Let's Not Forget Past Blues', that remembers City fans that have sadly passed away. On most match days, Eddie is at the ground early getting City memorabilia signed so he can either organise a raffle or auction it off for the various charities he is involved in. Over the years he has raised around £10,000 and his Facebook page has over 8,000 followers. For a few years Eddie lived over in Spain but even living overseas couldn't stop Eddie getting over to Manchester for the majority of City's games, Well done Eddie. If I was wearing a hat I would take it off to you but as I am not I can't! Instead, I am having a pint so I will raise my glass to you, all the best mate keep up the good work.

While nowadays the club is run on a very professional basis and everything is done to a very high standard, this was not always the case. Some farcical things have happened and at times we have had cock up after cock up which has at times caused even the most loyal of Blues to question their dedication to City. As loyal fans we have just taken the daft stuff on the chin and got on with the job of supporting City. At one time everything City tried to do was a fuck up; whether it was trying to buy a new player or trying to sell one of the players we had on our books, there was always a big chance the deal would go wrong. Even relatively simple things like installing a new roof or appointing a new manager presented a possibility that things could go dreadfully wrong. We even found it complicated to sack a manager and have embarrassed ourselves on more than one occasion when trying to do so. Things at one time were so bad that when Franny Lee was a player he said 'if there was a cup for cock ups City should win it hands down'. Unfortunately that tag stuck with us for many years. There has been much stuff written in the press and in City fanzines about our legendary mistakes and there was even been a book written called 'Cup For Cock Ups'. Like all City fans I feel we are blessed the way the club is run now but from time to time, when chatting with mates, it is not hard to recall some momentous cock-ups...

Going back to the 1970's we sold Franny Lee to Derby County which was a huge mistake. Franny was part of a brilliant City side that had just won a shed load of trophies and it was hoped we would win many more. Well for some strange reason we sold him and when he scored a spectacular goal for Derby County on his return to Maine Road, I remember commentator Barry Davies shouting 'look at his face, just look at his face!' The goal was replayed over and over on TV... not only did Derby County win the game but they went on to win the league as well that season.

Another clanger was dropped at Derby and although it involved City, it wasn't our fault, so we might as well have a little chuckle at someone else's expense for a change. We were playing at The Baseball Ground and already losing when we gave away a penalty. The referee went to put the ball on the penalty spot but as the pitch resembled a farmer's field there was no white penalty spot to place the ball on. Our goalkeeper, Joe Corrigan, disputed as to where the ref should place the spot and after placing the ball where he thought it should be, he got booked for his trouble. We then had the farcical situation where the groundsman came onto the pitch with a tape measure and a bucket of whitewash to measure up and paint a new spot. Derby scored the goal and went on to win the game but it goes to show that it is not only City that can drop a clanger or two and we don't have exclusive rights on cock ups.

In hindsight it was a huge mistake bringing Franny back as Chairman as he had been out of the game for a long time and although he tried hard, he made some terrible decisions and appointments and came out with loads of promises which built up fans expectations but the promises came to nothing. At first he had a great rapport with the City fans but there was just one mistake after another and soon the City fans turned on their former hero.

At one night game   loads of us went to watch City at Birmingham City's St Andrew's ground. The game was pretty unremarkable until about the 90th minute of the game and we scored so it looked like we were going to take the points back to Manchester. Don't be daft, this was City we are talking about and if anyone could fuck it up, we could and we did and ended getting beat 2-1 in the 95th minute.

The final game one season at home against Liverpool just summed up how City were all those years ago. A win would see us avoid relegation and a point would do if other results went our way. Late in the second half with not long to go the score was 2-2 when the manager Alan Ball mistakenly thought results elsewhere were going our way and that a draw would be enough to keep us up, so he instructed the players to keep hold of the ball and play for a draw, by the time he realised that we needed a win it was too late for us to do anything about it and we got relegated.

A couple of years later and numerous other bad decisions made by people at the club saw us in another last game of the season relegation battle. This time it was a battle to avoid the drop to the old division 3. We played brilliantly on the last day at Stoke and won 5–2 but results in the other games did not go our way and once again we got relegated.

One year the Prestwich and Whitefield supporters' branch had arranged with the football club that about 80 junior members along with their parents could go to the training ground to watch the players train then have photographs and autographs with them. The trip was confirmed with the club and arranged with military precision, nothing was left to chance so nothing could possibly go wrong could it? The youngsters were very excited as we arrived at the training ground only to be told that the players were given the day off as they had been on their annual Christmas party the night before. That was just another example of how unprofessionally the club was run back then.

Many fans reckon the sacking of Tony Book was the turning point for when things started to go pear shape for us. Peter Swales appointed Malcolm Allison to replace him. It was a huge bollock dropped as under Tony Book we had a great team but when Malcolm returned he dismantled a very good and promising team only to replace them with players who were not good enough. I am not even going to mention the fortune we paid out to one of the biggest flops of all time Steve Daley… oh shit I just did!

While we talking about flops the name of Lee Bradbury springs to mind. Now, as with Steve Daley it is not the player's fault that someone wants to shell out a small fortune for their services. Someone at City, in their wisdom, decided that a relatively unknown player from Portsmouth was worth around three million pounds. He wasn't, he flopped – what the fuck were the people in charge of making those decisions thinking of? To make matters worse, around the same time England International Paul Merson went from Arsenal to Middlesbrough after which both he and Middlesbrough enjoyed some good success. If Boro could afford him and his wages, I'm sure City could have. To rub salt in the wounds, over at the swamp they managed to buy England International Teddy Sheringham for just a bit more than we paid for Lee. There have been numerous other examples over the years where we have paid far too much for players. To make matters worse, as fans we can tell pretty quickly if a player is decent or not, it's just a pity some of our ex-managers couldn't.

One thing the club for many years would not and did not address was the club souvenir shop. While other clubs were investing in superstores and megastores to maximise profits by selling club merchandise, for years the only place where fans could buy things resembled a little corner shop and not many people could get in, with many people queuing outside usually in the cold and rain. We must have lost a small fortune back then as our marketing expertise was pretty non-existent.

Another thing I could never understand was because of our financial situation at the time why the club decided to demolish and rebuild the Platt Lane stand before the Kippax. In the wake of the Taylor Report, a wide ranging study to address ground safety brought about by the Hillsborough disaster, it was decided to abolish standing at all football grounds in the top two divisions and make the grounds all-seater. Luckily the Main Stand, Platt Lane and North Stand were already seated, so the only place where you had to put seats was the Kippax - simple is it not? Not for the head sheds at City is wasn't! Even though the seating at the Platt Lane wasn't the best it was in compliance with the new rules and regulations and could easily have lasted a few more years. The bright sparks running City thought differently, so instead of demolishing and seating the Kippax first then starting to generate money from the brand new facilities, private boxes and corporate hospitality lounges which would help to finance a new Platt lane stand, they did it the other way round and then wondered why the club was in such a financial mess!

When City played Gillingham in the play-off final at Wembley there was no system in place for fans to get their tickets in a civilised manner, so thousands of fans had to take time off work to go to the ground to queue for hours and hours to get their precious tickets. The ticket office was simply not geared up to deal with 37,000 fans wanting tickets in such a short space of time. Many were furious as not everyone could take time off work to queue up for hours to get tickets. The local radio station had many fans ringing up complaining and many people complained not only to the club but to local and national papers as well. It goes to show the appalling mismanagement of the club over many decades that we didn't even have a decent souvenir shop or a ticket office that was fit for purpose.

I am sure you could think of dozens of more examples but I am just glad that as City fans we took all the shit thrown at us and came through it with a smile on our faces and we are now reaping the rewards for our outstanding loyalty over the years.

It wouldn't be fair if I didn't mention a recent clanger dropped by our neighbours from Stretford .One Wednesday Evening in November 2017 a United scout who was based in Denmark travelled to Reykjavik to watch a friendly game between Iceland and the Czech Republic .When he arrived at the Laugardalsvollur national stadium he was met by some locals who kindly informed him that the game was being played 5,500 miles away at the Abdullah bin Khalifa Stadium in Doha .No one was sure which player or players he went to watch but try and explaining that balls up to the not so special one back at the swamp .Go on have a laugh I did

I will though just add one more to the list but pose it as a question: the subject has already been covered but ask yourself this. How did hundreds of Manchester United fans get tickets for the North stand in 1989 leading to the players being taken off the pitch? I remember the game was all ticket and fans had to have a membership card to purchase a ticket and all the United fans were grouped together so it was highly unlikely they were bought individually. There have been plenty of theories over the years of how they managed to get so many tickets together and one person's name comes up time and time again but I will let you ponder over that one.

5 - MANCHESTER CITY IN THE FAROE ISLANDS

WITH MANCHESTER CITY NOW becoming veterans of the European scene, we all know that that has not always been the case. Nowadays we are qualifying in our own right and playing the likes of Real Madrid, Barcelona, Napoli and a host of other European heavyweights. However, just 10 years ago, when City were drawn against EB Streymuir from the Faroe Islands, it was just our second appearance in a European club competition in 28 years. Before I go on about the game or more importantly some fans trying to get to the game, I will just waffle on for a couple of minutes about the Faroes.

I remember when the Falklands war broke out no-one had a clue where they were and while you will be glad to know the Faroes are nowhere near the Falklands and there is no chance of a war breaking out with the Faroes, well not to the best of my knowledge anyway, I thought I would give you a little information about the place. Now I bet you are thinking he has lost the bleeding plot (again) what is he going on about the Falklands for? Well, in 1982 when the war broke out, the majority of the population in the United Kingdom hadn't even heard of the Falklands, and if people had to guess, they were coming up with some great answers with many speculating that they were near the Shetlands, which as it so happens is nowhere near the Faroes or the Falklands, so it is a good job the Navy knew where to go or we would have dropped a clanger. I've not been to the Falklands myself but have been to the nearby Island of St Helena where Napoleon was exiled (well before my time I hasten to add) well when I say nearby it is about 6,000 km away but it is in that neck of the woods and they are both in the South Atlantic and as there is not much else out there they can be loosely classed a neighbours

The Faroes are quite small but it is a self-governing archipelago and is part of the Kingdom of Denmark but is a bit nearer to Scotland and Iceland. They consist of 18 Rocky volcanic Islands between Iceland and Norway in the North Atlantic Ocean connected by road, tunnels, ferries, causeways and bridges. The Islands attract bird watchers and hikers because of the terrain. The population stands at just under 50,000 and the currency is both the Danish Krona and the Faroe Krona. The weather is usually cold, wet and windy most of the year. Pretty much like Manchester don't you think? Ok maybe not then. The average temperature goes from about 38°F in February to about 52°degrees in August which is the mildest month, so if you're thinking of taking a visit there do not bother packing your factor 50. The climate has been classed as sub-polar seeing as even in the summer it is cold but surprisingly enough, in the winter the weather stays just above freezing. There is plenty of rain so visitors from most parts of Northern England will feel at home there, and any sunshine does not usually last long with cloudy skies being pretty much the norm.

While on the one hand between May and July the days are very long, in winter the weather is usually quite bad with it being predominantly dark so the days are quite short, especially from November to January. Even in the summer some parts of the Islands get snowfall.

In recent years many tourists from the United Kingdom have visited their nearby neighbours Iceland and by and large the climate is pretty similar but is more popular as a tourist destination.

If you like to swim in the ocean, beware as the temperature goes from 6°c (43°f) in February to 11°c (52°f) in August. Visitors tend to get over there from June to August as it is not as cold during those months and it doesn't tend to rain as much, September can be nice but can cop for a bit more rain. If you do decide to visit be sure to wrap up well and take plenty of warm clothes, waterproofs, a decent hat, woolly socks and most important of all a good old British brolly.

I visited Iceland during my time in the Royal Navy in the early 1970's. It was a lovely picturesque type of place with a very homely feeling and I imagine that is what the Faroes are like now. Iceland has of course been developed extensively to cope with increased tourism. I missed out on going to the Faroes when City played there in 2008 but I learned some really interesting facts about the place which over the next couple of minutes I am either going to educate you or bore you senseless. Please stay with me because I found out some good stuff so let's get started before you put the book down and go to the pub for a pint, so here goes. With such a relatively small population, there are more sheep than people (oh we are not heading in that direction?) The sheep are everywhere and even graze on top of people's houses as many roofs are covered in grass. If you end up hitting one while driving you have to report it to the police, so there is no chance of a bit of road kill there... No surprise that lamb is a favourite on the menu for the good folk of the Islands. They do have some weird ways of cooking it though, one such dish is fermented mutton called rast. The meat is hung outside in a hut for a few weeks to dry (hope the hut has a good roof), it is then either sliced up and eaten as it is or can be used in soups. There is even a deeper fermentation method where it becomes "skerpick" which has a very strong flavour and you eat it with a spoon, but I have been told it is an acquired taste which I believe is diplomatic language for saying 'it's hanging'. What the hell is wrong with a bit of roast lamb and mint sauce! Most people on the Island either own a boat or know someone that does as nowhere on the island is more than a couple of miles from the sea, so fish, shellfish and sea urchins are all regulars on the menu. Fishing and hunting is pretty much the way of life out there and lots of people are self-sufficient with many people having a basement where they slaughter and butcher their own sheep. Whilst the land is great for sheep, the water is great for fish and mussels which are caught and eaten daily but the land is not great for growing vegetables with the main crops being potatoes, turnips and rhubarb.

Puffins are regularly caught and eaten out there and the locals love them and before we get all squeamish about it, they have been eating them for hundreds of years. Thousands of puffins flock to the islands each year as the food, terrain and climate suits them perfectly. Campaigners have tried to stop the islanders catching and eating them.

Even in Iceland they eat puffin but again campaigners want to stop them being on the menu over there as well. Celebrity chef Tom Kerridge was accused of being colder than the weather in Iceland when he admitted eating puffin on a visit to Iceland. The BBC Food and Drink chef provoked anger after he wrote on Twitter that he was on his way to a "puffin lunch" before he admitted he had scoffed the seabird alongside guillemot, whale and horse.

The bird charity RSPB said puffins are protected at all times and safeguarded by law, well me thinks not everyone is "on message" as the politicians say unless something has dramatically changed over there in the last couple of years as it seems tourists as well as the locals enjoy to eat puffin meat in a variety of ways. In 2008 celebrity chef Gordon Ramsay was criticized for catching and eating one for the channel 4 show 'The F Word'. What happened to the saying "when in Rome do as the Romans do?" Well I hope you liked my little bit as a tourist guide? Now let's get back to the footy......

For our European Campaign in 2008 we qualified through the Fair Play league which gifts a place to the best team on the ratings of UEFA team values and fan behaviour and we only got the place by default as other teams in the Premiership had better ratings than us but had already qualified for their place in the competition by the more conventional route, i.e. finishing higher in the league but you can't look a gift horse in the mouth and in those days we had to take what was going. We were drawn against EB Streymur - a semi-professional team based in Streynnes. The club was only founded in 1993 when 2 clubs Eiois Boltfelag and Streymur merged. When City played them the team consisted of policemen, carpenters and accountants and no doubt a couple of fishermen. Their ground only held 1,000 people so for our visit the game was switched to the 6,000 capacity Torsvollur stadium in the capital Torshavn. To my Faroe friends I hope I have spelt all the words correctly and apologise for not putting dots and squiggles in as my machine won't let me do that. I also hope my few kind words about your island boost your tourist trade.

All the City fans as well as the journalists that went said it was a lovely place and the locals were great and yes some tried the puffin with mixed views on how it tasted.

Obviously it was quite a difficult place to get to, with ferries going but not on a regular basis, flights were limited and at the mercy of the weather and also quite expensive, and only specially trained pilots were allowed to fly to and from the Faroes, so with these factors in mind a group of City fans wrote themselves into footballing folklore by hiring a converted 72 foot fishing trawler called 'The Three Sisters'. The loyalty and dedication of the fans came to the notice of football magazine 'FourFourTwo' who were providing some sponsorship for the would be sailors who wanted to undertake the epic journey, which started from Manchester by car to Aberdeen before getting the ferry to the Shetland Islands on an overnight twelve hour crossing. From there they were to board the Three Sisters which had sleeping compartments for fourteen people and a fridge full of beer. The experienced skipper and crew were ready to welcome them on board when they received some bad news, and it would not be City if things didn't go to plan would it? The lads were left high and dry when the ship's skipper told them that the seas were just too rough with 16 foot high waves and Force 8 gales. And as the weather wasn't due to improve for at least the next 36 hours there was no way the lads would get there by boat.

While in the Navy I have experienced such conditions on a Royal Navy Frigate and a Destroyer. Even for experienced sailors on large ships it would have been bad enough, for inexperienced people on a small fishing boat it would have been a disaster waiting to happen. But all was not lost for the intrepid travellers as Magni Arge, the CEO of Atlantic Airways, came to their rescue by offering them free flights on one of his planes. He said he thought it was the least he could do as the lads had made such a gallant attempt to get to the island to watch the game. They were then able to get to the game and meet up with 250 other City fans who managed to make the long and difficult journey. They were rewarded with a 2-0 victory along with the brilliant hospitality from the locals, so all's wells that ends well and they were on to another winner as The Sun newspaper paid for the fuel for the flight and Thomas Cook put the lads up in a hostel. Bet the lads got a few pints back in Manchester while reminiscing what happened.

Well that's not all that happened to one of the lads, so please read on...

One of the lads, Dave Scally, stayed a little longer in the Faroes than anticipated and he became a mini celebrity when people heard of his problem following his and the other lads' intrepid journey to make it to the game.

After watching City cruise to a 2-0 victory Dave was feeling a bit ropey so he went to the hospital to get some pain killers before boarding his plane back to Manchester. Once the doctor gave him the once over they realised something was very wrong and within half an hour he was in the operating theatre having his appendix removed. Dave wasn't out of the woods yet though as he got an infection in his intestines and he was kept in hospital and the pain was so bad he was given morphine. Whilst in hospital feeling sorry for himself, he soon cheered up when lots of 'well wishers' came to see him, including a journalist from the Faroe Island newspaper who asked him for an interview which was then front page news; he also had a visit from Atlantic airline boss Magni Arge and Siggy Clementsen the manager of the football club EB Streymu who came loaded down with souvenirs and the offer of a lift home on the plane with all the team for the return leg which coincidently was the same time he was due to be discharged from hospital.

City won the 2nd Leg of the qualifying round 2-0 in front of about 7,000 thousand fans at Barnsley making the overall score 4-0. Hang about? Barnsley! Why on earth did City play a European home leg at Barnsley? Oh well they really wanted to play at Preston but the police objected citing 'safety reasons' as the excuse. Well this gets stranger and stranger looks like I asked the wrong question. I will start again... why did City want to play the game at Preston's ground in the first place? Well the reason was pretty straight forward, after all we couldn't play it at Eastlands as

Bon Jovi held a rock concert there and the turf had to be relayed. Oh silly me, why didn't I think of that? We can't let a rock concert get in the way of a European match can we?

By the way the population in 2008 of the Faroes could have, with a bit of a tight squeeze, fitted into Eastlands although they would have had to settle for Pukka pies though as there was no Puffin on the menu.

Well, all in all it was an epic time for all who made the long journey especially Dave and the other would be crew members. Another group went up to a place called Scrabster somewhere in Scotland and got a ferry from there.

Fair play as well to everyone who rallied round for Dave and the rest of the lads. So next time the train is delayed going to Stoke away just spare a thought for these lads.

6 – AROUND THE GROUNDS

SOME OF MY MOST MEMORABLE times watching City, have been when we played away from home. Nowadays City have a fantastic following on the road and also as we are now regulars in Europe, City fans follow the Blues over the seas and in the air in their thousands. Fair play to everyone who follows the team on their travels as it will cost a fortune over the season. Going back to the 70s and 80s some grounds were a magnet for City fans but at some grounds City didn't always take a big following. When you go to the same grounds regularly you become familiar with the area and the pubs, the chippies and also whether the home fans and more importantly whether the local police are friendly. In the 70s the West Midlands and West Yorkshire Police had a horrible attitude to football fans in general and away fans in particular and the treatment they dished out to the fans at that time was not good at all, many fans got arrested for all sorts of minor offences and even more got thrown out of the grounds for doing little more than enjoying themselves.

Some stewards at various grounds had a very high opinion of themselves and behaved in a way that on occasions greatly exceeded their authority. About 20 years ago I was on the receiving end of some jumped up official's over-reaction whilst watching City play at Charlton. At half time everyone on our row ducked under the barrier to go and get refreshments and to go to the toilet, so far so good. Just as the second half was about to start the City fans were already taking their seats and again the ones on our row ducked under the barrier as it saved walking about forty yards and then asking everybody to stand up while you went past them to take your seat. Again there was no problem – well there wasn't one until yours truly was about to duck under the barrier. A young female steward collared me and asked me not to go under the barrier but to walk to the end of the row then all the way back to about two feet away from where I was talking to her. I could literally touch my seat from where I was standing with the steward. What she was asking me to do didn't make sense then and it still doesn't make sense now. Everyone else on my row had already done what I intended to do. I politely asked the lady the reason I had to obey her absurd instruction and she informed me it was due to 'health and safety reasons'. It's just like politicians these days saying "it is in the interest of national security" when they haven't got a reasonable answer to a question. I asked her if I could see a copy of the regulations as I was convinced she was taking the piss. Instead of showing me the non-existent regulations she waved over a "senior steward", so I politely asked him for a copy of the said regulations. Without saying a word or giving me any warning he grabbed hold of me, turned me round, twisted my arm up my back and marched me past the bemused City fans who had witnessed what had happened, he then handed me over to the police, to whom he then gave his far-fetched version of events.

Fortunately for me the policewoman he handed me over to had a lot more common sense than he had, although she sympathized with my predicament she couldn't and/or wouldn't over rule the steward but she said she wouldn't arrest me either which I thought was pretty damn patronising of her as I had done fuck all wrong in the first place, so in a nutshell I got all the way to Charlton's grounds only to get thrown out and miss the second half.

Every cloud has a silver lining though as there was a pub open just near the ground so off I went to drown my sorrows and wait for my mates to turn up. After I returned to Manchester, I wrote a letter to the directors and chairman of Charlton Athletic Football Club to make a formal complaint about my treatment and to ask for a copy of the regulations. It didn't come as a great shock to me and probably won't come as a shock to you either, that neither was forthcoming. Oh well, it just reminds me to chalk it down to experience and it was never one of my favourite grounds anyway.

At Halifax in the FA Cup, 1980, City were beaten by the 4th Division side and when game finished, I was giving the players some stick and was arrested. The coppers had a sense of humour (not) as they put me in the cells with the Halifax fans that had also been arrested. When we were taken to the police station, they handcuffed me to a Halifax fan – however luckily it turned out the custody sergeant was the uncle of the lad cuffed to me! At least we both got a brew, although I would have rather got a pint ha ha!

Once I was let out, I went to a pub near to the train station, where it soon kicked off and the police turned up and arrested every City fan in there! I was on my own and was only guilty of having a drink. Luckily the copper dealing with me let me go once he saw my charge sheet, suggesting I ''get out of town quickly''.

I turned up in court a few days later and the policeman's statement said that I had led a mob of fifty City fans in storming the pitch. The copper must have been drunker than I was on the day to make that up! I told the judge that I went to the game on my own and watched the game on my own. All charges were eventually dropped.

On the way back from the Macclesfield Town v City game in 1998, me and my mates got off the train at Piccadilly station. The police were out in force and I said to Neil 'someone is going to get nicked here' as the police just look so confrontational. A couple of us walked to the left of the main mob of City fans and made our way to the exit. Just as we got there, a British Transport Policeman grabbed me from behind, stuck my arms up my back and forced me through the crowd and into the lift to take me to the police station, which is based at the train station. The first time he spoke to me was when we were in the lift and he shouted ''this will teach you for shouting 'you fucking twat'''. It was at this stage I realised there was a mix up as I knew I hadn't called my mate Neil or anyone a 'fucking twat'. However at the custody desk, the arresting policemen told the Sergeant behind the desk that I had been verbally abusive towards him. Now as I hadn't even seen the policeman before he grabbed me, obviously I hadn't spoken to him in any manner, never mind abusively but I just knew this incident wasn't going to end well.

I got charged with all sorts of nonsense, including threating behaviour, breach of the peace and other shit I have long forgotten. A few weeks later we had a supporters club meeting where a friend of mine – who happened to be a colleague of the arresting officer – told me the policeman who had arrested me was gloating that he had 'nabbed' the chairman of the Prestwich & Whitefield branch of Manchester City supporters club. Oops, I forgot to add that I was informed that the said officer was also a rag! My solicitor asked several times for the CCTV footage from the station as evidence to support my case – but the requests were ignored. I wrote to the police twice but I also received no response.

So I went to court and my mate Aide made a placard – 'FREE THE PRESTWICH 1' I had eight witnesses on my side and the only witness against me was the arresting policeman. As we were about to enter court, the prosecutor told us that the charges against me were being dropped. Of course I was mightily relieved – but at the same time I was livid. The policeman had lied and put me and my family through about eight months of stress and because he was about to be found out, the charges were dropped. So the moral of this story is the next time you read in *The Sun* or the *Daily Mail* about what a well-known individual or celebrity have been charged with, please take it with a big pinch of salt. People do not believe this kind of stuff still goes on – until it happens to you or a member of your family.

Carrow Road, home of Norwich City, has always been one of my favourite grounds as the pubs in the city centre are great and not too far from the ground and on sunny days it is great to sit by the edge of the water, having a pint and watching the boats on the Norfolk Broads. There is a great pub called 'The Complete Angler' and it's one where many City fans congregate.

I have actually had a couple of holidays on The Broads and it is a great experience until it pisses down and it's not much fun then but there are always plenty of pubs with mooring spaces where you can tie up and nip in for a couple of pints and something to eat.

I went to watch City play at Norwich quite a few times when I was in the Royal Navy, as it was a great place to visit and was not too difficult to get to from Portsmouth. One time I was going to hitch it from Portsmouth when I found out one of the stokers was going to drive to Ipswich in a hire car so I cadged a lift from him as Ipswich is only about 45-50 miles from Norwich. There was always a huge following of City fans there so the atmosphere was always good plus you knew it wasn't going to kick off as the Norwich fans are a friendly bunch and the police were chilled out as well.

Many City fans used to make a weekend of it and always had a good time. On a plus side there are some great chippies in and around Norwich and there is nothing like a load of stodge to soak up a couple of days' worth of beer. I wish all grounds could be as nice and as friendly as Norwich.

One year we were there and some Norwich City fans invited us into their supporters club for a drink which was actually a lounge inside the ground and we had a belting time.

Going to Birmingham and Aston Villa in the 70s were contrasting experiences. Birmingham's ground was a dump and some of their fans wanted to fight anyone and everyone, whereas the Villa fans were good as gold and very friendly. I always found the police though were very intimidating and aggressive and you could get thrown out of the grounds or arrested for the flimsiest of reasons. As soon as you arrived by coach or on the train you were met by riot police and of course great big Alsatian dogs – fuck me we were only going to watch a game of football. City used to always take a great following to Villa but it was hit and miss if many City fans went to Birmingham's ground or not. On one occasion we went to watch City at Aston Villa, we had just got off the coach and as we were making our way to the ground and we were walking past a few police officers, when one of them got a grip of my mate, who was stood next to me and when we asked what was going on we were told in no uncertain terms to fuck off otherwise we would get arrested as well. So my mate not only missed the match he spent a few hours in the police station, then he had to make his own way back to Manchester and return to court where he was given a £75 fine. Again, some of you reading this that didn't go to the away days back then might think I'm full of it and making some of it up but I know many fans witnessed similar experiences as the ones I have just mentioned – here, Phill Gatenby describes his experiences of the West Midlands Finest….

"Two of the many incidents that I won't forget relating to the WMP, one was at West Brom in 1983 and the other at Villa Park in 1980.

At the Hawthorns, City had lost the previous eight games. Right in front of us, early in the 2nd half, City (David Cross) scored a goal. We all went mental. I went double mental! I lost my footing on the terrace and fell backwards. Someone picked me up and I turned and thanked them – only for that person to twist my arm around my back and march me off to the police room. Loads of Blues around me tried to intervene and ask "what the fuck has he done?" but to no avail. I was in a police room surrounded by policemen. On my own, aged twenty. I kept asking "what did I do? I just slipped and fell backwards? Why am I here?". A burly cop in a white shirt and sat at a desk, who appeared to be in charge, looks at me and suggests that I keep quiet. I ask why I should keep quiet as I hadn't done anything. All I did was lose my footing on the terrace. I had driven to the game and hadn't had one drink of alcohol. Again I was told to keep quiet. I moved to the back of the room and lent against the wall, putting one foot up against the wall. The burly cop in the white shirt pushed his chair back and came at me with force. He grabbed my shirt collar and punched me in the face, stating if I continued (putting my foot against the wall) I would be in court on Monday for criminal damage to property. He then sat down and asked me for my name and address. To this day I have no idea where I got my answer from as I was still shaking from being punched in the face. I replied "I refuse to say anything unless in the presence of a solicitor". The burly cop put his pen down and looked up at me, surrounded by half a dozen officers. "What did you say?" he asked. I gulped and was shitting myself as I repeated my answer. "I refuse to say anything unless in the presence of a solicitor". The burly cop said "take his description down and throw him out". I then realised they had nothing on me and as I was being escorted out and the door was opened, I turned around and said "And I've got your number, I will be reporting you to the chief constable for punching me…" and the burly cop came running at me…. But the exit door was opened and I ran outside to safety and fortunately he didn't follow me! Outside were maybe fifteen or so Blues who had been thrown out for various reasons, mostly for things like swearing. We remained outside and with fifteen minutes to go, the gates to the Main Stand were opened, right next to where we were stood! We all went in and watched the game, ducking and diving at the top of a block entrance / exit steps . A steward came along and told us we were blocking the exit and instructed us to go on down into the stand and take a seat - and the next thing there we all were, in the corner of the Main Stand right next to the away fans, giving it the big wave and the City fans singing to us "Blues are here, blues are there, blues are every fucking where…." And in the final minute City (Kevin Reeves) score again (2-0) and every single blue who had been kicked out already – except me – jumps onto the pitch to celebrate with the players. The away fans were fenced in, but the Main Stand had easy access onto the pitch. Everyone was caught by stewards or police and for the second time taken to the police room! When the final whistle went, I was the sole City fan left in the Main Stand! I'd love to have seen the face on the burly officer in the white shirt when the same fans already ejected were brought into the room again!

The second bad memory of the West Midlands police is in the very early 80's at Villa Park.

I travelled to away games on, a coach, where three of us were punks – me, Loz Murphy and Alan Slater – and we wore studded leather punk jackets. At every away ground the three of us would routinely get picked out and searched whilst everyone else was just allowed off the coach freely. Alan had a jacket that had like twenty or more zips on it. Nothing could be put inside them, they were just zips. We would piss ourselves laughing as different police forces up and down the country would pull Alan to one side and search every single zip on his jacket. One time at Villa Park, it was pissing it down with rain as we got off the coach. The Alsatian dogs were barking like crazy and one City fan mockingly barked back and everyone laughed. I have no idea as to who it was, but the police assumed they did.... They grabbed Alan and demanded he sat on the wet ground and put his hands on his head. Dozens of blues protested that it wasn't Alan who had 'barked' and we were all met with the same response – ''do you want to sit on the ground with your hands on your head?'' The police closed ranks as the protests mounted. Alan, humiliatingly, had to sit on the ground in the car park in the pissing down rain with his hands on his head – until one cop said he could get up and continue on his way. An absolute disgraceful misuse of power and it came as no surprise a few years later when the 'Birmingham Six' were released having been stitched up by the same police force.....''

Just a bit further down the road, or to be exact further down the motorway, is Coventry City Football Club which had a great boozer called 'The Mercer's Arms' plus a couple of great chippies near their old Highfield Road ground. Apart from their accents, I used to always get on well with the Coventry fans probably because they also copied us and played in sky blue and like us they were also called City. Pity I can't be as complimentary about the police. One night game as we were being "escorted" back to the train station (which was was a fair old walk) out of the blue a copper behind me kept kicking at the back of my ankles in a bid for me to walk faster. If I could have I would have. I think the arsehole was goading me for a reaction. I think he wanted to arrest me so he could get back to the police station for a bit of warmth and a cup of tea. Luckily I kept my cool and managed to get to the train station with only sore ankles and no charge sheet.

I feel for the Coventry fans as they are a great set of supporters but they have been let down and badly treated by successive regimes and poor management. At one time they were a half decent team with a decent ground, but you never know, one day they might make a come-back.

Another club which has suffered greatly through bad managers and owners is the once mighty Leeds United. They had a reputation of being a hard football team and the fans also had a bad reputation as they had a hard violent following especially in the 70s and 80s, they even staged a pitch invasion when we were beating them in the FA Cup 3rd round at Elland Road in January 1978, in the forlorn hope that they could get the match abandoned and force a replay. The ref had other ideas and after a delay the game re-started and City hung on to win the tie. Their fans have been involved in some shocking incidents up and down the country, after saying that a lot of other clubs in that era had a following with an unsavoury reputation as well. I used to love going to Leeds though to watch City as it was always a tremendous atmosphere as thousands of City fans always made the trip over the border into Yorkshire. The Leeds fans are a very passionate bunch but there was always a chance of it kicking off on a massive scale and it usually did back then. The trouble is when violence breaks out it is all very random, anyone and I mean anyone; men, women or children could get hit by a flying bottle or brick or fall over and get trampled on and there was also a chance of getting bitten by a police dog or getting arrested for being in the wrong place at the wrong time. Then there was always a chance when you returned to your coach or car that it could have had its windows put through. Looking back, some people (I certainly do) must wonder why we kept going to games with the amount of shit we had to put up with. Many people will tell you that following your favourite team is like an addiction and to be honest they might have a valid point.

It must have been in the early 80s and City were at Everton on Boxing Day. I was working on the early shift but as one of the lads was going in his car I got a lift off him to Goodison Park. It was a rare occasion for me but I didn't have a drink before the game as it was a case of finishing work and legging it home for a quick shit, shave, shower and shampoo and a quick drive down the East Lancs to watch the game. We got in about fifteen minutes before kick-off and we were stood behind the goals watching the players warm up. Some of the players were taking pot shots at our keeper, they were off target with a couple of shots and a football ended up about ten rows behind me so the City fans started throwing the ball to each other for a bit of a laugh. For some strange reason the local constabulary took great exception to this bit of fun and four policemen with truncheons in their hands waded into our end to retrieve the football. Why they felt the need to be so heavy handed at such a harmless incident is anyone's guess but as they pushed and shoved their way to the back one of the policemen in his hurry to get to where the "offenders" were, wacked me in the face with his fist but as he was holding his truncheon in his hand I copped for that as well. Two City fans were arrested by the police over that incident. I wonder what they actually got charged with? It was just another bit of nonsense from the police, there was no need for them to get involved at all – plus I had a bit of a shiner for a few days!

I always used to love going to the swamp for the Derby but usually didn't like the end result. In the early 70s we did OK and I saw us win there in 1970 and in 1972, but I missed the most famous win at Old Trafford in 1974 when Denis Law scored the winner to relegate the rags. After that victory, we had to wait until 2008 for another win there. In between times we could only manage draws among the defeats. The most memorable game for me though since The 1970s was in 1990. I got my ticket from some bloke who was selling them outside the Kippax before one home game. He had wads of them for the Stretford End paddock. I didn't give a fuck where the tickets were for, I just wanted one. Apart from the official allocation of tickets for City fans (being behind the goal at the scoreboard end), there was hundreds of City fans in the Stretford End paddock and elsewhere in the ground. I wouldn't like to guess where the bloke got the tickets from but he must have done a roaring trade judging how many City fans were in parts of the ground usually reserved for United fans. The game ended 1-1 and Ian Brightwell scored a cracker of a goal for us and it went like a bullet into the top of the net. If you haven't seen the goal before, or in ages, get it on YouTube and I never tire of watching it as it was one of the best goals we have scored there.

Yes for many years we had to settle for draws at their place but that is not the case anymore and we get disappointed now if we don't get a win. I wasn't there when we won 6-1 but would have loved to be a fly on the wall in the United changing room as Fergie would have gone ballistic, though he left the ground early, just like 70,000 others. Oh well we waited a long time for something like that to happen, it was well worth the wait to batter them 6-1 in their own back yard.

So much is made of the great Liverpool fans and their "European Nights" are always highlighted by the media who love to butter up both the Liverpool fans and the football team. Well in the 70s and 80s it was a frightening place to go to as an away fan. Many fans were ambushed and attacked and some were robbed before and after the game. If you walked to the ground from the train station it was always a bit hairy. I was only sixteen at the time and had been to Anfield to watch City when I was home on leave from the Navy. It was an evening game and there was no trouble before the game as there were hundreds of City fans on the train and we all went to the ground together. On the way back though it was a different kettle of fish as the City fans were split up and walked back to the train station in small groups. I witnessed a small group of City fans being set upon by a large group of thugs masquerading as Liverpool fans. The City lads didn't stand a chance as they were hugely out-numbered and were attacked from behind but that is the way the cowardly bullies used to operate. Liverpool was another place where there was a good chance if you went by car or coach that your windows could be found smashed when you returned. I'm not saying the Liverpool fans were any better or any worse than other groups at that time but it did get on my wick when we kept getting told how great the Liverpool fans were. I have no doubt there were very many decent Liverpool fans in that era but they did have a large group of idiots who would attack away fans especially if they outnumbered them. They, like Everton fans, had an unenviable reputation for using Stanley knives to slash visiting fans. How many of the Stanley knife stories are true, exaggerated or just myth is anyone's guess. One of the worst outbreaks of fighting I witnessed at Liverpool was in 1981 in the League Cup semi final 2nd leg. Violence broke out big time as thousands of City fans had made the journey down the East Lancs. There were running battles before and after the game with many fans on both sides being injured and getting arrested.

Thankfully times have changed and there is rarely a hint of trouble and away fans are welcomed in many pubs near the ground with the away fans and Liverpool fans mixing well together today. Recently I was having a drink in a pub near Liverpool train station when Liverpool were playing Spurs and it was great to see both set of fans having a drink together just like it should be all the time really.

Blackburn is a great place to go to watch City and there is a designated pub for away fans but if you are staying in Blackburn for a drink after the game you can have a good natter with the locals without a hint of any trouble. One year I couldn't get a ticket in the City end for me and one of my sons so we ended up sitting with the Blackburn fans and we were treated well with no hassle whatsoever and the pies in the ground were great as well, as I said before, you need a good bit of stodge to soak up the beer.

Another club with a violent reputation back then was Chelsea but I loved going there because it was easy to get to when I was in the Navy based at Portsmouth. Although I was mindful of their reputation if I was going on my own, I would just keep my head down and keep my gob shut (Cath said I bet that was difficult) and I didn't experience any problems. In the 70s two of City's largest followings were at Chelsea, one was in the F.A. Cup and about 10,000 City fans roared the team onto a 3-0 victory and later on in the season an even bigger following was when we played them in the European Cup Winners' Cup Semi Final and there are estimates of between 15,000 and 20,000 City fans who made the journey. Unfortunately for us lightning didn't strike twice and we got beat 1-0 and we also got beat in the return leg at Maine Road so that ended our hopes for another European trophy. One year I went to Southampton to watch Chelsea when I was based in Portsmouth as it wasn't too far away. Chelsea won 3-0 and both the Chelsea and Southampton fans I was talking too were really good lads.

Tottenham and West Ham were two other London clubs I went to when I was in the Navy in the 70s. City didn't usually take many fans there, so again I just kept my gob shut and minded my own business. In contrast we used to always take thousands of fans to Arsenal and Queens Park Rangers. There was hardly any trouble at those grounds and there were plenty of pubs where you could have a drink and mix with the home fans.

I am well aware that other fans could have completely the opposite experience that I had in the 70s and 80s at various grounds up and down the country, some peoples experiences could have been better or worse than mine back then. Nowadays most people's experience of going to an away game is probably a laid back, no hassle, chilled out occasion. It is also probably true that some fans at certain grounds will have experienced the total opposite but I'm glad to say I can't see us ever returning to the dark days of the 70s and 80s.

I have to tell you this next story as it could never happen today. In the late 60s, one of our school teachers was a chap called Brian Grundy who also used to play part time for Wigan Athletic then he signed full time for Bury Football Club. Around the same time the football club used to give vouchers out to local schools in a bid to encourage youngsters to watch them play. In those days fans taking home made banners to a football ground was a common sight and we decided to go one Saturday to watch Bury play Barrow at Gigg Lane as City were playing away and our ex-teacher was now playing for the Shakers. The ground was only about four and a half miles from where we lived in Prestwich and was very easy to get to. Some of the lads had made a banner but I have not got a clue what was written on it but if I was guessing it would have been something simple like Bury F.C or the Shakers or because it was a large banner it could have said both. Now the banner was fastened on to two large wooden clothed props that would have been liberated from someone's washing line. Now can you just picture the scenario a group of kids getting on the bus then going into a football game holding onto two wooden clothes props, but like I said it was pretty normal back then. Once in the ground the banner was held aloft with pride.

Now I don't know who's bright idea it was but I guess I didn't need much persuasion, so about ten minutes before kick-off myself and another lad who will remain nameless (only because I cannot remember who it was) got onto the pitch at the Manchester Road end of the ground and proudly showed the banner off much to the delight and cheers from the Bury fans. What possessed me I will never know but roared on by the fans we ran across the pitch with the banner to the Cemetery end (Cemmy end to the locals) where the most boisterous of Bury fans were congregated. Half way across the pitch disaster struck and the banner came away from the pole I was carrying much to the amusement of the fans. I could do nothing else but just carried on running to the other end of the pitch just carrying a big wooden pole that was bigger than me. I must have looked a right nutter! I was nabbed by the local police and the reality hit me I was getting arrested and I was shitting myself. Just think what charges someone would get if they did that at the Etihad on a match day these days. The police could have thrown the book at me but because I looked like a tearful snivelling little school kid (because I was) all they did was throw me out of the ground minus the clothes prop. Wow! That was a near miss, especially when you see and hear what people get arrested for at football grounds now.

Most people who get arrested usually get a ban from attending football games as well. Fans in the Premiership and the Championship have a total of 1,127 banning orders, It has to be clarified though that just because you have a banning order it doesn't mean you've been involved in a fight or you are a football hooligan, you can be arrested and have a banning order for all sorts of minor offences like swearing, being drunk, ticket touting among a host of other things. It is hit and miss I suppose whether you get arrested, thrown out of the ground or just spoken to. It all depends on the attitude of the police or stewards on the day. Some can be heavy handed and that can inflame the situation while others can be as good as gold and defuse any potential situation from escalating.

Going to a football game should be and usually is a fantastic day out without any hassle or aggravation from other fans, police or stewards. Most supporters just want a good time free from stress and by and large football is a great spectator sport watched by millions and thankfully most people have those experiences, most grounds now are unrecognizable from what they were in the 70s and 80s which makes the 'match day experience ' so much more enjoyable. I am not sure if I like that term 'match day experience' I think it's something the PR people have dreamt up to convince us we are having a good time.

My match day experience in the 70s was getting pissed before the game, during the game and the same again after the game, and I just hoped I made it back home or to the ship in one piece without getting battered or arrested. I should imagine that's how it was for many other fans as well.

If I had to nominate my five favourite away grounds these are my pick Norwich City - Carrow Road, Newcastle - St James Park, Leicester - King Power Stadium, West Ham when they were at Upton Park and Leeds United at Elland Road. Okay, I will make it six as I really enjoyed going to Highbury as well which was the old ground of Arsenal.

OK, that is my bit done for now, I hope you enjoyed it and that it brought back some decent memories. Now is the time to put the kettle back on or get a beer out of the fridge as there are some fantastic stories by City fans spanning the generations.

7– KING OF THE KIPPAX
BY DAVE WALLACE

BACK IN 1955 WAS WHEN it all started for me, aged eleven. City were on their way to Wembley, we'd beaten United three times that season, we played in gorgeous sky blue, had Bert Trautmann in goal (I was a goalie albeit a very small one at that time!) and all the talk was of the Revie Plan and certainly not the Busby Babes. It was also the year that is generally recognized as the birth of rock 'n roll. City lost the final with ten men 3-1 against Newcastle United.

My dad was Irish and supported Bolton Wanderers and I had an older sister and two elder brothers, one of whom was a Teddy Boy with no interest in football, the other was a Blue but didn't influence me to support City.

Just after I'd started at Salford Technical High School, initially in Hanky Park, then Leaf Square, I attended my first game at Maine Road with a couple of Swintonian mates on October 15th 1955, watching us lose 2-0 to Preston. I can't really say that I was overawed with Maine Road but it was always going to be the place to be for me. That season we reached Wembley again, this time beating 'The Iron Men of the Midlands' Birmingham City 3-1. Bert broke his neck and played on heroically for the last 15 minutes and I was happy to be a Blue.

I also produced a City diary with reports and action shots of City games and player portraits, with ground drawings for a few seasons and like most schoolboys of that era I took pride in my City scrapbook, boosted by pictures cut out from Football Monthly. I also had my first letter printed in the Saturday Pink complaining about the publicity United got compared with that of City, for which I was paid the princely sum of 7/6d (about 40P).

In the following years I followed City all over the country until around 1961 when I started playing on Saturdays and Sundays and could only attend at the start and end of the season or midweek games.

By now, in the late sixties, I'd married and moved to Sheffield, as Sue was studying at Sheffield Art College and I played for a local club, so again my support was limited but we made regular trips over the Pennines in my Hillman Imp, dodging sheep on the Snake Pass, with the front end knocking and the head gasket blowing. The Imp once gave up the ghost on top of the Snake late one night on the way back to Sheffield, and we had to be towed by the AA to the garage and stayed the night at Glossop Police station!

It was now a good time to be a Blue and we enjoyed unprecedented success over the next few years. Into the seventies and the success continued with three Wembley visits, a loss to Wolves and wins against West Brom and Newcastle - revenge for 1955! By now we'd moved to Conisbrough, near Doncaster, where our first three kids, Marnie, Danny and Kaye were born. At the start of the 1976/77 season I purchased my first season ticket on the Kippax.

However, after moving to and living in Hull for a couple of years it was time to come home, and we moved back to the Manchester area in 1980. I was back in the old routine, going to games with my brother Frank and my eldest kids Marnie and Danny. There were Wembley visits again in 1981 (twice) and 1986, losses to Spurs and Chelsea (Full Members Cup!).

We attended Junior Blues meetings and Sue and I started to produce topical City cartoons, which we sent to the likes of Tommy Doc, James H Reeve, and Fred Eyre at Piccadilly Radio, with good responses. I'd also started to produce marquetry plaques which I thought would be more personal than the usual silver plates, pewter tankards or glass bowls normally given to players for certain achievements. With Sue's help I produced and presented or sent them to Colin Bell, John Bond, Joe Corrigan, Paul Power, George Heslop (meant for his pub on Hyde Road, though he said it would look nice in his daughter's bedroom!) Dennis Tueart and Alex Williams. I also have one which I did in 1986 for the FA

Youth Cup win, discarded from the City museum, which I hope to present to Stevie Redmond at some point if he'd like it. I was also requested to become the Junior Blues Father Christmas, which I did for about twenty years, including supporters clubs before the club forgot to tell me I was no longer required! Thanks to Wayne Norris, who produced the first sky blue Santa outfit which the club finally adopted a few years ago.

Then in 1985 football went horribly wrong. As we left the ground in triumph after beating Charlton 5-1 and gaining promotion, the news came through that there'd been a fire at Bradford. Later we learnt that there'd been rioting at the Birmingham v Leeds game when a wall collapsed on a fan, who was killed. A few days later we had Heysel. I had been in Belgium the week before the game on a business trip and I was advised by the locals that it was an accident waiting to happen as the stadium was crumbling and the local Italian community had snapped up all the tickets in the neutral section next to the Liverpool fans. UEFA were warned, well in advance, and the game could have been played at the Nou Camp or the Bernabeu, which were available, but they chose to ignore the advice. The game went ahead at that venue with dire consequences and English clubs were rightly banned from European competition.

So in the space of a few days we witnessed everything that could go wrong in football become horrible reality. Thatcher was PM, Moynihan the Sports minister, and we were threatened with ID cards, away fans were banned at Luton, we were fenced in, stewarding and policing left a lot to be desired and hooliganism was rife. Reporting throughout the media did not reflect the humour and experiences of the ordinary football fans, who were not the thugs or anarchists the press would have you believe but passionate football 'experts' with a point of view that was given little opportunity for expression. Indeed, one of the most infuriating things was to hear panellists on programmes like Question Time, who hadn't a clue, pontificating on football aspects and saying stuff like "we should make the hooligans join the army" (many of them were ex-army!) or Bernard Halford suggesting "we should birch the hooligans". Ken Bates even wanted electric fences at Chelsea! It was so inflammatory that if you went for a job interview, you couldn't admit to being a football fan.

At the time supporters' clubs were not particularly political, concentrating mainly on obtaining tickets, organizing travel and getting guests to meetings. Fair enough, but they were generally too close to their clubs to be objective.

Liverpool fans Rogan Taylor and Pete Garrett decided to form the Football Supporters Association, with a view to giving fans more of a voice. There was a lively branch in Manchester which included fans of many different clubs, of which I became an active member. We held regular meetings with guests such as Alex Ferguson (I know!), Jimmy Frizzell, Gordon Taylor and local footballers. We attended meetings in Coventry, halfway between the North and the South, and became a powerful voice on football fan related topics, getting exposure in the media.

At the time, football magazines, such as Match or Shoot were aimed at young fans and were generally in the 'what footballers have for breakfast' vein, but the Foul publication, eventually banned, inspired the fanzine movement, as did the music zines, and general fanzines like When Saturday Comes and Off the Ball were groundbreakers for the adult football fan. Club fanzines were appearing, the early ones being Bradford's City Gent, and Leyton Orient's Orienteer.

So, in the summer of 1987 I'd decided to do a City 'zine but we were busy moving house after Alex, number four child, arrived - registered as a Junior Blue on his birth. (He now owns a flat next to The Etihad!) However, at an FSA meeting I met Mike Kelly, who was starting to produce 'Blueprint' the first City fanzine. He'd beaten me to it but I already had a dossier of stuff Sue and I had produced plus new articles, which I gave to him. Unfortunately, the first two issues appeared late and out of date then, at the opening day of the new season at Hull, it didn't appear at all despite having the whole of the summer to produce it.

Talking to my mate Tony on the terraces at Hull that afternoon he said he could get inexpensive printing done at work if I fancied it. I discussed it with Sue who was supportive, so with what I had left we added to it and the first King of the Kippax was produced. I remember picking up a few hundred copies; it was pouring down, and I wondered if I'd be able to sell them all. It was daunting.

The first issue appeared at Barnsley on September 24th 1988, where you could park on the grassy slope next to the ground. I was on my own and nearly bottled out from selling but I'd sunk my money into it, so costs had to be recovered, and I sold about 80 at 50p a time. The 2-1 win helped sales. For the second issue I borrowed £400 from the bank for a 'wrap round' professionally printed job and increased the print run.

I wanted to publish regularly, with up to date and balanced views hitting the major issues; reflecting on events, supplying information, and most of all providing a platform for fellow fans to express themselves with humour. And they did. The fanzine gradually built up a team of regular contributors and sellers, plus a long list of subscribers from all over the world, some of whom we have met with and become firm friends.

Other City fanzines appeared, Electric Blue (later Bert Trautmann's Helmet), Main Stand View, Singin' The Blues, Chips 'n Gravy, The Fightback, This Charming Fan, Are You Blue or Are You Blind, Blue Print and the wonderful aptly titled City Til I Cry! And it's fair to say that there was much rivalry between fanzines, particularly when selling on the street but we're generally all friends now and can laugh at all the previous 'goings on'! In my opinion the fanzines and supporters' club meetings helped keep City fans' spirits up during the dark times.

In 1989 after City's 4-0 loss at Blackburn, news came through of the Hillsborough disaster, and once again it seemed the authorities had let football fans down, and worse, which has just been proven beyond doubt, there followed a disgraceful cover up of those events which has taken almost thirty years to be resolved.

Over the years we've been involved in various campaigns, against ID cards, Swales out, Franny in, Franny out, Free the 30,000, and have given our support to the safe standing campaign.

The Forward With Franny movement started in 1993 after

Peter Swales/John Maddock sacked Peter Reid and appointed Brian Horton, who to be fair generally won over the City fans. It caused a split in the official supporters club and the Independent supporters club was formed. Franny's henchmen were charged with getting supporters on side and visited supporters' clubs, advising us that among other things we need not worry about finances as "there is more money available than you could imagine" none of which materialized. The campaign went on until the following February, when the takeover was announced just before the cup tie at Cardiff which we lost 1-0.

One of the FWF's aims was to appoint a Fan on the Board, proposed by Colin Barlow the MD. I don't think Franny was particularly enamoured with the idea but this was duly actioned, though the method of appointment was criticized in some quarters. So I became that fan, which attracted much media attention and anger from some people who judged me by their own standards, assuming ulterior motives on my part. For the first board meeting it was agreed that the Sky cameras could follow me into the Boardroom, for the first Board meeting, as it was a ground breaking move for which football fans had strived for years.

When the camera man followed me into the Boardroom I don't think Franny had been advised of the situation and when he saw him Franny went apoplectic and frog-marched the poor fellow down the corridor into reception. Good start!

I was invited to attend the parts of meetings the Board thought appropriate, sometimes being left outside for a good while but I always had things to do whilst sitting in reception. At the time I was working as a Project Manager at Manchester Airport, on the design and installation of baggage systems, air bridges, lifts and escalators and I found it mildly amusing that the City Board members seemed to view me as a lowly manual worker, although the projects I worked on were valued well in excess of the turnover at City at the time! This was season 1994/95 and we didn't sign or sell a player in that time and the most beneficial meetings I had were with secretary Bernard Halford on fans' issues.

Probably my most satisfying achievement was when I persuaded

Bernard that, having had discussions with Rogan Taylor regarding the Hillsborough memorial service, that it clashed with City's home game with Liverpool. Bernard therefore agreed that the game should be moved to the Friday so that the Liverpool players could attend the service on the Saturday. I then had complaints from City fans on religious grounds, even though we had played on Good Friday for long periods in the past. Sue and I attended the service to represent City fans and, as expected, it was very moving.

I only intended to do the job as F.O.T.B. for 6 months or so, to hopefully kick the thing off and get it going for the next fan. So it was put out to the fans again and the leading candidate turned out to be Mark Bittner, who was even more bolshie than me so they knocked it on the head. However, I did persuade the club that if we formed a Fans Committee to gather fans' views, to pull together all the City fan groups and organisations, (and I made sure that all the fanzine editors were invited), so that the club could deal with one body in general. This they agreed to, with regular meetings held with club officials. This continues to this day as Points of Blue, fronted by Steve Parish, although instead of club officials attending we now only get a written response, so there's no debate, and it sometimes feels like responses are lip service only.

Things went from bad to worse on the pitch, we had manager after manager, and I became persona non grata at the club as I was supposed to be happy that we were on our way to the third tier. Eventually Franny went, David Bernstein came in with John Wardle, Dave Makin and Dennis Tueart and Joe Royle was appointed. We did go down, at Stoke, (where I was accosted by a Blue who thought it was my fault!) but bounced back with the Gillingham win and went up again then down again. Royle went, Keegan came in and we saw some of the best football we'd seen in years.

The move from Maine Road, where there were advantageous bottlenecks for selling, to COMS, meant a new approach to selling KK but we generally cover most ingress and egress positions.

By now all the other fanzines had long gone, though CTIC hung on in there for a while. Keegan imploded, Pearce came in and the club was sold to Thaksin Shinawatra. I didn't sell my shares, as I was uneasy with the new regime. It certainly caused arguments among City fans. Sven was appointed and I didn't rate him although he did give us the double over the rags and he went in the following summer, doing very little everywhere he went afterwards. The Leicester fairytale didn't happen for him. In 2008 the Sheikh came in and the rest is history.

Why on earth did he pick City with our 'typical City' DNA and the most obnoxious neighbours in world football, is anyone's guess. I'll go for our loyal fan base, the challenge, location near an International Airport, the stadium, supportive council, the availability of land in East Manchester, our history, and the publicity Abu Dhabi would get for being involved with a Premier League Club. I could say and the best fanzine in the land but that would be self-congratulatory and highly unlikely!

We're now approaching our 250th issue in our 30th season. We still get plenty of brilliant contributions and while sales have dropped (we peaked in 1991!) and sellers have dwindled, we're just about keeping our heads above water thanks to stalwart sellers Tom and Steve Parish, Ged, and brother Frank. The 'zine is more professionally produced with the help of our layout bloke Graeme and we still enjoy putting it together. Sometimes though, as Blueprint's Frank Newton once told me, by the time it's finished "you want to chuck it down the toilet!"

The main thrust these days is not on how badly the club is run but how prejudiced the media is and how bitter the established clubs and their supporters are. There's always plenty of material each month and it's wonderful to have positive contributions, especially after winning a few trophies and playing great football.

My first City away game was only down the road from where I used to live in Prestwich. It was against Bury in the old Second Division and guess what, City got beat! Nowadays Bury only get crowds of about three to four thousand but back then they were much better supported and at this game in 1966 over 20 thousand fans were packed into Gigg Lane. But in comparison to my short journey to watch City, Dave's first away game was an epic...

8- TALES FROM PADDY'S COACH

DAVE FROM WYTHENSHAWE

ROUND CHRISTMAS 1964 City were languishing in the bottom half of the Second Division. We had been playing crap and would endure our lowest-ever league gate of 8000 or so against mighty Swindon the following year – so it was obviously the right time to start going to all the away games…

I was sitting on the 102 bus outside Princess Road Bus Depot waiting to be taken back to Wythenshawe, yes I had left early but you had to, to get a seat on the bus and we had been battered once again. A friend sat next to me and told me in excited terms of his trip to the last away game on Paddy's coach. Paddy was the driver, not the name of the bus company.

I was informed the next away game was on 2nd January 1965 at Portsmouth. The coach would set off at midnight on New Year's Day from outside the Grand Hotel, Aytoun Street in the city centre and leave Portsmouth for the return trip at midnight the day of the game. One or two of my other Withy mates from the Red Lion pub were going so I agreed to give it a go.

I was 20 and my parents thought I was mad spending two days on a coach to travel to the other end of the country and back to watch a team of losers when most fans could not even be bothered to turn up to watch them at home but that's what made it an attractive proposition.

The Friday of the midnight departure started with a few beers in the Red Lion, then the 102 bus to Princess Road, Moss Side and then a walk through the alleyways to the City Social club for more beers. At closing time, 11 o'clock, we caught the bus into town and assembled outside the Grande. The Withy lot were joined by a motley crew from all over Manchester including Gorton,

76

Levy, Langley and Middleton. The age ranged from 17 to 23 and everyone without question was as pissed as a fart.

The coach set off dead on Midnight to a massive roar and load shouts of c- i -t-y, c-i-t-y etc. After all of 5 minutes the coach stopped as Paddy needed some cigs. Stupidly the keys had been left in the ignition and one of the lads decided it would be a laugh to drive the coach about half a mile down the road. Needless to say Paddy did not see the funny side of this particular prank but everyone else was in hysterics.

We all eventually settled down and set off again to loud cheers. The coach was a hive of activity and included various entertainments such as a return wrestling match in the aisle between two rather large guys, one of whom was known as The Vicar and no, he wasn't! Another group, including me, were composing City songs. Everyone swears the Jingle Bells song with the line 'Oh what fun it is to see City win away' was composed on this trip. There were a couple of card schools towards the back of the coach.

As the hours went by people started to doze off but nobody could because of the arguments and noise being made by the card players. The internal lights were turned off but the card players had come prepared with their own torches and flashlights. Despite Paddy's repeated requests for them to keep the noise down they got louder and louder. Paddy's patience had been stretched to the limit and finally he threatened to throw the card players off the coach. The noise continued, the coach stopped and the card players were booted off. Apart from Paddy no one had a clue where we were. The card players begged Paddy for another chance to which he reluctantly agreed providing they continued their journey in the boot of the coach. They surprisingly agreed to this and carried on their card games by torchlight in the boot. The rest of us managed to get the odd 5 minutes sleep.

We arrived in Portsmouth on Saturday morning, I think it was about 7-30 ish. We breakfasted on fresh milk borrowed from the doorsteps of Pompey residents. It was then a case of hanging around and keeping out of mischief until the pubs opened at 11. We reassembled in a pub right next to Fratton Park. We were joined by the only other coach load of City fans that travelled to Pompey for that game, most of both coach loads knew each other if not by name then to nod to. Lunch was fish and chips.

Due to the amount of beer consumed and little sleep I do not remember much of the game. I do remember we got a very creditable 1-1 draw, I always thought big Derek Kevan got our goal but it was Nelly apparently. The songs that were sung the most were Jingle Bells, Just like City (tune of Just like Eddie) With Kevin and Wag it's in the bag (I'm not even sure Dave Wagstaffe was still with us then but we sang that song, well I did) and also the Baguley B's song. Many of the Withy contingent played football for Baguley Boys and their song was sung for a couple of seasons at every ground in the Second Division. It always puzzled the fans of whoever we were playing but we thought it was great. City score and the chant of Baguley B's went up.

After the game we dined on pie and chips (no gravy in Pompey) and then off to Southsea to sample their pubs. The rest of the night is hazy but I do remember plenty of beers and chatting to the local talent. Most of the females loved our accents but they thought we were from Liverpool. As Beatlemania was at its height we thought it rude to disappoint the ladies as they seemed very excited about us being from Liverpool. To be fair we never said we were from Liverpool we just did not say we weren't.

Midnight finally arrived and somehow we all managed to get to the coach's departure point. The trip home was much quieter as everyone was pissed and knackered. No wrestling match and a much smaller card school.

As we approached Manchester Paddy was persuaded to detour via Withy and our lot were dropped off at the bottom of Hall Lane. There was a 15 minute walk home stopping off at the not yet open newsagent at Hall Lane Parade of shops where bundles of the Sunday papers had been left on the doorstep. A couple of papers were borrowed to read the match report and then home and bed.

Two weeks after the Portsmouth game was the famous Swindon Town home match, for which the attendance was a meagre 8,015 - only joking, everyone knows it was record attendance for any match in the world of over 200,000.

★

Fast forward a year to New Year's Eve, 1965. A group of the Wythenshawe Paddy's coach crew are at a house party in Brooklands South Manchester which borders Wythenshawe. Shortly after midnight one of the guys mentioned that Ralph Brand, one of the few failed signings of the Mercer/Allison reign, lived a few minutes' walk away. As he was a Scot and this was his first New Year in a foreign country we thought it was our duty to make sure he had a good Hogmanay. So 10 or 12 of us, all reasonably pissed, set off for Ralphs's home singing City songs at the top of our voices. We knocked on Ralph's door. I think it was Johnny Crossan who answered and surprisingly invited us in.

There were a few other players there as well as Ralph and Johnny, we had a drink with them, thanked them for their unbelievable hospitality and told them to make sure they won tomorrow.

The game the next day was a top of the table clash with Huddersfield. Although chasing promotion the City team comprised only two new players, Mike Summerbee and George Heslop, to the team that had struggled for years. Striker Ralph Brand had not adjusted to English football, which resulted in us being short of a striker. Defender and local lad Glynn Pardoe was used as a temporary solution. The team comprised a few other locals including Mike Doyle, Wythenshawe lad Dave Connor, Alan Oakes and Neil Young as well as Glyn Pardoe – all of whom formed the backbone of the team that would go on to win so many trophies in the following seasons. Colin Bell arrived the following March and a year later Franny Lee's arrival completed the team. The foreign contingent comprised Scot Bobby Kennedy and Welshman Cliff Sear.

At the game we assembled in our usual spot behind the nets in the Open End. This was the North Stand before it was redeveloped – first with a roof and then seats installed. There was a big crowd of well over 47,717 which was very good even then for a Second Division game particularly as not long before we'd had a crowd of 8,000.

As expected it was a tense game between the top two teams in the league but we manage to win 2-0 with goals from Mike Doyle and our new mate Johnny Crossan. However Crossan's goal is not the thing I remember him for in that game. By far the most memorable thing he did was to throw up in the middle of the pitch. Must have been something he ate.

Many thanks for that Dave. I wonder what the reaction of the present day players would be if a few fans turned up for a drink at their gaff the night before a game. Don't think Pep would be amused.

9 - VIENNA FINAL 1970

ALAN FROM WINSFORD

WHAT A SEASON THIS WAS for my beloved City! Having already secured the League Cup with a win over West Bromwich Albion at Wembley, it was now time for our final in the European Cup Winners' Cup - a trip that will live with me forever. People going to away games nowadays have a great number of options of how to get there. Many Supporters Clubs run coaches to all the away games and if you book early enough you can usually get a bargain on the train .Going to watch City in Europe is also very easy as Thomas Cook and Sports Options are just two companies that do charter flights plus there are great choices of routes and airlines if fans want to travel independently. Some fans, due to work commitments, can opt to go on a day trip so they fly back straight after the game, while others tend to treat the trip as a bit of a holiday and stay for a few days. However it has not always been as straightforward and going to Vienna turned into a longer holiday than first planned but I would not have changed it for the world, as when you are young and carefree life is just one big adventure and I was always up for a challenge. I used to go to many away games but the trip to Vienna was the longest trip I had undertaken back then.

That season I travelled all over the country watching the boys in blue with a hitch hike to Southport followed by a hitch hike to Bilbao with my good friend Lester Bebbington. After our demolition of Schalke 04 in the semi-finals (I think it was something like 6–2 on aggregate) both Lester and myself decided to take the high roads to Vienna, once again using our thumbs as a shout for "help, we need a lift".

We left our home town of Winsford on the Friday prior to

Wednesday's final and we eventually arrived at Dover on Friday evening for our ferry to Belgium. It was while we were on the ferry that we had our first bit of good fortune. An American Serviceman who was stationed in Garmisch, right on the German/Austrian border offered us a lift.

When we arrived in Garmisch it started snowing quite heavily and we made the decision to travel over the border and on to Salzburg via train. It was something we had never encountered in the leafy lanes of Mid Cheshire, as we were approached by a middle aged couple at Salzburg Railway Station asking if we were looking for a room for the night! How strange, we thought, but we were so tired and had no other plans so we took a gamble and travelled only a few miles to their home, where a wonderful comfy bed and white linen sheets were a pure welcome.

The next morning the weather was wonderful and we continued our journey to Vienna… or so we thought. We decided to have a rest. We had a large sheet of cardboard with the words WIEN scrawled in big letters. The ignorant Austrians only flew passed us in their cars, shouting obscenities and tooting their car horns. Three hours later and finally someone stopped and we shouted "YES GET IN" as we thought we were well on our way to our final destination. The driver then got out of his car and starting to talk in broken English. It transpired that we were not getting any lifts as we were going in the wrong direction to Vienna! Oh come on, we were only 18 at the time.

Finally we reached Vienna on the Monday afternoon and reached the ground, to be met by other City fans who also had nowhere to stay. The Vienna Stadium was in fact a multi-purpose sports ground and with no security, seven of us decided to take a gamble and climb over the railings and sleep inside the stadium. You have no idea how comfy those Pole Vault mattresses can be and we managed to spend both Monday and Tuesday evening in there without a soul knowing.

On the Tuesday, the two of us went into Vienna central and spoke to an Austrian guy who told us where the City players were staying. Our funds were dwindling by now but we decided to take a taxi and hopefully see the players. I had started supporting City in the very early 1960`s as our neighbour's adjacent back garden was home to none other than Glyn Pardoe. My Dad knew Glyn's dad well and asked him if it would be possible for him to take me to a City home game.

Can you imagine a teenager travelling with the centre forward for Manchester City (that was Glyn's original position) to a game in which he would be playing? It was unreal at the time. I thought it was brilliant though and I loved all the attention I got as my friends were quite envious of the fact that a City player used to take me to the home games. After I left school I began to organise away trips via a mini bus and we always ensured that we reached the away grounds before the City bus; as the players came scurrying down the steps we looked out for Glyn and his cousin, my namesake Alan Oakes. They would come over and ask how many of us there were and they would try their best to secure as many complimentary tickets as they could, with Mike Doyle also giving us his share.

Anyway back to Vienna… We went miles up into the mountains and finally arrived at City's Hotel. We asked if a message could be sent to Glyn informing him of our arrival. He came down and couldn`t believe we had hitch hiked this far. He went away for a few minutes and came back with Alan and Mike Doyle and another person I did not recognise who happened to be a photographer from the Daily Mail by the name of Peter Potter.

We had our photographs taken with the three players and Peter told us that this would be inside the sports pages of the Daily Mail. That thrilled me no end as my Dad was an avid Mail reader and I thought of the look on his and my Mum's face, when opening the paper the next day.

We thought that was the end of our wonderful day… but no. Glyn asked Joe Mercer could we travel down to the training ground with them on the team bus. Joe came over to us and said we were more than welcome. Can you imagine two teenagers travelling on the bus with their heroes! Other players came over and shook our hands and onto the team bus we travelled in awe of the company we were in.

At the training ground me and Lester had a kick around between ourselves and we stood on the training ground touchline with Big Mal putting the lads through their paces, twenty-four hours before the big match. One thing will always stay with me at that training session was watching one of my heroes virtually reduced to tears… Mike Summerbee failed a fitness test and was ruled out of the final. It was only when we arrived back home, that we realised we never made the sports pages with our photos as Mike's injury was the big back page headline.

Finally, that Wednesday night arrived and we stood inside a stadium with a capacity of 40,000, with 4,000 + City fans and a handful of Gornik fans as a block was put on Polish fans travelling to Vienna. After about twenty minutes the heavens opened and all 4,000 of us got soaked to the skin as there was not one piece of roofing in the stadium. But who cared! After another fine display we had earned our first bit of European silverware.

Unfortunately on our way out of the stadium myself and Lester were split up and the next time I saw him was back in Winsford, as we arrived back separately with myself getting back some twenty-eight hours later than my travelling companion.

And finally one piece of memorabilia that I brought home with me… a football from that Austrian Training ground, which was used every Sunday for 4 years, on our local recreational park. It never left my side until the wear and tear of those long Sunday games finally saw that piece of leather finally come to an end but not my memories of a wonderful eight days.

The fans that travel abroad now have no need to participate in a bit of hitch hiking as getting everywhere is so easy and I envied the fans who travelled to watch City play Napoli and witnessed Sergio Aguero become City's highest goal scorer of all time as the blues became the first British team to beat Napoli in a competitive match in the San Paolo .Well I hope you liked my little adventure, it brought back some great memories. Let's hope it's not too long until we pick up another European Trophy. You never know, it could be sooner than you think!

Come on you Blues!

10 - MY FIRST AWAY GAME

SEAN RILEY

I'D BECOME A BLUE thanks in the main to the Pritchard family from Moston - Joe and Beryl were good friends of my mam and dad and had a few children; two of their elder daughters - Sandra & Tracey - used to babysit us in the early 70's. On one such visit they gave me my first set of football cards, orange backs (ABC '72-73 series for all you fellow anoraks out there!) and I was hooked, I had watched intently on ITV as we lost 1-0 at home to Sheffield Utd (Geoff Salmon scoring directly from a corner kick I remember, much to commentator Gerald Sindstat's surprise) two weeks previously I'd watched the highlights of our hugely disappointing League Cup Final defeat to Wolves where their rookie keeper, Bury born Garry Pierce (from a family of Blues – Ste Pierce attends City games to this day), sporting a red goalkeeping jersey kept out everything we could throw at him. The month of April saw us lose heavily by 4 goals to nil at Anfield, as Liverpool challenged Leeds United for the title, the goals being shown on Granada Reports, we looked like lambs to the slaughter in front of the Kop, it was as though the scousers were sucking the ball into our net. I later found out we'd drawn 1-1 against them at Maine Road a couple of days earlier, our away form jinx would plague the club throughout the 70's.

'My first game' was a fan initiative started by the Club not long after our current owners came on board and thousands of Blues, myself included, eagerly recited memories stretching back decades in some cases, it's a very personal thing after all, and that first experience often shapes that young boy or girl for the rest of their lives. Mine was no ordinary first game, most young fans get taken to a home game by their family or relatives but mine was away (albeit only a couple of miles or so outside the city of Manchester, but it still felt a million miles away) and the stakes could not have been any higher.

Saturday 27th April 1974 was the day to be precise – it was a real baptism of fire in the white hot heat of a Manchester Derby. I had just turned 9 years old and football hooliganism was rife, no more so than among the infamous Red Army, masquerading as Manchester United fans, who were busy trying to dismantle every town and city unfortunate enough to be in their way. Surely this was the last place on earth you'd want to give your son his baptism in the far from beautiful game? Well, not if your dad was of Ancoats stock (Jersey Street) and a highly rated amateur boxer, scrap metal dealer and doing what dads did in those days, taking his eldest son to his first football match.

My City scarf was wrapped/tied securely around my neck, there was no writing on it, a simple but nonetheless very smart combination of thick sky blue and white, punctuated by narrow maroon lines. I was so proud as I walked down Warwick Road holding my dad's hand, completely oblivious to the tension, the simmering undercurrent of hatred from those in red, towards those in blue, what could possibly go wrong! At one point my dad turned round and talked to a group of men (late teens/early 20's hard to say) as we approached the turnstiles at what we all now know is the Scoreboard End of Old Trafford. Innocently, naively I thought, they must be dad's friends, otherwise why would he be talking to them? He told me later that the far from innocent group of United fans were plotting to relieve a boy of his City scarf, the boy in question being me…

'But why dad? Why would they do such a thing? What had I done to them?'

My dad could see I was genuinely shocked upset by what he had told me, I had mates in school who were United fans, my best friend was a United fan, why would they want to do this to a little boy. My dad said 'Son, there are good people, and there are bad people, and these were bad people, but don't you worry about it, they wouldn't have dared lay one finger on you.' I knew this to be true in as far as I don't remember getting battered and I still had my scarf, even standing on my seat holding it aloft when Denis Law scored the first goal I ever saw live.

So how had my dad talked them round? He smiled and with gritted teeth, told me what happened next. As he turned round to confront them – at this point they would have seen a short man of 5'-7" with a muscular build and arm muscles bulging and hands like shovels, helped by years of carrying steel and loading skips and a pair of eyes which could cut through the very steel he used to carry. He greeted them with the following words of wisdom "If you attempt to do what I think you're planning to do, I will put you all in the concrete mix for the M62…" I checked this out years later and realised my dad was referring to the last leg of it which remained incomplete towards Leeds. Now anyone reading this who knows my father will fully appreciate the gravity of the situation these young United hoodlums had landed themselves in by their own actions! One thing is for sure, he never made idle threats and I don't think he was in the kind of mood to give them a choice – it would be straight up to the Tilcon Road Stone depot on Oldham Road, Miles Platting and straight in the back of a cement mixer!

Anyway, with their cards well and truly marked, I thought nothing of it and said goodbye to my new found 'friends' and skipped off with 6 new pence in my hand to buy my first ever football programme from the old man with a flat cap wearing glasses outside the Scoreboard End of the ground. I wasn't sure who had marked it in pencil on the front cover, probably numbering how many had been sold, but it has survived remarkably well and still graces my collection over 4 decades later. We took our seats looking down on the Scoreboard Paddock, the noise was deafening, much louder than I envisaged it was going to be, I didn't have a clue where the City fans would be located, this was the era before segregation of fans, although it definitely came in for our League Cup tie there the following season. I was completely oblivious to the importance of the game in terms of what it meant to both sides. Anything less than a win for United meant relegation from the First Division, and even a win didn't guarantee them safety. For City, it was nothing more than personal pride in terms of a disappointing season with no League Cup trophy, but for the likes of Mike Doyle and the local lads in the team, it was a rare chance to rub plenty of red noses in it and to afford the City fans the same opportunity to do so, there was no way they were going to pass on it now.

Memories of the game itself have faded, mainly due to the fact it was a hugely disappointing affair, with so much at stake. United looked like a team who were already doomed, whilst City defended stoutly and didn't take the couple of chances they created, my boyhood hero Dennis Tueart coming closest by hitting the post. Then, in the 82nd minute, Francis Lee, who, unbeknown to City fans, was playing his last ever game for the Club (at least I can say I saw him play for us!) sent in a low cross from the left and Denis Law (also playing his final league game in domestic football) with seemingly nothing on, connected with a back heel which saw it deceive United keeper Stepney and roll in the net! From where I was sat, it looked unbelievable, he seemed so far out from the goal when he did it, commentator Sinstadt's iconic words 'Denis has done it!' would soon appear on the back page of every newspaper. As for me, well I instinctively climbed on my seat, and held my scarf aloft in celebration. The sporadic punch ups around us in the seats and on the terracing below seemed to go on for an eternity, among the bedlam the referee led the players off the field of play as the Stretford Enders invaded the pitch to attempt to have the game abandoned with six minutes left un-played.

Tommy Docherty (who had repaid Denis Law's faith in him by releasing him from United which enabled the Lawman to have a second stint at City) and former City player and legendary United manager Matt Busby pleaded with the Neanderthals to get off the pitch but they were having none of it. The fighting continued as we left the ground but nobody came up and confronted me or my dad and I was celebrating seeing my sky blue heroes' victory, not realising there would be an appeal to try and play the outstanding 6 minutes after the referee had taken the decision to abandon the game. Fortunately common sense prevailed and the result was allowed to stand and United were condemned to second division football, where a good number of their 'fans' would continue to wreak havoc up and down the country. The controversy around that goal and the myths which still live to this day, are written in folklore. Denis was once quoted as saying it was the one goal he almost wished he hadn't scored. That's an interesting statement and of course that's his prerogative. He served both clubs with great distinction but for my part (and any other Blues making their debut in the stands that day) he scored the FIRST goal I ever saw in professional football. It was a moment for me to cherish and I still do to this day. If I get the opportunity to shake Denis by the hand and tell him, I will do.

Since that day back in 1974, I've been fortunate enough to see City lift 3 League Cups, 1 FA Cup, and 2 Premiership League titles, and win promotions, including the unforgettable play off Final in 1999. To cap it all, I met a Moston Blue by the name of Jane Taylor back in the mid 80's, and married her within 12 months. Now in our 32nd year we continue to enjoy the rollercoaster which is Manchester City Football Club, and as I'm sure I speak for most of us when I say, quite simply, there is no other Club quite like it.

While I was addressing what sort of stories I would like included in the book, I remembered a newspaper article where two City players turned up at my old mate Sean Riley's house some got in touch with Sean and asked him if he would like to write an article for the book. He said he would love to but he had already written a piece for the August edition of the City fanzine King of the Kippax So many thanks to Dave and Sue from the fanzine for letting me use the following article and of course to Sean who has also written about his first City game.

"SOMEONE'S KNOCKING ON THE DOOR..."

SEAN RILEY

WHO CAN FORGET the unmistakable dulcet tones of ex-Beatle Paul McCartney and Wings in the opening verse of their catchy single 'Let 'em in' all the way back in the scorching hot summer of '76. Life was good in the Riley household; at the tender age of 11 I'd been privileged enough to see City train on the Maine Road pitch a week before the League Cup Final and then meet and greet all the players one by one as they finished the session and have my double page Manchester Evening News souvenir colour pull out autographed by them all, if memory serves (sadly the newspaper poster didn't survive but I can vividly picture it now). We had once bumped into Joe Corrigan visiting a family in Blackley as a few of us cycled to Heaton Park; we nearly fell off our bikes when we realised it was him. And my biggest claim to fame was when Kenny Clements, who had recently moved into a brand new house built on the Fairways in Moston, came to our house and played snooker on the three-quarter-sized table with my dad and his pals one night. It felt like royalty had been, we were so excited to know a City player we knew was standing there, as me and my younger brother gazed on in disbelief in pyjamas with our glass of milk, ready for bed but allowed downstairs momentarily to see the man himself. I remember thinking his perm looked even bigger in real life than it did from Block C in the Main Stand…

Meanwhile Pat and Win Power were busy running the Woodman Pub just down the road in Hollinwood, where the Failsworth OSC was born, and their son, better known as Paul Power to a generation of Blues, would become another player to visit our house. I was living the life of Riley and not even a teenager! Of course technology being what it was then, no photographic evidence exists, more the pity, but I can put myself back in the picture ingrained on my memory in a split second. Also the disappointment of not getting my boyhood idol Dennis Tueart's signature initially, legend has it he either didn't see me or body swerved me to get down the tunnel into the changing rooms, I was blissfully unaware as my dad's pal promptly ran down the tunnel and gently persuaded Dennis to go back out and 'sign the bloody kids poster' and he duly obliged (but knowing the reputations of both men, I suspect he was fearful of reprisals if he didn't do the decent thing – no damage done – I forgive you Dennis!).

So fast forward 41 years, and on the Wednesday before we played at Watford, my missus Jane receives a telephone call from Lee Kenny of Cityzens asking if we would be available for the Monday morning immediately after the Watford game. Of course we both had work but Jane can book the time off as she is her own boss, her call to me was to say the Club wanted to film my City memorabilia room. Knowing it was short notice and having received some coverage about it recently, I would be lying if I said I was in two minds (would people want to see the same stuff again?) and the half a day's holiday I would need would be needed for a midweek game next season but just something in Jane's voice and the fact Lee had asked, made me think I didn't want to let Jane, Lee, or indeed anyone down, so I quickly checked with operations and my holiday was duly granted….

So the Watford weekend and stay over was duly completed, and we returned home Sunday night, I hadn't mentioned the planned visit to anyone, being keen to keep it all low key, but little did we, or other lucky Blues know, what the Club had in store for us on Monday morning, 22nd May 2017.

As mid-morning came and went, both Jane and myself were anxiously looking at our watches, I was committed to be back in Sheffield for an afternoon meeting starting at 1pm prompt, whilst Jane was almost ready to leave for work. I'd nipped up to the toilet for a pee but no sooner had I got to the top of the stairs when Jane shouted up to let me know 'they're here!' Deciding to hold on to nature's call, I about turned and walked down the stairs, just before I reached the bottom step in readiness to open the front door which leads out to our porch, I will never forget the tone in Jane's voice as she uttered the words "OH MY GOD….!"as I simultaneously opened the door, to see Ilkay Gundogan knocking on the porch window!

"We've got a bell it's on the left hand side feller!" I joked.

I looked again, and realised Leroy Sane was also at OUR front door, together with the rest of the Cityzens team and film crew (Lee Kenny you 're a legend…!) and Rob Pollard from the MEN. My initial shock soon disappeared as I greeted them all with a 'Morning!' before pointing politely in the direction of Leroy and saying, 'I saw you yesterday…' Ilkay then went on to say they were here to say thank you to us in person for our support and they wanted to show their gratitude (our season tickets and tickets to every away game will be covered by the two players for the whole of 2017/18, I kid you not), talk about knock me down with a feather! I was stuck for words temporarily (unusual for me I know) but tried to convey how deeply grateful and humbled we were by their magnificent gesture, what a great initiative by them and our beloved Club….!

Contrary to the snap video shots which didn't show it, we did of course invite the players and the staff and film crew into the house. No sooner had they stepped through the front door (all £60 million quid's worth of them in transfer fees – arguably the most high profile visitors to these parts of South Chadderton since Lady Diana re-opened Princess Park 30 years earlier!) than I was explaining if they had told us they were coming we'd have had bacon butties and brews ready for them, which brought a laugh and a smile. As did Ilkay's response to telling him we named our cat 'Silva'. Quick as a flash he replied back, "you will have to get two more cats then…"

It broke the ice perfectly, as did our offer of bacon sarnies and a brew had we known they were coming, they laughed (as I nervously looked at Jane thinking had I put my size 9 in it without thinking there may be reasons other than Pep's diet plan that may have prevented consumption in any event – no harm done though!).

Unbeknown to us as the players stood in the hallway, our neighbour and pals who live across the road (Marie is from a big family of Blues, her husband Al an old school Blackley Red) had clocked the fancy limousine type Merc pulled up outside our house. Alan just happened to be in his garden and thought it must have been a Birthday surprise or something, but when Sane got out of the car, he looked, and even though his eyesight isn't what it used to be, he said to himself that looks like bloody Sane! Although he didn't have the same success identifying IIkay!

As I waffled on without a care in the world, Jane was hastily finishing off her bits of make-up whilst being the perfect hostess, before plucking up the courage to ask if it would be okay to take a selfie with Leroy, one of the crew quipped, "well Jane it is YOUR house, you can ask and do what you want" (within reason naturally!) and our fleet footed winger was only too happy to oblige. Unsure what to do next, and still thinking well they've come to see the memorabilia room, I led them there but not before IIkay was interviewed in our kitchen as Jane panicked about the cat litter tray being in there, to which I replied, "well the Cat's got to shit somewhere!" which raised a few smiles again.

So up to the box room which is now converted to a shrine to all things football, not a trace of decorating or paint to be seen, just wall to wall covered in City memorabilia. The thing that struck a chord with Jane and I were the impeccable manners shown by Leroy and IIkay throughout. They are well educated, grounded young men with none of the apparent baggage which comes with some young players who think wealth and status gives them power to do what they want. Their command of English is perfect and it always makes me conscious of the fact I didn't try hard enough to learn a second language when given the opportunity at school. As the camera continued to roll, I was soon back on my soap box singing the praises of my boyhood legend and all-time favourite City player Dennis Tueart, before swiftly adding our esteemed visitors were of course our modern day equivalents, once again the comment brought a few smiles. Whilst IIkay was busy talking to the rest of the ensemble, I was able to have a good one on one chat with Leroy, and there were so many things I wanted to ask him! Why did he sign for City when he had the pick of several top European Clubs? He didn't hesitate to tell me he knew Pep from his time in Germany and that when Pep wants to sign you, then you want to play for him, it was really that simple! I explained how Pep was everything you would want a manager to be, whilst Mourinho is one I would personally avoid, I cited his public slating of his own players as one example of why I didn't rate him as a world class manager or a likeable person, that lack of man management skills in any other industry would see him fail, Leroy appeared to listen intently. I asked him about how many photos and autographs he had given, it must be a lot to cope with, he said it is but he didn't mind doing it, and I told him it was best not to keep count, to which he smiled and laughed.

IIkay joined the conversation again and asked what it was like following City during the tough times. I explained the fact that the worse we got on the pitch, the more City fans would simply turn up, which to me highlighted how big a club Manchester City really is. I explained that players like Dennis Tueart, who got what the Club and the fans were about, brought out the best in us, and vice versa. I said to Leroy, if there was one thing I could convey as a fan to the players, it would be to remember us when you need that moment of inspiration in a game, and quoted an example of God Forbid, when we are 1-0 down in a Manchester Derby and you found an inner strength and belief from your relationship with the fans, to give that little bit extra, to go and score the goal which either rescued the game or enabled us to go on and win it….

We viewed the other Club badges on display, and the Schalke

poster from our Europa League game there (courtesy of Anthony Sudworth – cheers fella!) certainly caught Leroy's attention, being the club he joined us from, I then went on to explain to both players how Germany was the favourite destination in Europe to see football (both at club and International level) for not just us, but many other Blues, with special praise for Southern Germany, although they both politely reminded me the Western part of Germany where they hailed from was just as nice too. Our visit to the Faroe Islands and a poster recovered from the Manhattan Pub in Streymur were next up for conversation, as I went on to explain how difficult and expensive it was to get their despite its reasonably close proximity from Britain. How the Danish Police came to the island which normally doesn't have a police presence, such was the importance of our visit, and despite there being fewer than 200 Blues present, we still managed to drink the town dry (and again I emphasised how similar England and German fans are in the way they support their Clubs and their social habits etc.).

A few photographs were subsequently posed for, although I've always argued my face is far more suited to radio. I've never known just under an hour to pass so quickly in my life and I've no doubt Jane will say the same. Because we weren't prepared, we had nothing ready for signing by the players for nieces and nephews, it was a missed opportunity, although Phil Dooley managed to tweet Jane and get his Watford programme in our possession signed before they left. The handshakes to both players turned into a man hug on my part, and as I hugged Gundogan, I instinctively said I was being very careful not to injure him! Again it brought bouts of laughter from everyone, it had been that kind of meet; informal, relaxed and leaving fond memories which we will carry with us to our graves. I think the players enjoyed it too, and having seen the other videos where other fans received similar surprise visits (my particular favourite being the players turning up in a school playground and playing football with the kids) it certainly helped promote the Club and the players in a positive light and if they can make this a regular occurrence in seasons to come and reach out to as many City fans as possible, then it can only be a good thing in my opinion.

We said our goodbyes and thanked everyone for making it such a memorable occasion and as for my United supporting pal across the road, when I confirmed who he thought he'd seen outside our house the day before, his look of jubilation that his mince pies hadn't failed him, and that he could go back in work the following morning to tell his Red and Blue pals alike that he was right and they were wrong to doubt him, well I couldn't deny him that, he's not a bad lad, for a red anyway…

FOOTNOTE

A huge thank you to former Blue and Club Ambassador Alex Williams MBE. The Peak District has always had a history of good solid support for City, and when a friend contacted me to see if we could help him to find a 'Name' to open Buxworth Children's play area, Jane said why not try City in the Community, bearing in mind this was less than 2 weeks to go before the event. So an email was duly sent, and to our surprise Alex himself replied to confirm he could step in at short notice but that he would not be offended if we said no! Now anyone who knows of Alex Williams knows it is an honour and privilege to have the big man around, and we duly replied to tell him in no uncertain terms how grateful we were, and that we weren't sure who would be more excited, the kids, or the parents! So the day before we played away to Middlesbrough, Alex duly turned up, right on cue and was the life and soul, dishing out Tee shirts to the kids and was bombarded for autographs and photographs by old and young alike. It was a great turn out and the organisers (some of whom don't follow football) were genuinely thrilled to see how popular Alex was. It was a great afternoon, made possible by a bloke whose services to football and the community are without equal. Alex Williams embodies everything that is good and decent about Manchester City Football Club, and we are very lucky to have him on board, cheers fella – you did us proud! #mcfctogether

11 - CITY v ARSENAL

Ian McMahon (11 Years old at the time)

SATURDAY 8TH OCTOBER 1977 - 3PM

OFF TO MAINE ROAD AGAIN two buses to get there, only 2p per trip. I sit downstairs as can't be doing with the smoking upstairs. 204 to Belle Vue get off just before the amusement park. Get on the 53 will get off on Lloyd Street and walk down to Maine Road.

Will have a quick look round the souvenir shop while it's quiet, maybe buy a programme from last week's away game, it may come in handy for using as a token should we get to one of the cup finals like last year.

Looking round to see if the TV camera vans are here; can't see them, so won't be able to watch them later on Match of the Day or on The Big Match tomorrow. Be good if the cameras filmed all the games but guess the TV companies can't be at every league ground. Be good if they could also have more live games as we only get to see clubs in the FA Cup Final or European finals. Least there's a World Cup next year to watch plenty of live games, hope England can qualify though Italy look favourites to go through so may just get the Home internationals live on telly.

Off round to the Kippax… that man is here again with his sign "The End of the World is Nigh" he had that last season as well and smelling the onions from the burger vans by the walls behind the nearby houses. I had a burger from there once, not very good, waste of 20p.

It's nearly one o'clock, said I would meet my cousin at turnstile 56 at one, no sign of him… will give him 5 minutes after they open the turnstiles up, don't want to miss a place on the white wall at the bottom.

Let's see what the number is…

7

Thought it would be 5 as it's the 5th home game, wonder why they don't' go in order. Think mum said it cost her £7 for the season ticket.

Well I can't see my cousin and I gave him 10 minutes. Oh well, no way of contacting him now hopefully see him inside. Better get a wee first as I will be on that wall a long time if he doesn't show. Don't want to lose my place.

I'll get a programme to read while I'm waiting for kick off. 15p this season!

Bit of a wait now till the teams come out. The stand is slowly starting to fill up, tend to get a lot that don't get to their places till just before kick off. There's a man who keeps moaning that his pint of Greenall's is now 40p.

Well they just announced the team, one difference to the programme – Brian Kidd replacing Joe Royle at number 9. It did say in last night's Evening News that Joe may miss the game but I suppose they've had 24 hours since that was printed so he may have improved – no way of knowing till they announce the team.

1 Corrigan

2 Clements

3 Donachie

4 Owen

5 Watson

6 Booth

7 Barnes

8 Power

9 Kidd

10 Hartford

11 Tueart

12 Channon

7 locally born players in the team– that's good to see.

10 English and 2 Scottish players won't get to see any foreign players here this season as we're already out of the UEFA Cup

which we got into by winning the League Cup last season.

Our record signing, Mike Channon, is on the bench even though he cost £300,000. Heard he is our top paid player as well on about £500 per week. Was shocked to see Hamburg break the UK transfer record in the summer paying Liverpool half a million for Kevin Keegan, wonder if there will ever be a million pound player?

The teams come out to a big roar from the Kippax. Love joining in the songs like Dennis Tueart, King of all Geordies, Oh Asa Hartford Asa Hartford Na na nan na na nah, Oh Willy Willy Willy Willy Willy Donachie.

My dad's not here so I can sing all the Tommy Booth song…

Big Joe Corrigan's just gone to get his lucky heather from Helen in the North Stand and a quick kiss. Will soon hear the song Helen, Helen ring your bell.

Kicking off towards the North Stand… come on City.

Looks like a big crowd, Kippax is quite full been getting over 40k each home game this season so far.

Corner to Arsenal Super Mac Malcolm McDonald left unmarked – 1-0 to Arsenal

Kippax fans not happy singing 'you're gonna get you're f★★king heads kicked in'.

Chance for City – goal, Peter Barnes makes it 1-1.

Well 1-1 at half time better get my programme out to see how the other ten Division 1 games that kicked off at 3PM are doing. Be a few minutes while they put the scores on the ABC board in front of the North Stand. Not got my transistor radio so no other way of knowing.

Here we go…

A 1-1 Bristol City v Leeds

B 0-0 Leicester v Villa

C 1-0 Liverpool v Chelsea

D 1-0 Birmingham v Coventry

E 1-0 Middlesbrough v United – YES!

F 0-0 West Ham v Forest

G 0-0 Newcastle v Derby

H 1-0 Norwich v Wolves

I 1-2 QPR v Everton

J 0-0 West Brom v Ipswich

Could do with West Ham beating leaders Forest who were 2 points ahead of us before kick off. If that happens and we can go on to level points, then we will have a top of the table clash at Forest next week.

Teams coming out for 2nd half to a big cheer.

Arsenal fans try singing but drowned out by the noise of the Kippax fans.

Foul on Peter Barnes in the box by Pat Rice. Big shout from the fans in the Platt Lane stand and the ref's given the penalty.

Dennis Tueart against big Pat Jennings – come on Dennis!

Yes! He sent him the wrong way – 2-1 to City.

Full time and City have won, hopefully someone will have a radio on the bus so I can hear the other results though they will be in the Pink Final later with the match report.

12 - THE TRIALS OF A FEMALE FOOTBALL FAN

BY LOZ SOUTHON

I'M NOT ENTIRELY SURE where my love of the "beautiful game" came from. I was born in Salford in 1961 and I am (shock horror) a girl! My family didn't go to football. In fact I can't recall anyone I knew actually going to games. But I was (and still am) a tomboy. Also we didn't have practically 24 hour coverage back then. I was probably too young to watch Match of the Day and probably Cup Finals were the only games televised live. Maybe I was subliminally aware that England won the World Cup in 1966. Maybe I was subliminally aware that City won the League and the FA Cup and the Cup Winners' Cup in 1968, 1969 and 1970. What I do recall is seeing City on TV and seeing… Rodney Marsh. Yes I know some people reckon that he lost us the League, but I just kept thinking "wow" and that was that, I was a City fan. I don't recall seeing the 1974 League Cup Final defeat but I did watch the 1976 League Cup win on TV and Dennis Tueart's overhead kick! Wow!

I envy young girls today. I used to try and join the lads in the park for a kick about, but had very little impact as I was largely ignored, probably due to being a girl and a very small girl at that and just used to run about trying to get a touch of the ball. My moment of shame being when Barney Daniels (he went on to play for City) joined in and he actually passed to me, probably because I was in front of goal and everybody was ignoring me, so it seemed a no brainer, except that I was so surprised that he actually passed the ball to me I just panicked and booted it and it was one of those misses that if You Tube had been around, it would have had hundreds of "hits." Nowadays of course ladies football is played in schools and ladies teams are common. Who knows, I could have been the female equivalent of Lionel Messi!

When I went to secondary school I used to watch the school team play. Each weekend I would turn up and get on the bus with the lads and teachers. I was once dribbling the ball on the touchline at half time and the coach/teacher said in exasperation "there's a girl here showing you how to control the ball!" At the time I was quite proud. Thinking about it now, it was bloody patronising.

As a football fan though I have two problems: 1) My height. I peaked at 4" 11 (1.5 meters) and 2) I have a memory like a sieve so am unable to retain facts and figures. I would dearly love to be one of those people who can remember who we played and when and where and who scored and how, but sadly, except for certain events (Kinkladze's goal against Southampton for example, being one of them) this eludes me.

Which brings me to attending my first ever game. Had I known at the time how important it was to remember this, I would've done something to preserve the memory, however all I remember is it was a Derby at Old Trafford and Steve Coppell was playing for them. I only remember that because I was outside waiting for autographs, I asked someone for their autograph, he went to oblige and I realised it was Steve Coppell and I said "oh no, I don't want yours."

So, whilst I know that many people reading this will have been taken to their first game when they were still in single figures by their dad or probably somebody else from the family. I was approaching 18 and was still a Maine Road virgin. So, when I was asked what I wanted for my 18th birthday, I asked for a season ticket for Maine Rd. Unfortunately, again, I can't remember what my first home game was (and I didn't even drink before games then!) but Google is our friend and apparently it was a 0-0 draw against Crystal Palace, that might explain why I don't remember it.

As I didn't know anybody else that went, I used to happily go on my own on the "special" bus, from Salford Precinct. My next away game was the FA cup semi-final at Villa Park. At one point, some lads helped me up onto a wall so I could see, which I regretted when I saw the drop on the other side, then some policeman told me to get down, for which l was actually grateful.

I also went to Wembley for both finals, on my own. Once again I couldn't see much but I was there but at one point something happened, the crowd in front of me surged forward and I could see the whole of Wembley, just as Steve McKenzie struck the ball for that brilliant goal. I can't remember whether I actually saw Ricky Villa dancing round Tommy Caton or whether that's just seared into my memory because it gets shown on TV year after year!

At this juncture, I really don't recall many other girls of my age going to football. Not to say they didn't, but if they did, I didn't come across many on my travels or at least I was not aware of them. So, when I went to games, I would attempt to strike up conversations with lads or blokes. Some of them indulged me, some were patronising, some just ignored me and some were downright hostile! I remember once having the audacity to voice an opinion and this lad said to his mate: "Just ask her how many studs football boots have, that usually shuts them up." Charming!

Then of course there was the attitude that we must only go because we fancy the players or just want to look at their legs, never quite understood the latter. Once some bloke said, with some surprise, that I clearly knew my football because I knew who had been promoted from the (old) second division to the first.

1989 seems to be the point at which blokes actually started taking me seriously as a football fan. I got a seat in the North Stand, so was sitting with the same people each week. I guess attitudes in general towards women had evolved and some of these blokes had daughters who they had brought up as (or tried to, in some cases) City fans.

It was also around this time (so I'm nearly 30 at this point) as I was a late starter actually attending games, that I started attending away games on a regular basis. My first away game (besides the Cup games I mentioned) was a bit of a disaster (I do actually remember this!) I had arranged to go with a mate, another girl, to see Arsenal v City. We were going to get the special from Piccadilly but my mate's train into Piccadilly was late, so she missed it. Of course I didn't know this at the time because we didn't have mobile phones, so I just got on the special, went to the game and we came out in a bright yellow kit and got beat 4-0. Also, the lad I was sitting next to kept "breaking wind", so not a good day. Transpired that as my mate had missed the special, she had got the next London train and she was standing whereas I was sitting, so we went to the game together but never saw each other!

Calling them "specials" was something of an oxymoron though. They were invariably old stock trains with no heating so were usually freezing and using the same toilet as a train full of blokes, especially a train full of blokes who have been drinking, is not recommended. This doesn't even come close though to using the toilet on a coach which is full of blokes. If possible, I try to avoid going to the toilet on a coach, however sometimes needs must. As any female will know, sometimes when you go to the loo, the best option is to "hover" which isn't easy with short legs on a moving coach. Once, the toilet was blocked so was practically full to the brim. As I was desperate I hovered, the driver braked suddenly and I finished up sitting in several blokes DNA...

Also around this time I started seeing someone who was a City fan. Strangely, he didn't go out with me because I was a City fan, it was just a co-incidence. In fact he was very hostile to any of the female species watching football and used to get quite cross if I attempted to discuss the game with him. However, I went to an away game with him and some of his mates and that was it, I was hooked. I enjoyed the games better going with a bit of company. For the record, no I can't remember which game that was either but that was the start of me going to games both home and away on a more regular basis. As a result I met loads of lads who actually didn't seem to have any qualms about me being a girl so from then on I had a load of mates to attend both home and away games with.

Going back to the bloke I was seeing he hated Clive Allen whereas I thought he was brilliant. I think that he probably liked him even less because I liked him! We went to Port Vale away in the cup and, of course, he came on and scored with his first touch. I went ballistic and he just looked really annoyed and said "for f★★★'s sake!" How can anyone be cross that their team has scored? He also got annoyed once watching an England game because I voiced an opinion that Tony Adams was having a good game and he got annoyed because apparently that's what he was thinking. So he wasn't only annoyed if I disagreed with him, he was also annoyed if I agreed with him!

One good thing is, of all the years I've been going to football with all these blokes, they mostly just saw me as one of the lads. I once stayed at someone's flat after an away game. He asked me if I wanted to get in his bed but I wasn't sure whether he meant with him or instead of him, so rather than ask the question, to avoid any embarrassment, I told him I was fine, I'd sleep on the settee. Someone who did make a pass at me was Eddie McGoldrick! He was a guest at the Prestwich Branch. I asked him to sign a shirt (which I was wearing) and he said: "I don't want to press too hard" so I said, joking, "Please do" and he leaned in and said "not in front of the children, come and see me later," at which point I ran off! I am sure he was only joking but I did not ask for another autograph just in case.

A barrier for me to watching football is also my height. I've missed many important moments simply because I couldn't see. I once went to Oldham away, the end was packed and I was right at the back and literally didn't see a single ball kicked, unless it went up in the air. I think that we won 5–2, if memory serves.

I sometimes wonder how we managed to plan away games before mobile phones. We had to ring round everyone's land lines and agree to meet at the train station or the first pub nearest to the station, which mostly worked fine, except for once when I arranged to meet someone at Bradford train station, being unaware that there were two stations in Bradford I was waiting at one station and my mate was at the other.

I once went to an event at work where the manager doing a presentation, said something like, "excuse me ladies, this is an analogy for the gents" and proceeded to talk about football. I made my feelings clear on the feedback form at the end. My friend (another girl and also a football fan, who supported Blackburn Rovers) attended future events and said he didn't use it again.

Obviously I had no issue with the analogy, it was the assumption that we ladies wouldn't understand it and also that the men would. For instance my (male) colleague who was sitting next to me at the time has no interest in football whatsoever and what he knows about the game would probably fit on a postage stamp!

One of the downsides to going to football is the occasional violence. I can never quite comprehend why grown men, some married with children, some with responsible jobs, instigate violence. I was once in a pub in Sheffield (I think it was New Year's Day) when a load of Sheffield fans ran in and started fighting. There were families eating in there. One lad smashed someone over the head with a chair, a woman nearby was hysterical. At Burnley a lad just walked into this pub and punched a lad in the face. What the one who threw the punch didn't know was, he'd just punched another Burnley fan who was talking to us. At Huddersfield away last year, their fans were waiting for City fans to come out of the pubs and make their way to the ground. A City fan (who wasn't young) stood there and said "come on then" and this Huddersfield fan just punched him straight in the face and put the City fan on his arse. Then there are the ones who don't instigate violence but if it starts, don't hesitate to join in. I went to away games with the same lad for a number of years until he got banned for three years for getting into a fight after a pre-season friendly at Doncaster! I used to spend a lot of time and effort trying to keep him out of trouble. We were once in London having played Spurs and someone threw a bottle towards me and it literally touched my hair and smashed on a bus stop in front of me. That was very scary as well as upsetting.

Being a girl occasionally had its advantages. At Rotherham away in the second division, as we got off the train, the police made everyone stand in front of a video camera and give them their name, address and date of birth. They waved two people through. Me and… Nick Leeson. Nick was the original Rogue Trader who brought down Barings Bank in 1995 and he spent four and a half years in a prison in Singapore. Nick has always been a City fan and when he was arrested he was wearing a City shirt at the time.

While in prison Dave Wallace made contact with him and when he was released from prison and back in the United Kingdom he attended a King of the Kippax event that Dave had organised; he soon made friends with loads of the lads from Prestwich and started to attend their meetings and to go to away games with them. Nick used to tell us half the stuff the press wrote about him was in his words " a load of bollocks " Nick is still in demand as an after dinner speaker and has written a few books, the most famous being 'Rogue Trader'.

My first supporters' meeting was at a branch set up by a mate of mine. Quite frankly they were boring so I only went to a few as they were in Winton which was a pain to get to if you didn't drive. Then I joined the Prestwich Branch. The meetings there were always entertaining and I met some great people there. I met Nick a few times there as well as many players, ex-players and managers. I met loads of managers as City used to change them at regular intervals. Kevin Keegan came a few times and he was great to listen to plus he made sure all the kids got as many autographs and photographs as they wanted. I would love to see Pep at a meeting but I doubt that will happen any time soon, having said that he is working wonders with the team at the moment and that is far more important than attending supporters meetings plus I have already met him as I saw him once near his hotel and even though I went all shy and girly I managed a quiet 'hello Pep' and he said hello back. I was buzzing for the rest of the day and could not shut up at work about my encounter with him.

Going to the P&W meetings was great for me as I started meeting loads more females who like me loved City with a passion, plus there was always a good drinking session at the meetings. I don't know how Don and the rest of the committee members managed month after month to get so many great guests to attend plus they ran trips to many away games and organised charity fundraising events, race nights and Christmas parties for the kids. James H. Reeve, who was a local radio presenter, used to come and chair the meetings and was great at interviewing the guests. I still see many of the branch members on my travels and it is great to catch up with them and unlike in the past we never seemed to have much positive to talk about as City were quite poor for a long time, it is a completely different situation nowadays, and some of the football we are now playing is breath-taking.

It's great that attitudes have changed and many women and families go to football, it is pleasing to see so many young girls go now and the club seems to do a lot for children and families unlike when I first started to go. I often wonder if some of the lads who were patronising and hostile to me when I started going went on to have daughters and whether they brought them up to be City fans and took them to games? One thing I would say is that most grounds and football clubs are now geared up and cater for women and children which is very pleasing.

13 - THE FOOTBALL WIDOW

CATH PRICE

I HOPE THE TITLE of this chapter isn't too morbid, but for many years I was the stay at home wife, while my husband (the author of this book) and our sons used to go and watch Manchester City play.

I have always liked football as many years ago as a young girl back in the 70's my dad was a football manager of a few local pub teams and I used to go and watch them play now and again, and what I do remember it was they were usually always on wet and windy mornings, but I think this is when I became a fan. I also loved watching Match of the Day on the black and white TV – in those days the commentator would say "for those of you who don't have a colour TV so and so team is playing in the white shorts and the other team is playing in the dark shorts" or words to that effect. I remember one night watching Match of the Day with my brothers and sisters and my dad said there's something wrong with the new TV he had just bought and whacked it on the side (something we always did to fix the telly back in the day). We were all shouting "leave it Match of the Day is starting", next thing he turned the TV knobs and we had colour! It was amazing! We all screamed and shouted at the telly laughing. It must have been so hard for my mum and dad holding that little secret in all day, we just thought mum and dad had just bought another black and white telly.

Just going off the subject for a minute, while I'm wandering down memory lane, when I was a kid we used to turn the colour button down on the TV by adjusting the colour settings and guessing the colour of the dresses on the show 'Come Dancing'. Coming from a big family we used to end up arguing as to who guessed it right first time – oh well, small things amuse small minds but they are great memories – now back to the football.

When I first met my husband Don in 1977 I knew he was a fanatical football fan and it was after a Manchester City v Bristol City game so he tells me. Funny how he remembers football dates... for our second date he took me to a City Supporters meeting (how romantic!). Our first row was a couple of weeks later when he turned up drunk as a skunk after going to watch City play Nottingham Forest away, well it wasn't much of a row, I left him to it in the pub and I went to another pub with my friends, it's funny how he remembers events around when City were playing. If anyone asks him which year we got married he won't say 1981, instead he'd say "the year City got beat by Spurs at Wembley!"

A few years later our two sons, Steven and Sean, were eager to go to the games with their Dad and Don used to take them to City reserves and junior games, as well as watching the first team. They used to come back talking about the game and how good or bad the players were. I then had to wait for Match of the Day to start before I could watch the highlights. I remember they came home one time and they were buzzing after they had been to Bolton to watch City juniors play Bolton juniors and a young Gary Flitcroft was sat behind them and they got his autograph.

Steven was only about five or six when he went to his first game at Maine Road, Don had got tickets in the North Stand which was right behind the goal and had a great view, I got every detail from them when they arrived home. They arrived at the ground early to soak up the atmosphere, however there was a slight problem as a gentleman and his wife turned up and informed Don that he and Steven were sat in their seats, Don double checked the tickets and they were definitely in the correct seats, however the man produced his season tickets and the club had only gone and resold the man's seats – talk about a cock-up! Well at least some things haven't changed at the club. Anyway, with some fans moving and swapping seats for them they eventually got sorted in their new seats and enjoyed the game and City went on to win.

When the new Platt Lane stand was built a section was

allocated as a family stand and Don got one adult and one junior season ticket and the lads took it in turns to go to the games with him. They used to sit next to Sue Wallace who is the co-editor of the long running Fanzine King of the Kippax and if one of her children could not go to the match Sue used to give Don a ring so both our lads could go, which was very nice of her. So most Saturdays and if there was a midweek game I was left at home to do the housework or ironing while Don and the lads enjoyed themselves at the game and then when they got back they spent ages telling me how good or how crap the game had been, in those days it was often crap but they always seemed to enjoy themselves.

When Don started running the Prestwich and Whitefield (P&W) I used to help out and I got talking to other wives and some also got left behind while their other halves went to the game. Having said that, some were glad to get rid of them for the day, whereas I wanted to go, so one day I thought 'sod this' and told Don I wouldn't mind going to a match with them, Steven and Sean looked at me as if I was an alien asking for mission impossible, it was like "really mum are you sure?" Well, after a bit of persuasion, I went to my first match with them, it was an evening game against Spurs and I claimed I was their lucky charm as City won.

The buzz I got going to my first game was special, just seeing so many people hurrying about to get to their part of the ground, the noise, even the smell of hot dogs and onions and the atmosphere. I made sure Don held on to me for dear life as I didn't have a clue where to go if I got lost plus I kept telling Steven and Sean to stay close to us but all I got from them was that "Yes Mother" look. This was the 90's and more and more women and children were attending games and the grounds were changing to all-seater and the 'facilities' were getting better as people around me said they used to be awful.

One thing I do recall was the attitude of the police towards some of the football fans and their very negative attitude towards the fans. One game we all attended as a family I remember getting in line behind the lads to put them in the turnstiles, this policewoman on a horse was shouting abuse (not instructions) to the fans and she then shouted at the top of her voice to me "Move!" But where could I move to? She only went and rammed the frigging horse into me and nearly sent me flying. I didn't have chance to say anything, she was just barging her way through the fans, that's the first time I thought 'frigging hell them horses are massive' and it made me quite nervous. I was thinking 'was there really any need for that?'

Another occasion as a family we were walking towards Wilmslow Road after a game to get the bus home when we heard loads of shouting. The police were on horses and charging down the road and on the pavements into a load of the City fans, they were running towards us so we had no alternative but to run as fast as we could to get away from the police as they were swinging their batons at anyone who got in the way. It was the first time I had been genuinely frightened at a game. Luckily we got away unharmed but it was a scary moment, Don informed me later that that was the norm in the 70's and 80's (I was glad I didn't go back then).

One great day that stands out for me was when Sean won a competition to be club mascot against Bolton Wanderers and as it happened it was the first game City had won all season. When Sean came out onto the pitch with the music blaring he was holding the then captain's hand, Keith Curle. I was a blubbering wreck, I wanted to shout as loud as I could to the crowd "that's my son out there." Sean then went to have a kick about with the goalie Eike Immel and he managed to chip one over him and scored, all the fans behind the goal was cheering and clapping Sean and shouting to get him into the team and again I was a blubbering wreck.

On another occasion Don wrote to the club as it happened to be Steven's birthday on an evening game when we were playing Ipswich. Don asked if Steven could meet the players and to be honest he didn't really think he would get a reply but he was chuffed to bits as not only did he get a reply but also four tickets to watch the game in the Main Stand but also the four of us were to be allowed to meet the players and to get autographs and photographs of them in the changing room before the game.

Well to say Don, Steven, Sean and myself were chuffed was an understatement and we were really looking forward to it. Sod's law intervened however as I hadn't been feeling too well for a couple of days beforehand and come the night of the game I wasn't well enough to go, so my sister Jackie went in my place. They had the time of their lives and Jackie (who is a red) was nearly converted to being a City fan, oh and she took great enjoyment in telling me they met the players, got autographs and how she had her photograph taken with a couple of semi-naked footballers while they were getting changed but they kept their shorts on! Jackie even had one taken with my favourite player at the time Keith Curle, she took great delight in showing me the photographs once they were developed. 'Pig sick' doesn't even come into it. Jackie was impressed though at how polite and professional the players were. There were also other children and families in the changing room and the players made time for everyone.

At the time going to the game was quite affordable as match tickets were relatively cheap and as a family, besides going to plenty of home games together, we started going to away games, sometimes Don would drive and we would stay overnight in the Premier Inn. Other times we would go on the supporters coach. The first time we went on the supporters' coach it was funny seeing and hearing grown men, women and kids singing City songs. As Steven and Sean were only young I used to say it was only on football days they could sing them as most had swear words.

"Yes, Mother" they would say.

But win, lose or draw we would have a great time and I got to meet other women who were City mad, we got to meet so many characters that it usually made a great weekend. Another great weekend away was at Swindon where Don had managed to get four passes for the players' lounge after the game. We had something to eat and drink and talked with the players and of course got some autographs as well as getting some photos taken with the players. As City were not very good back then it was more of the social element that people enjoyed and I got to meet loads of great people, fans and players.

When Don and I were in London for the Royal Tournament, Lucy (Kit Symons' wife) invited us to her house near Wimbledon for something to eat and drink which we thought was really nice of her.

As a family we went on some pre-season matches and went to Ireland and Scotland. Scotland was great because I have family there and we stayed with them. We also went to Thailand and that was brilliant as we just treated it as a holiday.

We went to Hamburg one year as well but just as we arrived in the big square where all the City fans were meeting we got attacked by a load of local idiots who were throwing bottles and glasses at us, they were not even Hamburg fans. We legged it into a Burger King to get away but a few of them followed us in and shouted abuse and one of them hit Don a couple of times. The lad was off his head on something and it was only about 11am. He must have thought he was really hard attacking a 50 year-old bloke who was with his family. Luckily the manager was a huge bloke and he ushered the idiots outside then ordered a taxi for us so we went back to the hotel to chill out. Although the incident was over very quickly at the time it was quite frightening as you always think what could have happened. Anyway, after a couple of drinks we put the incident behind us and went on to enjoy the weekend.

Helping Don and the others run the P&W branch was a lot of hard work but very enjoyable and at times it was like a madhouse at home with the phone ringing almost 24-7. Many City fans phoning up thought we were part of the club or the ticket office, some of the things they asked me about City and went on about were unreal; why they thought we could sort their problems out was anyone's guess but that's another story. I used to think 'why me?' I remember the first time Don asked me to contact the players and ex-players at City to see if they could attend a meeting, I was a nervous wreck as some of these players and ex-players were Don's heroes, but after a couple of times I realised that all of them were just ordinary people and most were very pleasant and polite. Anyway, after a few phone calls, I became a dab hand at it. I also helped out at family fun days, race nights, children's Christmas parties (we had a blue Santa) and charity fund raising events where I got to meet other female football fans such as Joyce, Debbie D, Lillian, Jackie, Leslie, Lynn, Loz, and Jane R and loads of others. It was great being a City fan even though the football most of the time wasn't the greatest. We had some great social events and I really enjoyed the race nights as it was great fun being a 'dolly dealer. 'How we ever managed to sort the bets out and pay the winners their correct winnings I will never know, as everyone kept buying us drinks...

The stand out game and weekend for me was when City played Gillingham in the play-off final at Wembley in 1999. Obviously tickets were in very high demand and the lads were chuffed to bits when theirs arrived. We went by coach on the Saturday and stayed over in a hotel as the game was on the Sunday, everyone was in good spirits when we arrived at our hotel in Hemel Hempstead. Dave and Sue Wallace plus many other City fans were also staying there. After a few drinks and a good night's sleep and a hearty breakfast it was back on the coach and off to Wembley. Steven and Sean were as excited as me, as it was the first time we had ever been to Wembley. We went into a social club not far from Wembley (I cannot remember the name of it) and we had a good few drinks with the City fans in one room and Gillingham fans in the other; there was plenty of singing going on and good banter between the two sets of fans. City fans were in good voice as we were expecting to win. We soon left the social club to get into Wembley early (even Don did) which was a surprise to his mates because often he gets in football grounds late. We wanted to make the most of our time in the stadium and to soak up the atmosphere and savour the occasion, it had been a long time since City had played there and knowing what they were like, it would be a long time before they played there again.

The noise was electric and it brought a lump to my throat when the players came onto the pitch. The game seemed to go very fast and it soon became obvious that it wasn't a foregone conclusion that City would win. Then the unthinkable happened and City went 1-0 down, things soon went from bad to worse and with not long left on the clock we were 2-0 down. Unbelievably loads of City fans started to leave, I get they were disappointed and they pay their money and can do what they want but it's not every day City get to Wembley and the last thing players want to see is the fans leaving in droves.

Well one thing City have never lost is their fighting spirit and Kevin Horlock got one back seconds before the ninety minutes were up .While Don was disappointed and thought it was too little too late, I was positive we could do it (I felt it in my water as they say). The noise from the City fans was incredible when the fourth official indicated there would be five minutes of extra time. Well the City players seemed to get a new lease of life while the Gillingham players looked to be deflated. Then something remarkable happened, with only about a minute to go Paul Dickov fired in the equaliser. Every City fan in the ground went crazy and those that had left early must have been kicking themselves. It was on to thirty minutes extra time which, to be honest, was a blur and I don't remember much about it. Then it was all down to penalties. It was not a nice way for Gillingham to lose the game but it was very exciting and nail-biting stuff to say the least. We had a couple of scares but went onto win 3-1 on penalties and then the party started with many fans waking up the next morning with sore heads.

I've not been to a game for a long time now and I have become an armchair supporter but I still get excited whenever City are on the TV. I watched the Carabao Cup game against Wolves in October and again I honestly believed when it came to the penalty shoot-out City would win and we did, although the new format of the shoot-out takes some getting used to.

With all the new stadiums that have been built and with the upgrading of existing stadiums I hope the clubs up and down the country keep the ticket prices reasonable so that families can afford to go to the games and share some of the great experiences we had as a family. Ticket prices can be kept down as City have done time and time again as tickets for cup games are great value for money. Away tickets have been capped at £30 each after a campaign by supporters of several different clubs. I only hope that helps families enjoy away games together as well as the home games.

Most season tickets are very good value for money. Don was telling me that City have always had some great deals on season tickets going back to the 70's when he got his first one. It is pleasing in this day and age to see more women and children attending games and that facilities for them have greatly improved. I could mention how bad toilet facilities were back in the day, but Jane and Loz have covered that. God help any women if they have to go to the toilet on an away coach, especially if all the fellas have already been. Urghh… it doesn't bear thinking about!

Women's football has recently been getting loads of great publicity and Manchester City has invested a lot of money into City's female team and I hope they continue to be successful and more fans start going to support them, the future looks bright. To finish, I would just like to say that I hope females and families going to the matches have as great a time as I did when I used to go.

14- MY FIRST MANCHESTER CITY GAME

BY JANE RILEY

M Y FIRST CITY GAME was a night match. I was 14
and my brother agreed to take me to Maine Road
where he'd already had a season ticket for around 5
years. I have a vague memory that we played Liverpool. It was
1981. I've checked since and it was Liverpool in the League Cup.
We lost. Of course we did.

I had no idea then that this was pretty much the default setting
for City in the 80s and 90s. I only recall a feeling of slight fear of
the noise and crowds around the stadium. It was dark and grim
and edgy. I remember the smell of the burger carts and horseshit.
I remember thinking outside the stadium that I slightly regretted
persuading my brother to take me, and my mum to let me go. Then
I walked out onto the top of the Kippax. It was a sight I knew
then I'd never forget; an infinite sea of tightly packed bodies in
the gloom of the stand and the brightness of the illuminated pitch
glowing in the floodlights. It was terrifying but it was tribal and it
was brilliant.

The match itself I recall none of, other than we lost – unluckily
that night as it happens. There was a feeling of c'est la vie amongst
the fans. I asked my brother what happens now. He shrugged, "we
come again next week"

I remember the mocking from schoolmates; "City are shit, what
you watching them for?" Taunts heard by every City fan around
Manchester in those days. It served to make you determined to be
a Blue. This was the opposite effect, no doubt, from that which was
intended. If truth be told I understood little of football in those
days. I was a 14 year old girl in a somewhat rough secondary school
where the easiest way to survive was keep your head down and

hope for the best. Inviting ridicule wasn't my ordinary intention. But my brother was in the same school, he could look after himself, and he was a City fan. That was good enough for me.

I went to a few home games that season. Paying into the stadium felt like the most daring thing I'd done in my life. My brother went in a separate entrance with his paper ticket out of his season ticket book, and I still remember the thrill of bravery I felt, floundering amongst a mass of giant strangers pushing through the turnstiles. Then it was over to the programme seller, followed by a strange tasting burger or pie and to take up our position at the bottom of the stand. I was then (and still am) not fitted in stature to stand anywhere at a match but at the front. Not if I wanted to see it anyway. My brother gave up his favoured position in the middle of the Kippax to accommodate me.

We went to Wembley that season. I wasn't allowed to go, or rather my mum asked me not to go because of the potential for trouble. My brother went on one of the many coaches City laid on. It went from Hollinwood and I remember going to meet him on the Saturday after the first game, with my dad. He was optimistic about the replay. Looking back now, I think the disappointment of that replay and the real pain I could see in my brother, is what led to me drifting away from attending games. I was annoyed at City and there were then other demands on my time. The demands of teenage life.

I met my future husband Sean Riley whilst working in our local pub. Sean and his mates would come in on a match day and I learnt they were all avid match going Blues, home and away. I didn't realise then just how devoted to City Sean was. My love/hate for City was resurrected. I went with Sean to many home and away matches that season – 1985. It was a very different experience for females back then. Stadiums were dilapidated and female toilet facilities it seemed were discretionary. I principally remember the outhouse with no roof at Southend. Outside toilets had largely been eradicated in households by the late 70s. I know my grandparents were compulsorily re-housed due to having no indoor facilities. I believe their former outdoor toilet ended up at Southend.

To be fair, I think we were then, and are now, spoiled by the relative majesty of our own stadium. Very few other grounds in those days could compare to the facilities at Maine Road. It was ahead of its time. I believe the Etihad to be so too. Our new stadium is largely splendid in terms of facilities in most of the stands although the South Stand facilities for non-corporate spectators are inexplicably paltry. If you are not lucky enough to afford tickets to the 93:20 Club, then the sustenance on offer is an overpriced pie and suspect tea.

Alarmingly we also appear to have a growing issue with access to the stadium. Unspeakable queues and issues with under enthusiastic jobsworth stewards- many of whom lack basic common sense. I'd hazard a guess that both standing and swearing have been synonymous with football since the game began. Whilst they are technically now offences, I don't believe either justifies the heavy-handed approach increasingly dished out by stewards at the Etihad to deal with either 'offence'

Nevertheless the stadium is a beacon of magnificence in east Manchester. I hope the club do not lose sight of ordinary fans' value and their contribution to the growth and current prosperity of this club of ours. It's a hackneyed phrase but it remains true. Without the fans this club is nothing.

The grim era of City was so very different from these days of present. We all have the stories of Cardiff away. Charlton at home, Gillingham in the play-off final and the dark times of York and Lincoln.

The journeys, adventures and labours of watching City throughout the 80s and 90s are now being squared in spades. This is our time and long overdue. For my part, compensation came in 2011. My mum had died 4 months previously and we were facing United in the semi-final of the FA Cup. It could have gone so terribly wrong. It could easily have finished me off there and then.

Perhaps moments like that and the inexpressible euphoria of 'Aguero Day' 12 months later, are something fully enjoyed only by coming from the dark times preceding them.

I'll leave the relating of the many episodes of hilarity and

Left: The author as a 15 year-old serving on the HMS Ganges
Right: Don and his beloved wife, Cath
Below: Our granddaugher Ayala, one of the next generation of blues.

Above: Don serving on the HMS Devonshire
Below: An evocative picture of the old Scoreboard End at Maine Road which later became the North Stand.

King of the Kippax editor Dave Wallace (the lad with the bobblehat on) with City fans as they prepare to depart for West Brom in January 1958.

The pubs surrounding Maine Road did a roaring trade on match days. The Clarence was one of the most popular for blues. Sadly, these pubs have all but disappeared since the club moved.

Jane and Sean Riley were delighted to receive a visit from Ilkay Gundogan and Leroy Sane at their home.

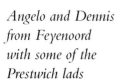

Angelo and Dennis from Feyenoord with some of the Prestwich lads

Mark McCarthy cousin of former City captain Mick and his son Harvey at a City home game last season

The fishing boat hired for the Faroes trip. Sadly the plan had to be abandoned due to rough sea conditions

The club recognised the loyalty of the fans when City were at their lowest ebb in the Third Division.

City fanzine stalwart Phill Gatenby started the Safe Standing campaign after a visit to a Portuguese Second Division game. On returning to England the campaign mushroomed to include supporters of all the big clubs and even reached the desk of the Prime Minister.

*'Gentleman' Joe
Mercer holds aloft
the European Cup
Winners' Cup trophy
following City's 2-1
win in Vienna. A game
attended by Alan from
Winsford who slept in
the ground*

*Dante Friend with former
Piccadilly Radio City commentator
Brian Clarke.*

*The pitch invasion in the wake of Sergio Aguero's injury time winner
against QPR in 2012.*

Battle of the Fanzines: a friendly rivalry that sometimes spilled over into acrimony

Two legendary Blues: Helen the Bell lifting the 1976 League Cup and Pete the Badge at a recent Premier League game.

The huge Blue Print banner that was seen at Maine Road during most home games in the early 90s; contributor Phill Gatenby gets the chance of a lifetime to be Moonchester!

The 1894 group are attempting to bring the atmosphere of Maine Road to the Etihad…

camaraderie to those who can do them better justice. I will say this: Somebody (my dad actually) once said to me, on the subject of following City everywhere, every week, "get a life" but Dad, this is life.

City is life.

15 - FROM A FOREIGN CITY FAN BACK THEN

ERIC JONKER

GETTING MYSELF A CITY-SHIRT

I N TODAY'S WORLD it's actually quite easy to become a City
fan. Wherever you are on this globe, if you have a mobile phone
you can be a Blue within a few minutes – you can get the latest
news by simply pressing a few buttons, watch the highlights (short
or extended version), listen to the manager's pre and post-match
comments, player interviews and all the latest news on every other
department within the club or any other club you are interested
in. Between social media and the internet today's technology is
simply made for football fans. Even watching City play is easy as
there is hardly a place left on earth where there is not a television
with a satellite connection to watch whatever match you want and
Premier League games in particular.

So, let me take you back to the year 1976. Early that year on
28th February 1976 to be precise, City beat Newcastle at Wembley
with the famous Dennis Tueart overhead kick. In June that year, the
Sex Pistols made their debut on stage in Manchester and among
the crowd were the likes of Peter Hook, Bernard Sumner (Joy
Division/New Order) and Steven Morrissey (The Smiths), as well
as the founders of the record label Factory Records. Meanwhile I
was 17 years old, living in The Hague in a small apartment on the
4th floor with no lift. My dad served in the army and my mum
worked in a home for the elderly while my sisters were still living
at home.

I played football at VUC, nicknamed The Penguins due to the
kit of black tops with a bright white vertical strip, black shorts and
black/white horizontal striped socks. Football was not an unusual

choice of sports as both my parents loved to watch it whenever there was a game on telly. They didn't support a specific team, just enjoyed the beautiful game and supported the Dutch national team or any Dutch team that played in Europe. I can't remember supporting any team myself to be honest. I loved watching Johan Cruyff so I watched a lot of Ajax and it is hardly a surprise I still rate my late countryman as the best all-round player of all time. Pep Guardiola will agree.

I was very interested in foreign leagues and England in particular. The FA Cup final was shown live on Dutch television and these games impressed me. I remember keeping up with the scores and tables I got from football magazines or the daily paper that printed results and tables. I knew foreign clubs by name, where they were from, the stadium, what their kit looked like and most of the players.

In those days, 1976, owning a football shirt from a foreign club was special, from an English club it was even more special. The Admiral ones were popular. I think West Ham and Manchester United seemed to be the main ones seen around. You could actually buy the West Ham ones in a specialized football store. I was keen to try and get an Umbro one. Why? Because I like to do things differently, I guess. As shops didn't sell Umbro I decided to look up the addresses of the English clubs that played in Umbro kit, City being one of them. I wrote a letter to these clubs stating I was interested in trying to buy myself an Umbro shirt of an English club and asked if they could explain to me the best way to get one. In those days English was taught at Dutch schools from the age of 12 and although I wasn't really a great student, English never seemed to be a problem. Anyway, I sent off my letters and waited.

After a few weeks, City were the first to react. I remember a brown envelope with weird foreign stamps in the corner and airmail sticker! On the back it read Manchester City Football Club. I quickly emptied the post box when I got sight of the envelope, ran up the 4 floors to our apartment, and ripped open the envelope. As the package felt soft I even imagined City had sent me a football shirt straight away. I was quite naive.

Within was a letter, in English obviously. And yes, there was more. Not a football shirt, but a silk white scarf with sky blue prints saying Manchester City F.C. with the round badge similar to the one we have it these days and Junior Blues on it. The envelope also contained a single badge that you could sew onto clothing. I was thrilled and even now I don't really know why I got that excited, just that I remember I did. The letter was from Lorraine Firth who in those days ran the Junior Blues Club. Even if I was a year too old to join, she had made an exception for me being foreign. I didn't save the letter and I still pity that. I read the letter numerous times, and I clearly remember the club was pleased and honoured that someone from abroad took an interest and advised how I could become a Junior Blue. Finally there was a list that showed the prices of merchandise. Not a giant one in those days.

A few weeks later I got a letter from Bristol City, in those days playing in the old First Division – and that was it! Other clubs either didn't bother to reply or never received my letter. By then I was already following the City results in the paper, it was the season when City did really well finishing runners-up to Liverpool in the league.

However I still didn't own a football shirt and that was still very much on my mind, and I had already decided that I wanted one from City. I ordered one by post and was eagerly waiting for it to arrive but I had to be patient. Where can get one within a week nowadays? Even from outside the UK, in those days it took weeks. Whenever I did training at my football club, I sort of envied other guys wearing the top of an English club team.

One of my team mates actually was a United fan with a United top. He was English and from Flixton in Manchester. Two other teammates of mine asked him to get them the shirt and he took care of that through his family. They knew City had contacted me and it brought some kind of friendly rivalry amongst us. City lost to United twice in the '76-77-season. One of my teammates actually travelled to see the derby at Old Trafford. Despite the banter not being too serious, I didn't like it, I didn't like United and I didn't like their top. I met the guys who owned the United shirts about thirty-two years later at a football reunion. They had never been back to England or Old Trafford and stopped supporting United a long, long time ago. Typical I would say. They were stunned to find out I was still very much a City fan and what it had actually brought to me in my life.

Finally my City-top arrived, again in a typical brown envelope with an airmail sticker. I carefully unwrapped it, put it on and I immediately fell in love with it. The Umbro stripes on the sleeves were fantastic, I loved the badge and the shirt fitted perfectly. I remember the faces of my teammates when I entered the dressing room and put on my City top for training. It was a classic and very much worth the wait. I'd like to think I was the only person in The Netherlands who owned the Umbro shirt of Manchester City F.C.

During the spring of 1977, I received another letter from City, saying they were doing a pre-season tour in the Netherlands, visiting Arnhem and Zwolle. I had no hesitation visiting those matches. On the day they played Vitesse, my dad drove me to Arnhem. He had planned a work trip nearby, so it should've been a comfortable trip. It wasn't really. My dad simply couldn't understand why I wanted to attend the game. City were a foreign club and other than a couple of letters, the silk scarf and a City shirt, he felt it was a waste of time. And he was probably a bit worried as hooliganism was quite common in those days. Anyway, I was happy he dropped me off and I could go my own way. As it was way too early for kick-off I simply wandered through the city centre, not particularly looking for a pub or a pint, but hopeful to run into a few Blues.

I passed a pub with City fans in without me noticing. One of them stepped outside, yelling 'Hey you! Blue!' I waved, hesitated a few seconds but decided I might as well say hello. The guy was Alan Edwards from Denton. We are still very much friends and I like to think that is for life. We often make fun about this incident as neither of us expected what kind of friendship would arise. It was a moment when there was no particular reason for him to step outside as I passed by.

I was quickly introduced to another City fan inside that pub called Alan Potter. He is probably one of the most famous names amongst City fans and especially the Norwegian branch. For the ones who know Alan there is no need to describe this big man with a great sense of humour.

The City fans were very curious about me. I suspect that in those days a City fan being foreign, as opposed to being born and raised in another country, was quite rare. However there was already the Scandinavian support in those days. I had no problem joining in. I was actually surprised as nearly everyone was wearing a different City top, either a t-shirt, a top from another year or an away top from former years. They all looked great to me. And despite wearing my fancy silky Junior Blue scarf, I didn't hesitate to accept one of the knitted scarves I was offered as well as the beers that the City fans seemed to enjoy.

I can't remember a lot from the game other than it being a typical pre-season friendly. It was impressive to see the players on the pitch from such a short distance. I enjoyed their reaction to the fans when they sang. I quickly learned a few lyrics from City songs to join in the singing although it was sometimes hard to understand that Manc accent.

A few days later City travelled to Zwolle to play PEC Zwolle and I met up with the guys I met before in Arnhem. Obviously there were no mobile telephones but we could do without them in those days and still tracked each other down somehow.

We got in the stadium early. Players from both teams were kicking footballs in the stand. Again there was this relaxed pre-season atmosphere. However I did notice some Zwolle fans were kind of provoking City fans without the City fans actually reacting because whatever what was said to them was in Dutch! I simply didn't bother to translate. It was weird and I couldn't really understand why they did that, other than they must have thought wherever English fans were travelling in those days, they were automatically looking for trouble and therefore aimed to be provoked.

At half time me and a few City fans started to play a bit of football in front of them on the pitch using one of the footballs that had been kicked into the stands before the match. Soon someone did a Tommy Booth and hoofed the ball over the fence into the stand where the Zwolle fans were standing. City fans who joined in the play asked for the ball back, without any response. I walked up to the fence and politely asked in Dutch if they could return the ball. That hardly helped. I explained in Dutch that as the ball was kicked by a City player, it obviously meant a big deal for the one who caught and owned it. Again it didn't work. What happened next was that when they noticed I was Dutch and they started to provoke me. The denigrating remarks from my part, and by that point actively translating what was said in Dutch to the City fans around me who joined the debate, didn't ease the atmosphere and I got on the nerves of a few of their fans.

In those days, and especially at a pre-season game, there were hardly any stewards and it was easy to step from one stand to another which is what these fans did after the final whistle. They were somehow offended by me, calling me a traitor for supporting a foreign team and when they finally stood right in front of me in the away end, my mate stood up and told them to shut up and f**k off. The next moment he was sat back in his chair bleeding after he was hit on the nose. All of a sudden a few fights broke out. I was absolutely stunned about what had happened from simply asking for a football back that had landed in the opposite stand by accident. Police soon settled matters and I was questioned for a few seconds. In the end we didn't get the ball back.

From then on I regularly corresponded with both Alan Edwards and Alan Potter, who took turns to write to me, one reacting immediately, the other one testing my patience. They would inform me about the games they visited and send me programmes or City stuff. It was just great receiving a letter from them or the club once every few weeks. Reading the programmes gave me a lot of information about the club and players you couldn't get otherwise back then.

Up until the summer of 1977 I can't say in all honesty that I felt like a true Blue. It was hard to get a connection like you can today, although today's social media more easily accommodates the glory-hunting fan rather than the one who actually cares for the club. Despite being formally a Junior Blue, wearing a City top when training and now specifically watching the City results and their position in the table, there was something missing. The pre-season games and meeting up with City fans in the Netherlands changed a lot obviously but my interest in the club could have easily waned.

One of many tips I got from the City fans was the live match commentary on Saturday afternoon on BBC Radio 2. You could also get the latest football flashes a few minutes before the daily news in the afternoons during the week. There was hardly any news about City but I still listened whenever I was home. If I wasn't playing football myself on Saturday afternoon, I was stuck to the radio trying to pick up the second half commentary. The sound was horrific and faded regularly but it didn't stop me from listening for at least three hours to what was happening around the grounds. The one thing that got through in clear sound was the reading of the final scores just after 5pm (that's 6pm in the Netherlands). I quickly recognized if City had either won, drawn or lost by the way the final results were read, the announcer would change his voice from high to low for a home win, building it up and down for a draw and start low and get higher for an away win.

Every time the commentary switched to the ground where City were playing or when the final results came through without me knowing this result, my heartbeat rose. As for second half commentary, we weren't on much but I do remember we were on when we played United and Liverpool in the 1977-78 season, when we won both home games 3-1. I recorded the commentary of the second half on my cassette recorder. I think I must have played the cassette numerous times as I could practically recite the exact words after a while. I loved the English commentary, the way they described what was happening on the pitch, and sometimes you could hear the City fans singing.

The goals from the Liverpool game were shown on a Dutch football programme. In those days we couldn't get English television at my house, although I knew about Match Of The Day and I knew with the right cable connection one was able to get English television. Soon after my parents decided to get the package that included BBC television, watching Match Of The Day and Jimmy Hill soon became a weekly highlight.

So after nearly a year since City replied to my first letter, we were able to get English television and I had seen the Blues live twice in a pre-season friendly, had a City shirt, owned a knitted scarf and a silk scarf, listened to the radio, and saw the goals being scored against United and Liverpool in a 3-1 win - Mick Channon doing his windmill. It's hard to imagine the impact of this nowadays.

MY FIRST VISIT TO MANCHESTER

Eventually, Alan Edwards invited me to come over to England. I chose to visit during the Christmas fixtures. It was school holidays and I was able to see two matches within the space of three days. Not that the goings-on at school had my attention, it was all about preparing to go to England. Living close to the Hook of Holland, the ferry to Harwich was the obvious choice, then by train from Harwich to Manchester. In those days there was a direct connection from Harwich to Manchester albeit the train would stop at practically every station it passed. It took about eight hours but I never had to get out or change trains. I could simply sit back, relax and enjoy the food I brought with me, and I read a few programmes that were sent to me. I had already read them but it was still good to do it again… and again.

As romantic as the journey by train might sound, my first trip to England was far from that. On December 24th at 22.00 the ferry left Hook of Holland in quite stormy conditions. I'd never been on a ferry. In those days you could either spend the night in the public rooms or book yourself a cabin. I booked myself a cabin as I didn't know what to expect in the public rooms. Just playing safe, I guess. The plan was to check in my cabin, have a few beers at the bar and then on to bed.

As soon as I had finished my first beer, it must've been the first pint come to think of it, the ferry hit open sea. I'd had a full meal at home before my dad dropped me off at the ferry station. Within seconds I felt sick. I tried to stay in the bar but I knew this wasn't going to last long. I walked (more or less wobbled) back to my cabin, unfortunately unable to reach it. The first toilet I passed was mine and I started to throw up straight away. So much for the beer and the meal my mum had made.

The sick feeling didn't wane, nor did the throwing up for that matter, so I simply stuck to the toilet. And that's where I stayed up until the moment the ferry sailed in to the River Stour and the tide was calmer. That was about seven hours after we had set off. I went to my cabin, freshened up a bit, and waited for the announcement to leave the ship. As soon as I left the toilet where I had spent the whole night, I witnessed the public rooms full of sick people that had obviously missed out on a toilet. The smell was like any of the toilet rooms used at Old Trafford, despite it being one of a very few stadiums in England I haven't visited (and I doubt I will ever to be honest).

Anyway, I was happy to step off the ferry and walk up to the train station only to find out there weren't any trains. They never run on Christmas Day apparently, although nowadays you can get a few, although they are very limited. I tried to contact one of the stewards to find out what options I had, when a big fat copper tapped me on the shoulder and told me to keep moving to the bus platform as I was obstructing the people going there. The helmet impressed.

I stepped onto one of the coaches that drove us up to London. I'd guess 95% of the people were going there anyway. We were dropped off at Liverpool Street Station. OK, London was the capital, I had read many things about it, I knew loads of football clubs were based in London but I was far from interested in any of those things at that particular moment. I asked around what to do when the only option appeared to be taking a taxi to Manchester. I walked up to the nearest taxi platform but none of the taxi drivers were interested in taking me and that was even before I asked how much it would cost me. They either knew I couldn't afford it or simply weren't interested in giving up a full day driving. Fair enough.

I ended up in some kind of taxi garage. As I walked up to the desk there were three guys about my age who appeared to have the same problem. They needed to go to Liverpool. I told them I had to go to Manchester. They were happy to add another one to the party to keep the price within reason. Then this man turned up and seemed interested in taking us all the way. We agreed on the price, I think it was about 50 pounds each and before I knew it we were on our way.

I remember it being an old uncomfortable vehicle, with me sitting on the back seat with two Scousers (that's the word you use when you are talking about people from Liverpool, I was educated by my Manchester mates). The third, the fattest and ugliest one, was sat in front next to the driver. It was far from comfortable but I was relieved I would end up where I wanted to be. I couldn't understand this weird accent that didn't sound like English to me. I still wasn't feeling well, although I slowly got hungry. The drive up north took ages. Nobody was interested in football. I'm not even sure what we talked about, if we talked at all.

The driver was a nice bloke and he made sure he dropped me off at Piccadilly Station as that is where I would arrive by train in normal circumstances. The streets were deserted, so it didn't waste too much time for the others. It was Manchester before Liverpool for drop offs, just the way it should be.

So there I was, standing in front of Piccadilly Station on Christmas day, late afternoon, and not a clue where to go other than that I agreed to ring Alan as soon as I had arrived at Piccadilly Station – if only I'd had a mobile in those days.

I walked up to Piccadilly Gardens to one of the famous red phone boxes. The phone didn't work. On to the next one. Damaged. Welcome to Manchester. The third one did work and I was happy to have a few coins in my wallet to be able to use the phone. There was not a soul on the streets that might be able to change money if I had to.

I rang Alan. He told me he and his dad would drive straight down to pick me up. Great. I didn't realize it was still some way down from Denton to the city centre. I was starving and it was getting dark. I didn't feel that comfy after what I'd been through in the last twenty-four hours, being on my own in the middle of a deserted city centre in Manchester.

In the end I had nothing to worry about. I soon found myself sitting at a dinner table accompanied by Alan and his parents, enjoying one of the best Christmas dinners ever. They'd already had theirs. I was so hungry I simply ate whatever Mrs Edwards put in front of me. She simply stuffed me. And all these stories I got from others that the English food was horrible? Rubbish. It wasn't. Well, not what had been served by her that night.

Later Alan's parents went out and Alan Potter came over to say hello. I was to drink my first Guinness. Let me say that I had to get used to that kind of beer. I drank a few and a few more, talking City kept me going, obviously unable to keep up with the tempo these guys were drinking from their cans. The talk was mainly about Colin Bell's upcoming return from injury. And to finish the night, I started to feel sick. Again. Too much food, too much Guinness...

The toilet was upstairs. I nearly made it. It was some introduction to the people who invited me over.

I was soon introduced to the pre-match warm up. After breakfast and a coffee (might have been tea) we soon headed for the pub where we had a few drinks before we would drive up to the stadium. We headed for The Windmill down at Hulme Road. I was introduced to several City fans and friends, with everybody taking an interest in me for being foreign. They were impressed the way I spoke English and even more impressed when I did a few words in German and French. I skipped the Guinness and went for the lager. Pints were reduced to halves and by recommendation by one of the ladies in there, I had the lager with lime. It was hardly a drink that impressed the males, but whatever. I enjoyed that drink!

I couldn't wait to get to the game. My ticket was in the Kippax. City were playing Newcastle and results hadn't be overly good in the past few weeks. We discussed the possible line-up and again the main talk was about Colin Bell. Many told me why he was such a great player for City, how he got injured, and how great it was if only he could play that day. The atmosphere in the pub was fantastic.

It was already darkening when we drove up to Maine Road. Soon you could see the lights and we were dropped off about ten minutes' walk from the stadium. I remember the old neighbourhood, the typical Manchester houses in lines as seen in Coronation Street, all these City fans walking up to the stadium, coming from all directions and wearing their scarves. It made me feel like there was no way City could lose that game.

And there it was - Maine Road in all its glory. Like an old fort, happily taking in another full house as she had done for decades. This was exactly how I'd imagined an English football stadium should look like. I got myself through the small corridors, wondering how people bigger than me could manage. No security checks in those days unless there was a definite reason to do so.

I walked up the stairs and there I was - standing on the Kippax. The roof hanging over the Kippax was huge, darkening what was underneath it. A packed crowd stood beneath it, most holding drinks and smoking cigarettes. I'm not a very tall person to say the least, so it was hard for me to see the players warming up. I read through the programme to discover the line-up and what was said about the players taking the field. I realized I was actually a few moments away from watching my first City league match, only a few months after I met City fans in Arnhem.

Only a few months ago before writing these memories, Peter Dootson, dad of Lewis Dootson who runs the Dutch branch, asked me about the first match I visited and if I bought myself a programme. I did, but I didn't save it for whatever reason. It turned out he collected match day programmes. He was happy to give me the programme of that game, City versus Newcastle played on 26th December 1977. It was not hard to imagine I was thrilled with that gift. And going through the programme I remembered a lot of what was in it.

The programme had the usual starting 11 in those days: Corrigan, Clements, Booth, Watson (captain), Donachie, Power, Owen, Hartford, and up front Tueart, Kidd and Channon. City wore sky blue shirts, shorts and stockings with white diamond trim. Newcastle were playing in black shirts with white vertical stripes, arms white with black motifs down the seams, black shorts with white motifs down the seams, white stockings with two black hoops on the turnover.

How about that! And obviously the token was taken out of the programme which I now carefully keep.

Again in the stand it was all about the substitute – that was Colin Bell. I think for most fans it was more about Bell coming on rather than the result in the end.

When the first song came up I was impressed by the noise from the Kippax. But the sound wasn't nearly as loud as the one when the players ran out on to the pitch. Colin Bell was the substitute.

The first half ended in 0-0 and due to my height and the packed crowd, I could hardly see any action. Then again I was more occupied by the Kippax, the City fans, the songs, the moaning (yes, even back then) yet still applauding nearly every move by a City player right or wrong. It was simply a great experience and it was only half time.

At half time the rumour was Colin Bell would come on. And the more it seemed a reality, the louder the noise in the crowd became. It was like everybody was building up the noise for the moment he would actually enter the fray.

It was much louder than expected. The roar that came out of the Kippax and probably all of Maine Road when indeed Colin Bell came on as a second half substitute never has been overtaken in all my visits to Maine Road or any football stadium for that matter. Now maybe when Aguero scored that famous title winning goal might have surpassed it, from where I was in the Kippax I doubt it. Or maybe the Kippax roof was echoing the sound to make it even more spectacular. People were hugging and crying even before the second half got under way. When Bell touched the ball for the first time the sound was like we'd scored. And we soon did. It was game over for Newcastle. A Tueart hat-trick with Kidd scoring the fourth made the return of The King as memorable as a football match can ever be. In all the years I have seen City play, looking back at it I think there has never been a more dramatic moment at Maine Road. Although, in all honesty, I must admit I had never seen Bell play before that day and I didn't have the same emotions about the player. But it was impossible not to understand the emotions every City fan was going through when he came on.

After the match I tried to stay in the Kippax for as long as possible. Hardly realizing at that particular moment what an important piece of the club's history I had witnessed these last few hours. As we passed a chippy I was introduced to the famous fish and chips. I was handed over in a piece of paper with the fat combining with the ink and dripping down… English food was horrible.

We ended up in great spirits at The Windmill again to discuss what had just happened. Giving marks to the players, discussing their performances and so on. It was simply great to be a part of that and it made me forget all about the previous day. And everybody made me part of it, thankfully we were able to communicate by language and the fact that I was somehow special for supporting City as a foreigner, coming all the way over from The Netherlands to watch them play, with everybody telling me I was lucky to have witnessed the Return of The King.

The thing I can't remember is if we got home in time to watch Match Of The Day that night, if the City match was on (must've been) or that we just stayed up for no reason other than looking back at what was simply an unforgettable day.

In hindsight I think this day definitely made me the City fan I am nowadays. A fan that is passionate not just about the club, but the fans too.

Two days later we travelled to Ayresome Park, Middlesbrough. Colin Bell started from the off. And so did Peter Barnes, my favourite City player in those days. We won 2-0. Late in the game all of a sudden, Middlesbrough fans got into our stand and started fighting City fans. Before I could even intervene, and I'm not sure if I was going to, police came in and drove their fans out of the stand. It must've been a two minute riot at most. Other than that incident, it was a great trip with loads of cans in the car, to what in those days was and surely many decades after has to be one of the shittiest places I have ever been (excuse the language, but it's the most fitting word to describe Middlesbrough and their stadium in those days).

The next day I travelled back home by plane. My parents agreed to the extra cost. I can't remember much of that so it must've been a smooth one I guess. It was some experience and even now I love talking and writing about it.

THE PINK FINAL AND ALL THE WAY TO WEMBLEY

Since that couple of games in 1977 I came over whenever I had saved enough money, with the Edwards' agreeing for me to stay over. That never seemed to be a problem and with Mrs Edwards spoiling me and serving me her homemade cherry-chocolate cake, I simply couldn't imagine there was a better place to stay.

I also joined in for the following pre-season tours in the Netherlands (again) and Belgium. The one I remember best is a tournament in Edinburgh where City played Hearts and Hibs – a bit different to the pre-seasons of today in other parts of the world, but you can't stop the world from changing. There I met loads of City fans all eager to know more about me being a foreigner supporting City. It was easy to meet up with the players and manager before and after a match. And when it was hard, I used my 'being a City fan from The Netherlands' patter to get my way and it often worked.

Normal matters resumed at home. Writing letters to my mates and the club, listening to the radio and watching Match Of The Day on Saturdays. There was one change though. I subscribed to the Pink Final. Every week it was delivered on either Wednesday or Thursday. It overtook Match Of The Day as the highlight of my week. Every Wednesday I cycled as quickly as possible to my house and checked the post box, only to find out if the next edition either was or wasn't there. If it wasn't I was always disappointed but happy to know it would arrive the next day. And it would make me ride home as fast as possible again the very next day.

I enjoyed reading the Pink Final. Always skipping the United part or whatever there was written about that club. But reading the City match reports, anything else that had happened that week, and I also started to take a firm interest in following the results of the other clubs in Greater Manchester, as I still do.

Many would agree with me today that information about the club is by far easier to get through the internet but I still pity the day the Pink Final delivered its final edition. Living abroad and not able to visit all the matches, the Pink Final somehow gave you the idea you had actually been at the game. The habit of grabbing the latest edition from out of my post box every week and the warm feeling you got when reading the match report will never be beaten by the reports on the website of the M.E.N. Those reports are cut, to get more 'clicks' via the website. But it has definitely lost the romance and deep match analysis of what was printed in the Pink Final up until the last few seconds of the game that was printed on the back page. Things change, some for the good, some for the bad. This one belongs to the latter.

In 1981 I got a ticket for the FA Cup semi-final versus Ipswich Town at Villa Park. In those days I was a member of the Denton branch run by Alan Potter. In the 1980-81 season Malcolm Allison had been sacked and whereas many raised a few eyebrows for the money spent on young kids, Allison was and always has been ahead of his time and that often worked against him. He had already recognised the talent of kids like Tommy Caton and Steve Mackenzie that many of us failed to see. Despite the look of the team, it didn't work out, mores the pity for a man who had meant so much to City in the past.

John Bond took over and brought experience that made the team play well again and made the talents of the younger players' blossom. It was the year when a fantastic and very interesting documentary about City and the 1980-1981 season was released, named 'Manchester City - A Club in Crisis!' It was broadcasted on Belgium TV, with Dutch commentary from the legendary Belgian football commentator Rick de Saedeleer. By that time my parents had got themselves a video recorder so I could tape the documentary and watch it over and over again.

I finished school, was working and got my driving license. Soon I got myself a second hand Citroën 2CV, unfortunately painted red. I soon covered the car with City-stickers. It wasn't fast, didn't drive very well, broke down a lot of times, cost a fortune and looked anything but a sports car. Pretty much a description of any United team for that matter but it enabled me to drive rather than rely on public transport. A smooth trip overseas was enjoyed by ferry and then the long drive to Manchester, avoiding the main roads. The weather was fabulous and I soon found myself having a full English breakfast in a double decker bus that had been rebuilt into a restaurant. Driving on the other side of the road wasn't a problem. Sitting on the opposite side in the car when stuck behind a slow vehicle was. As I was unable to see if there was any traffic coming up from the opposite direction. So I had to be very patient again and wait for the other vehicle to change direction to see where I was going. As for finding my way? Again there were no mobile phones in those days. Just a map and road signs rather than a navigation system telling you where to go.

On semi-final day I was part of a group of coaches full of City fans driving down the M6. There was a lot of drinking on the bus and soon the song broke out that we needed a wee. Apparently the Bus drivers had picked out one wee-stop, as I witnessed about one hundred men standing next to each other pissing down the hedge of the car park, with another few hundred waiting. Never mind where the ladies were.

I'd never been to Villa Park and to be honest I was impressed by it. Villa and Ipswich were top sides in those days with Ipswich having two Dutch players in their ranks, Arnold Mühren and Franz Thijssen. The atmosphere was great in an amazingly packed end where all the City fans were standing. I think the match itself wasn't too exciting but the tension was certainly there and all that the City fans wanted was that trip to Wembley.

I missed the decisive goal by Paul Power in extra time from a free kick. I knew we got ourselves a free kick but was unable to see him taking it, let alone the ball hitting the back of the net. Our end erupted and I was lifted and dragged down a few stairs to land on my feet again. I had to work my way up again to where I'd been standing a few seconds before, with every City fan celebrating and hugging me. I had already caught a bit of a cold on the day and due to all the singing, I completely lost my voice much to the relief of those travelling with me.

The Edwards' agreed that I could stay at their house until the FA Cup final on condition I make myself useful. Of course I would. I rang work to take up whatever days off were left that year, rang my parents to say it would be a while before I returned home and booked my trip home the day after Wembley, meaning I would drive up to London and straight on to Harwich the day after the match to get the ferry home again.

Obviously everybody had to work during the week and I made myself useful as promised. So as soon as I got out of bed, I made my own breakfast if Mrs Edwards was out working. If she was at home, breakfast was served the way I wanted it. She was such a lovely lady and looked after me as well as possible even though I was twenty. Most of the time I either drove to the city centre, to the Peak District, or to Maine Road. Even if there was nobody there I loved to just walk around the ground and through the empty stands. The groundsman was always willing to let me in because… yes, I was a foreigner. Or I just went to the souvenir shop across the road and talked to the couple that owned it (not sure if they did actually) or have a coffee.

Quaffers night club was a well-known place to go out to at night, a typical 80's disco. Being foreign didn't harm me getting the attention from the ladies. I also went away with a girl I knew for a while and she was another one on the list of City fans that I wrote letters to in those days. She lived with her brother in New Mills in quite poor conditions. So she was happy to go out for a few days to family in Derby and a B&B in Blackpool. With her sitting next to me in the car it was easier to overtake slow vehicles. Although I enjoyed her company and the days out, I was happy when I got back home at the Edwards' and looked forward to whenever City had to play. This included trips to Wolves (an easy 3-1 win, and Wolverhampton hardly making an impression as a city to go back to) and Ipswich (weather conditions had turned to winter, and we sang Wembley songs for 90 minutes despite losing 0-1) with home games against Everton and Crystal Palace to finish off the season and prepare for the FA Cup Final.

I had to wait until the last few days to find out if I'd got a ticket. Even Alan Potter and his network tried but it seemed every Blue from wherever wanted to go, and rightly so. There was an evening event just a few days before the FA Cup Final at the supporters lounge at Maine Road, but I can't recall what it was about. Just that I got tickets to visit and ran in to Steve Mackenzie who was eager to have his picture taken with me, when I soon found out he was totally wasted. It was a great night with many players around, and it was then when I was told a ticket for the Cup final was arranged for me. I was just thrilled.

The day before the Final, the coaches drove down to London. I followed in my red car.

Despite the City stickers on it, I got a lot of banter from the City fans about it and rightly so. Just before we entered London someone who knew the roads came to sit next to me to guide me to the hotel just in case I wasn't able to follow the coaches. Well, I lost them and the guy next to me hadn't a clue where we were. We just drove around when all of a sudden we saw the coaches again. Just that they were on the other side of the road and coming up towards us. Even though we weren't allowed to do a U-turn as the road was divided by a verge, I simply stopped the car, took a turn, drove over the verge and put my car in front of the traffic to end up just behind the coaches again, causing a traffic jam on both sides and pissing off quite a few Londoners. This was much to the liking of the City fans in the coaches. The guy next to me panicked when I told him "Hey I'm Dutch. So what do I know?"

I don't need to go over my first Wembley experience and the final result as about everyone was there. I like to think by that time I was as much a Blue as every other City fan in there. I didn't really want to say goodbye after spending time in England for over four weeks, but there was little choice left. I soon drove to Harwich and home.

When I got home, the next day I went to see the travel agency to book a return flight to London (there was really no other way in those days) for the replay. This time a match ticket was easier to get as unfortunately many City fans couldn't afford to travel back to Wembley for a second time in a few days. The atmosphere was fantastic again, maybe different to the first game. Even now I don't understand why Steve Mackenzie's goal has not been deemed the best ever scored at Wembley.

Back home I needed a few days to get rid of my half English-half Manc accent and started to speak Dutch again. By then it got through to my dad that City wasn't just a one day love affair. He didn't agree, but he understood. I was totally broke and had to start to repay my debts to my parents.

The extended stay was one of the best ever periods in my life. If I wasn't a Blue when I arrived, I have certainly felt like one ever since. Being a City fan has brought to me so many fantastic memories I could easily write an entire book about it. I am so lucky that one of many letters was answered by City and that Alan Edwards took the trouble to walk out of that door in the pub in Arnhem to get my attention. I have met so many interesting people, it has taken me to several interesting places (no, not Middlesbrough or Wolverhampton) and as of today it's an ongoing love affair.

It took a while before my next visit to England as I bumped into a girl who now happens to be my wife and started building a career and building a life with her. Happily she's a footie fan and she loves City. Up until the internet it was still hard to get news about City. Now I try to catch up by watching a game live as much as possible, and watch every game on telly in a pub in The Hague where we have formed quite a strong following over the years of diverse nationalities that makes it probably the most interesting group of people ever with the one thing in common: Manchester City Football Club.

I met ex-Republic of Ireland manager and former City captain Mick McCarthy quite a few times when I was Chairman of the Prestwich and Whitefield Manchester City Supporters Club. Mick was great in supporting our charity events and often sent me signed shirts that we could auction off. I always found him to be a down to earth bloke who came across as one of the lads. He used to come out with some cracking stories and nothing seemed too much trouble for him. Mick comes from a big family so let's see what his cousin Mark has to say...

16 - WHY I BECAME A BLUE

BY MARK MCCARTHY

A SUNDAY VISIT TO MY grandad's house in Aylesbury, which was a twenty-five minute drive from our home in Milton Keynes, was something I always looked forward to. Grandad Danny would always have a story to tell but this particular afternoon in 1983, he proceeded to tell me about my cousin Mick McCarthy who had recently signed for Manchester City. This kicked off a fixation for City which is still going as strong as ever some thirty-five years later. After producing a pile of City match programmes that Mick had sent, most signed by the entire first team, I was hooked. I'd never really been into football before and certainly had never supported a team but I now had a real focus in life… CITY. I truly believe that you don't choose City as they are either chosen for you or City chose you.

Growing up in the South during the 80's and with City not setting the football world alight, gathering information on the Blues was a difficult task until I discovered City Club Call, 'Keep up to date with the Blues' the headline read and the 0898 12 11 91 will be forever etched in my memory, I would call this at all hours looking for information and all through the summer desperate to know how we got on some pre-season tour of Norway. It would take at least 5 minutes before any information was actually given and I was brought crashing back down to earth when returning from school one afternoon to discover my parents had sold both the TV and video player from my bedroom to pay for the mammoth phone bill I'd rung up calling 'City Bloody Club Call'!

I got my first chance to see City live in November 1985 as we were due at Luton Town, which was only about half an hour from our home. Manchester to me in those days was just a place I could dream of going to, and Maine Road seemed a world away. After badgering my dad for many months before to take me and with no chance of a fixture change in those days, he finally relented. My Mum kitted me out from head to toe in blue and white City stuff and I couldn't be prouder on my way to watch the Blues. The walk to the ground felt amazing and we entered the first turnstile we saw. After a few minutes and constant dirty looks we could feel something wasn't right as the crowd around us seemed to be moving further away and we appeared to be on show. As the chants of 'City....City' went up from the opposite end of the ground it dawned on us that we were in the wrong end of the ground and needed to move quickly. This was 1985 and it was certainly an experience for a ten year old! The stewards promptly threw us out and my Dad was seething as we headed back to the van to go home, I was distraught but he finally saw sense and we headed back to the ground where he had to pay again at the right turnstile and again I was hooked. The atmosphere in that tiny away end was electric and I couldn't help but watch the many characters I was surrounded by, everyone seemed to know each other and I wanted some of it. For the record we lost 2-1 - typical City!

Once I was old enough I would travel from Milton Keynes on my own to watch City as soon as I'd saved enough money for the train which would take about four hours in those days and I simply couldn't wait to get to Maine Road. I'd jump on the P11 bus from Piccadilly and the buzz of excitement running to the ground I can still feel it today, as soon as the Kippax opened its doors, I'd be in and belting up the steps. This idea soon wore off as it was a full hour before kick-off but at first I was transfixed by the stadium and used to love watching the Kippax fill up on a Saturday afternoon. The excitement of us attacking was electric, as you knew if we scored all hell would break loose and you could end up anywhere and in any condition, I'm so pleased I'd experienced Saturday afternoons on the Kippax, something that will never be seen again.

I eventually joined the London supporters' branch and began travelling to games with a few members who lived close to me and we would often pack a car out before heading off to games.

I recall driving to Bristol Rovers midweek for a League Cup tie that went to extra time, it was played at Bath City's Twerton Park ground, with the Rovers fans singing 'Where's your caravan?' to Ricky Holden and the stadium announcer introducing Garry Flitcroft as 'Garry Flipflop' when he came on. You went to the games knowing you'd have a fantastic day out win, draw or lose and you already looked forward to the next game before you were home from the present one.

My favourite memory of the Kippax was Wednesday 21st August 1991 when we beat Liverpool 2-1 thanks to a couple of David White goals. There was a tingle in the air that night and Maine Road under lights was something special. Wins over Liverpool were a rarity to say the least in those days but this evening was electric, speaking to David White earlier this year he told me that night was the best atmosphere he'd experienced at Maine Road and also his favourite Maine Road night.

I stopped going for a good few years as I started playing a decent standard of semi–pro football and captained Milton Keynes City FC in Southern Premier for over 400 games, I was also part of the famous (well in MK that is) Wishing Well Sunday team who became the first non-league side to win a trophy at Cardiff's Millennium Stadium by winning the National Carlsberg Cup in which over 900 teams had entered. We played the Semi–Final at Anfield, won the Final in Cardiff and went on to finish runners up in the European Pub Cup after losing to Norway on Porto's old ground. We had virtually the same side as our Saturday team and finished the season with 6 trophies overall. I then retired on the back of that season due to constant knee trouble but it was some way to finish, so in 2002 my passion returned for watching the Blues again.

I now travel home and away with my 14 year-old lad Harvey-James who is as City daft as I ever was. The atmosphere at games is different now and the characters seem to have gone as football has changed dramatically over the last 10 to 15 years but one thing that will never change is the supporters' passion.

Harvey has attended over 120 games, visited over 50 grounds

and I can't now imagine going to a game without him, I used to dream of what I do now; watching City and the bond we have travelling around the country and Europe watching City together is something I will treasure forever.

We were in Iceland in August 2017 for City's pre-season fixture against West Ham at their National stadium. I'm not good with booking things so I have a travel consultant I use. Flights were delayed so we were eventually dropped off by our private transfer at our hotel at 1.30am only to be told at reception that this was not our hotel at all. With the transfer long gone and armed only with a map I couldn't read and the young fella in tow, we set off to find our hotel. It was pitch black, bloody cold and I had no idea at all of how to find the hotel the bearded guy had told us was only five minutes away. A good forty minutes or so passed and I'm starting to question "How the hell have I ended up lost in Iceland" when Harvey says to me "Give us the name of the hotel Dad and I'll put it in my phone in Google maps". Ten minutes later we are checked in and I'm recovering from the next culture shock which was the price of the much needed pint I had just ordered! The trip was made worthwhile as Joe Hart made his West Ham debut against City and came over after the game and gave Harvey the gloves he wore in the game and had a quick chat with us.

After receiving programmes from Mick McCarthy on a regular basis, delivered via my grandad's house, I became a keen collector and now can boast having almost every home City programme from 1945/46 to the current season (three missing) and almost every away from 1949/50 to current season (25 missing) in all competitions. I recently purchased the first ever Maine Road match programme for the ground's inaugural game against Sheffield United from August 1923 and I also own every cup Final programme we have played in apart from 1904. Well a man does need a hobby! I also started up a Facebook page dedicated to City match programmes while also featuring nostalgia articles and quizzes which is aptly named Manchester City Match Programmes and can now boast over 2,500 members.

I rarely get to see Mick and unfortunately it's usually at a big family funeral or wedding when I get the chance to talk City with him, although I have constantly reminded him when we've spoken that it's his fault that I'm a Blue to which he once replied with "it could have been worse as I nearly signed for Notts County before City, so you could have supported them!"

Although these days supporting City there is very little to moan about in the way there once was and I'm enjoying every second of it.

Once a Blue always a Blue!

Cheers for that Mark! What a great programme collection you have. Hope you have them insured and that you soon get your missing ones. It must be like a full time job running the Facebook page. Next time you go on a trip I think it'll be favourite to let your son suss out where the hotel is at least you will get there quicker!

17 - BACK IN THE DAY

DANTE FRIEND

W E WERE SAT IN THE BAR at Euston Station waiting for the train home back to Manchester. It was April 1997 and we had just drawn 1-1 away with Charlton Athletic at The Valley. I will always remember this because people nowadays forget what it was like to be a Blue in the bad old days. Two Blues sat opposite me and we were talking about the state of football back then, examining where we were compared to the "elite" in the Premier League at the time.

We had dropped out of the Premiership the year before and our fixture list this time around had been very uninspiring – Grimsby, Tranmere, Barnsley. You'd try and get yourself "up" for these games. A chance to tick off a new ground perhaps or you'd convince yourself that we had to be there, that the club needed us – in that we had to escort City back up to the top no matter how long it would take. Following City all over the place was the norm for us coming from Blue families but in a way it became a badge of honour too.

"All that will happen now," said one Blue to the other, "is that the clubs at the top like United will always have the money and no one else will be able to compete… but at least it will be obvious to everyone that nobody else can possibly compete. That's the way football is now."

So for all those Lad Bible following, new era SKY fans who slate City fans for only filling 54,000 seats in a 55,000 capacity stadium and think we are somehow "plastic" fans, it's worth reminding people that we kept going year after year, home and away whilst we went up and down the leagues, whilst we had to play Macclesfield, while we lost away to Crewe on Boxing Day, when we had five managers in as many months, when we had numerous chairmen and whilst the other lot were bringing home European trophies – we kept going and we knew back then, long before we had the takeovers, first Shinawatra and then Sheikh Mansour, that football was about money and the only way you could really compete at the top level was to buy big.

If the Premiership is a world league and shown in every country worldwide then quite obviously any of the teams in the Premiership could have been taken over by rich consortiums. That's what the Premier League wanted. It happened to be us. We found a new source of money. Why should we turn that down? After all, Manchester United, the club who we helped keep going by letting them use Maine Road, who we were bigger than for decades until their cup win in 1948, even they had a rich benefactor come in and save them. So it's alright for them to have investment... but not us?

First of all everyone laughed when they saw City fans with tea towels on their heads outside the ground. Then they revelled at our early failures, losing in semi-finals, failing to land Kaka. Then the tide turned. We won something. The FA Cup. Then we won the League. Then it became, you only won it once. You only won it on goal difference. The Arabs will get bored and you'll be back to Macclesfield soon enough.

Then we won the League again and got to the Semi Finals of the Champions League and of course, it goes on and on. The laughing stopped. It then became fear and then became loathing. We hate it when our friends become successful... and if they're Northern that makes it even worse.

City fans knew the score. City fans of a certain vintage are happy now that the club is successful but maybe something from those "bad old days" has been lost forever – but then it's lost for everyone – as the age of innocence in football; the Charles Buchan era, the Roy of the Rovers era, whatever you want to call it, has long gone. It's gone for all of us but it's unfair to single out City as being the reason why football is falling apart.

Juventus are only where they are through FIAT. PSV are backed by Phillips. AC Milan were backed by Berlusconi and Mediaset before being taken over by Chinese investors. Paris St Germain, Chelsea and clubs such as Zenit are all of a sudden changing the status quo. Yet I would also argue that Blackburn Rovers and Wigan should also come into the group seen as "ruining football."

Let's remember when City scraped up in the play offs in 1999 – we did not even have the biggest budget in that Division. Fulham, bankrolled by Mohammed Al Fayed and managed by Kevin Keegan, were the big spenders and Wigan, bankrolled by Dave Whelan, tried to buy success and went all bitter when they missed out to us after Shaun Goater scored a perfectly good and legitimate goal in the play-off semi-final at Maine Road – as if they were somehow entitled to just buy their way through the leagues. No one in the media seems to pick up on that point. When we went up against Gillingham the players knelt down to worship the fans. It was the fans that kept our club going.

So we are where we are but I was a young City fan in those days and already very frustrated about things. I was only a few months old when we won the League cup in 1976 so there was no memory there. My earliest memory of City was the '81 Cup Final – I can't recall the game itself on the Saturday but I do remember the replay – being allowed to stay up and watch and being distraught the following morning having to go to school. A heartbroken 5 year-old.

I remember daft things – listening to Brian Clarke's commentary on Piccadilly Radio on a Saturday afternoon in 1982. Joe Corrigan dislocated his shoulder and was carried off against Watford and Bobby McDonald went in net. We actually won 1-0 and went top of the league! We were relegated that same season and the cycle of decline continued. I can also remember that football on TV that year was split between the BBC on the Saturday night with Match of the Day, and Granada on a Sunday afternoon.

I went to Worthington Road Primary School in Sale Moor and Paul Power came along one day to hand out prizes at the school sports day. My dad was talking to him non-stop on the touchline and Power shouted encouragement at me when I did the beanbag race. He became my first idol, then Paul Stewart, Paul Moulden, then Whitey, Lakey, Colin Hendry, Clive Allen. Later on, through supporters club events, you get to meet some of the former players; Roy Little, Tommy Booth, people who had blue blood and had so much time for you and had so many stories from the old days. It kept us going.

Football was great as a kid. I remember watching the Spain World Cup on TV in 1982 and dashing home from school to watch England v France and Italy v Brazil. Then there was Spain v Northern Ireland and Scotland v Brazil. Hot summer days and nights watching great teams and great players like Zico. England were unlucky. They didn't lose a game and could have won it.

Panini sticker albums helped with the learning of the names of all the players from all the teams. Also that was when I first found out that the England flag was the cross of St George as until then, with Charles and Di's wedding fresh in my mind, I'd always thought it was just the union flag and when the score came up in England matches I had to ask my dad what that flag was next to the word England.

That's when I really fell in love with football. Who couldn't? Sunny days, bright stadiums, great football and the games on at normal times so young kids like me could watch. Top kits as well. I remember the semi between France and Germany and Battiston being taken out by Schumacher – those dirty Germans were at it again!

Then at school playing football and everyone would religiously collect and swap Panini stickers – Football '83, Football '84, Football '85. Shoot, Match and all the other annuals by now replacing The Beano and Whizzer and Chips. Staying up late to watch Sports Night when City were on in the Second Division and seeing us win away at West Ham in the League Cup – the shock of the round! Watching Match of the Day and listening to the sport coverage on Radio 2, the predecessor to Radio Five Live. That amazing music used to come on at 1.30pm and you knew the football coverage was about to start. Begging my dad to take me to a game. Finally – City versus Leeds, April 1985. We lost 2-1. But I have been a regular ever since.

Back to 1997 and I was a regular at away games and had been for almost a decade by then. I had never seen City experience any success unless you count promotions and a trip to the Full Members Cup Final.

Francis Lee had fought a tough campaign against Peter Swales and finally forced him out after Ian Niven, one of Swales' staunchest allies, swapped sides and gave his vote to Franny to give him the edge 4-3 on a split board. I was part of a group – Free The Manchester 30,000 – that felt that the club was going backwards and heading for the third tier (we were right) under Lee's leadership (or should that be lack of leadership). There were demonstrations outside the ground and it was all borne out of pure frustration.

We suffered under Peter Swales. We flickered briefly under Howard Kendall but then one by one the boy Blues who won the 1986 FA Youth Cup were sold off. Kendall (Judas) resigned and went back to his "wife" Everton and we had two top five finishes under Peter Reid however the football was appalling, the fans wanted his assistant Sam Ellis gone and quality players such as Clive Allen, Colin Hendry, Michel Hughes and Neil Pointon were let go whilst expensive players were brought in and sadly did not improve the team.

We had players in that squad, like Curle and McMahon, who used to blank the fans. They thought they were bigger and better than everyone else. We had David White bombing down the wing and what a player he was for a while, we were so proud of him. He was one of us. When he was swapped for David Rocastle we got a little bit of cream for once, some amazing footwork and the odd glimpse of what Arsenal fans would have enjoyed back in the day at Highbury. We then had Gaudino and Kinkladze; Uwe, Beagrie and Paul Walsh. We had Niall Quinn who carried that club for years and was then sent out to face the media after relegation when others like the chairman and manager hid. He was then sacrificed which is probably where his sly digs as Sky commentator against us have originated from. Perhaps he didn't feel the club had been as loyal to him as he had been to the club. It's a shame he is not a City fan anymore because he was a hero to many Blues who followed his career.

We had the fans telling Francis Lee 'do not appoint Alan Ball' and Franny saying it was a great appointment. He got us relegated and it took us 4 years to get back. We also fell through the trap door to League 1 (real name division 3).

We had Brian Horton and his kamikaze defending – losing 5-0 at Old Trafford on a humiliating night where we were exposed for being so far behind. Whilst we had not been successful over many years United had not won the league either. In fact we always had the fall back line of "Last Manchester club to win the league." When they did in 1993- aided and abetted by the disappointment of the Spurs quarter final and subsequent riot – it made the fans demand Swales resignation. We were not competing with them anymore. Telling us Alphonse Groenindijk was the new Arnold Muhren didn't appease the fans. Swales promised us £6m for new signings which didn't materialise. 1993 was the summer of discontent.

The atmosphere looked after itself in those days, it really did; there were no hangers-on in the crowd then. Maybe in the 1995-96 season we saw a few lads bringing their girlfriends to away games, people you hadn't seen before. Oasis fans rather than City fans. But they were soon gone the year after once we'd been relegated. It was a hardcore.

'We never win at home and we never win away. MCFC! OK!'

That's what it was all about and why it is sung now so our past is not dismissed.

City fans had gallows humour. "We'll win again... don't know where, don't know when" was a regular chant back in the day. We had a good sense of humour. Impulsive chants, those days have gone in the main now because of the type of supporter that football wants to attract into the stadiums. Clubs also are filled top to toe with careerists – people who are working for us because of our name and our profile, not because they are necessarily Manchester City fans. Something is lost in the link between the club and the fans.

We have always had a nationwide fan base but it was really the local support that kept our name going during the dark days. It wasn't just about going to the match, it was about having a day out. A knees-up. A gentleman's morning at Bernard Manning's, a quiz night or a question and answer with a player at a supporters' club meeting would be just as much on the agenda as standing outside The Sherwood waiting for the away fans to be walked past. When you look back it was all daft. What was it all for? Meeting Kit Symons and Gerry Creaney might not sound like everyone's cup of tea – and believe me it wasn't – however it was something to do. It kept us going.

Singing "Wonderwall" for Alan Ball... We didn't sing it because we liked him. We sang it because it was something to sing… and it rhymed with Ball.

Football was still typically Saturday at 3pm. You could plan your weekend better in those days. The cup final was still a real highlight of the season and most of the time the last domestic game of the season played after the league championship was completed.

City fans had demonstrated against Swales in '83 and '87 and then '93 but only in 1993-94 did we get him out. It was when the media started making football such big news and later rolling news that it became obvious that if fans got themselves organised and pushed their agenda then the media – usually lazy bastards who want someone to write the story for them – would just pick that up and run with it.

If Francis Lee had taken over in the late 70s after retiring he would have been perfect. That would have been unlikely anyway given the way he was booted out of the club and off to Derby – another decision which cost us a league title – but by his own admission Franny had fallen out of love with football and had not been to a game in 15 years, so he was completely out of the loop. Franny came in just as tactics were changing and just as the money in football was getting even bigger. We also had the Kippax to redevelop and once that stand went, something inside the ground died.

Stevie Lomas kept the ball in the corner and we went down.

The Liverpool fans cheered when the other results came in. I remember feeling utterly frustrated with my club whilst we were getting turned over in every single derby but when we got relegated we were getting turned over in the mini–derbies; by Stockport, Oldham, Wigan, Bolton and Bury. I think all the Greater Manchester clubs bar Rochdale turned us over in that period and that was only because we never dropped low enough to play them!

Manchester United never ruined my life. Manchester City did though in those years. It was horrible in those times it was like living in a nightmare and not being able to get out of it. Yet we were 'everyone's second club', a fact now long forgotten. 'Stand up if you hate Man U' would be the first song an opposition club would sing at Maine Road, seemingly to get us on side.

The City fans were desperate to see the back of Swales. Eddy Shah was linked with taking over the club in the 80s. Then someone called Mike McDonald (no relation to Ronald). Then finally Franny Lee. The QPR game in September 1993 was the day of the Swales Out protest. The fans blockaded the main entrance before the game and at full time the whole of The Kippax did a sit in – a protest aimed at raising coverage in the media. It could not go unnoticed. Imagine that now - everyone staying behind at the end of the game? A lot of fans leave the stadium 10/15 minutes before the end these days!

I was then part of the campaign to get rid of Francis Lee from the club. I wasn't blinded by his previous history as a player as many fans were. I never saw him play. I judged him on his record as a "hands-on" chairman. There was a chemistry problem. There was a rumour Coppell never picked the side once during his short stay. We were going nowhere and just because he was a former player I felt he should be judged on his present record not his past as a player. There was no discipline at the club.

The agent Jerome Anderson brought a lot of players through the door, a lot of the Georgians. Perhaps he was on a retainer. For Kinkladze the fee was officially given as £2m. Privately it was mentioned that the fee was £250,000 – which would have been more like it given the state of the club's finances. We had players who were allegedly threatening the manager, threatening to have him killed. I was getting phone calls from people inside the club at the time, they wouldn't give their name but it could well have been the manager's secretary, someone like that giving me snippets of information saying, "make sure you have a big turn out on Saturday outside the ground" – this was before the Bury game at Maine Road which we lost 1-0 and the crowd finally turned on Frank Clark and Francis Lee in a big way. 3,000 people were outside the main entrance and that gave John Wardle and David Makin the chance to make their move. Eventually David Bernstein came in.

I remember working at Cable and Wireless in Wythenshawe. We were on a works do, on a Friday night. It was when we were really poor. We were stuck in the third tier and not looking like we were going to get out of it either. We had Reading the next day at Maine Road at 3pm. The Reading players were in the night club we were in: Fridays in Didsbury. I had been hoping to "get off" with one of the girls I worked with that night and when I popped over to see her, there she was wrapped up in the arms of a footballer, Andre Williams, snogging away. Frustrated I went home. But at least I had the match to look forward to the next day...

Word reached me that the Reading players had been seen jogging down Palatine Road on Saturday morning, sweating off their night on the beer after Tommy Burns – the former Celtic player and then Reading manager, read them the riot act. I felt confident that we would win now, knowing that the opposition had all been out on the piss and the pull until silly o'clock...

Needless to say the final score that day was: City 0 Reading 1 – Goalscorer: Andre Williams.

There's plenty I don't miss from the bad old days, yet there are some things I do miss. Will my kids have the same passion for City as I did? Will they want to get up at 4 am and get a train at 5 so they can arrive in London at 8 and drink all day and get home at 3 in the morning after going clubbing after the game? Probably not. When there is so much dough in the game and you haven't got the same bond between the players and fans, it can never be the same.

I used to miss going to The Parkside for opening time, standing outside some times and drinking cans from the shops opposite if I was skint – the game starting at a proper time - 3 o'clock, finishing at 5, then walking up Oxford Road into town stopping at various places before ending up in a club, 5th Avenue, Brickhouse, 42nd Street or The Boardwalk. Those are days you can't get back.

Yet my life still revolves around Manchester City.

I help out with The 1894 Group now as some of us are trying very hard to get the atmosphere back. We are swimming against the tide and have a monumental task. We also try to reflect the traditions of the club that have been lost in the post-2008 re-writing of the club's history.

18- TYPICAL CITY... NO MORE!

DAVID WALKER
READ BUT NEVER RED - www.readbutneverred.com

IN THIS AGE OF SOCIAL MEDIA where #footballbanter can easily and regrettably escalate into online abuse, some of the milder insults hurled in the direction of many a Manchester City fan is to label them as 'Plastic' or a 'Glory hunter'.

It's by no means a term reserved exclusively for City supporters but it's one regularly trotted out by keyboard warriors keen to undermine the loyalty of fans, many of whom have been through thin, thinner and positively anorexic times, following the often Not So 'Super City from Maine Road'. It goes hand-in-hand with the ill-informed or just pig ignorant chants of the imbecilic ranks of opposing supporters who are forever asking City fans: 'Where were you when you were shit?'

Obviously these misguided morons never do their research, otherwise they'd know that when City slumped ignominiously into the third tier of English football in 1998/99, average home attendances at Maine Road were well in excess of 28,000, in a stadium with a capacity of about 34,000.

Whereas City used to be heralded as 'everybody's favourite second team' – based on the sympathy vote of being in the shadow of the 'Dark Side' at the Theatre of Screams – that all changed on September 1st 2008, when Sheikh Mansour took ownership of the Sky Blues. Literally overnight, City became the focus of every green-eyed, disaffected football follower on the planet.

Instead of Mario Balotelli's famous question 'Why Always Me?' supporters of clubs the length and breadth of Britain, especially in Liverpool, London and Newcastle, were querying 'Why Not Us?' It's a bona fide question but every other club's disappointment was far outweighed by the incredulity and joy of those associated with Manchester City Football Club.

This was an intensely loyal fan base who had ridden a football rollercoaster like no other for decades with more lows than highs, one which took every proverbial kick in the 'spherical objects' and turned it into a perverse badge of honour. Tom Cruise and the Mission Impossible film franchise would've more than met their match if they'd gone in search of any glory hunters bedecked in sky blue, prior to the Abu Dhabi takeover in M11 3FF.

As for finding hordes of 'plastics' – that would've been limited to local landfill sites or environmental recycling plants. Rest assured, if you were a City fan prior to 'The Money' your loyalty should never ever, for one nanosecond, be questioned. Your credentials are 'impeccable' – you are a true Blue – well versed in your understanding of the self-deprecating term, 'Typical City', with all the scars to prove it.

But what are the origins of allegiance to our beloved City? The answers are manifold, some obvious, some slightly more obscure. The big ticket answer for many who have suffered through decades of under achievement will be that they're Manchester born and bred, blessed with parents who bestowed a blue blood birth right upon them, flowing from generation to generation.

Undoubtedly being a City fan has – at times – been a very heavy cross to bear. It's an analogy light years removed from the modern day play on words where not one but two Jesus's have risen to prominence in City's match day line ups. Whereas Navas became a City Premier League Champion and two-time League Cup winner before returning to Sevilla, he never quite nailed the art of crossing. Fast forward to the here and now and a certain Gabriel Jesus is shaping up as a potential world-beater, a Brazilian superstar in the making, who will crucify opposition defenders for years to come.

It's a joyous prospect as Pep Guardiola prepares to take City to hitherto unknown heights with a squad awash with skill, speed, youth, creativity, belief, guile, spirit, experience and resilience.

But City being City, there'll always be a niggling element

wondering if a group featuring Jesus, Sergio Aguero, David Silva, Kevin De Bruyne, Leroy Sane, John Stones, Raheem Sterling, Kyle Walker, Benjamin Mendy, Bernardo Silva, Ederson, Fernandinho, Vincent Kompany, Phil Foden, Ilkay Gundogan, Danilo, Nicolas Otamendi, Fabian Delph, Brahim Diaz and Yaya Toure could somehow contrive to snatch defeat from the jaws of victory, embracing trauma instead of triumph.

Surely the answer from even the most cynical and battle-hardened Blue would have to be an emphatic NO!

The transformation from 'Typical City' to perennial title and/or cup winners has still to happen, but it's well underway, with Pep only a quarter of the way through his second season at the Etihad. In the midst of what could turn out to be a record-breaking Premier League season and the prospect of even better to come, it's the easiest thing in the world to be a 21st century City supporter. But what of my own humble origins and why did I swear a lifetime of allegiance to the City cause?

Having been 'created' in Cleethorpes on the East Coast, I cannot claim Mancunian origins. Indeed, my first experience of watching football was from the terraces of the Osmond Stand at Grimsby Town's Blundell Park back in the late 1960s. My Grandad Anderton took me to see The Mariners play Doncaster Rovers in the old Fourth Division. I'd just started at primary school and Grimsby lost 2-0. My abiding memory was that of a pink and white coconut bar my Grandad bought en route to the ground, for me to eat at half-time. Such were the levels of 'excitement' as Town plodded to inevitable defeat, I kept mithering my poor old Grandad, asking when would it be half time?

A lifelong Grimsby fan, the ageing John Lovell Anderton must have been disappointed by the disinterest displayed by his one and only grandson, handing over the confectionary with barely 20 minutes played! I've always maintained a healthy affection for my hometown team but my true football love is Manchester City and it stems from one woman and one man – my best friend's Mum and Francis Lee.

As kids we all played street football and would assume the

identity of various star players of our time. My best mate was Stephen Scott and he supported Queen's Park Rangers, hence he was Rodney Marsh. His mum, Margaret, had a bit of a soft spot for Franny and, for some unknown reason, I became Francis Lee in the highly competitive knockabouts in Braemar Road and surrounding streets. I shudder to think how different it might've been had I opted to be George Best, Bobby Charlton or any other non-City icon from my childhood.

As a six-year old, I was 'Franny' despite never having seen him play or knowing that much about City. Mrs Scott (she'll always be Mrs Scott to me) is now in her late 80s, and she couldn't have known the course she was inadvertently setting for me over the next five decades. But that was it – there was no going back – Manchester City was my team. It also helped that Bobby Kennedy, City's left back just prior to the glory years of Joe Mercer and Malcolm Allison, was Grimsby Town's Player-Manager at the time and his daughter, Lorraine, was my first 'girlfriend' at the tender age of just seven.

As a kid you were really lucky to catch a glimpse of your team if they featured in one of the two games highlighted on Match of The Day – all on a glorious black & white TV screen. My first ever City match was Crystal Palace away at Selhurst Park on August 19th 1970 – a 1-0 win with Alan Oakes getting the winner. My Dad – an eminent journalist – had written to Joe Mercer a few weeks before the game, explaining it was to be my first City game and asking if it would be possible for me to meet the players.

He received a typed response, personally signed by Gentleman Joe, in which the City Manager was delighted that '...young David was a Blue...' and that City would do all they could to beat Palace on the night. However, Joe stated, if City were to lose the game there might be some 'industrial language' that wouldn't be appropriate for the ears of a 7-year old boy, so regrettably he couldn't accommodate my Dad's request. It was a lovely letter – sadly lost a long time ago – but one which only served to enhance my Sky Blue passion.

I can recall TV footage of City winning the League Cup against

West Bromwich Albion in 1970 on a mud heap at Wembley. Even more vividly, I remember seeing a brief black and white clip of Tony Book holding the European Cup Winners' Cup aloft in rain soaked Vienna, courtesy of the BBC TV news. I was at Wembley with my Dad in 1976 when Dennis Tueart struck that wonderful bicycle kick winner against Newcastle and, like every other City fan, never for one moment envisaged the 35-year wait that was to follow before City once again won 'major' silverware.

Of course as any long-suffering City fan knows, there was plenty of drama along the way between the mid-1970's and the dawn of Arabic ownership, some of it pleasurable, but most of it pretty painful. The unlikely 1999 Second Division Play-Off comeback from being 2-0 down and staring into the abyss of another season in the third tier of English football was 'Typical City' in reverse. City played two Get Out Of Jail cards thanks to Kevin Horlock and Paul Dickov, followed up by Nicky Weaver's penalty shoot-out heroics, as Joe Royle's men, bedecked in that loudest of City shirts, sent the massed ranks of City supporters into unexpected ecstasy.

It was a marvellous high amid a myriad of desperate lows as City bounced up and down the divisions, almost as quickly as the Maine Road managerial doors flapped open and closed with managers arriving and departing.

Having ravenously devoured Wembley wins over Manchester United and Stoke City to lift the FA Cup in 2011 nobody – absolutely nobody – could have prepared themselves for what would unfold 12 months down the line, as City were crowned Champions of England after a 44 year hiatus.

Pep Guardiola's City may have Jesus in their ranks in 2017, but Roberto Mancini's City of 2012 resorted to a revival of biblical proportions to resurrect their Premier League title bid when all seemed lost. Far from rising from the dead on April 8th Easter Sunday, 2012, it appeared Arsenal had laid City's Premier League ambitions to rest as Mario Balotelli was sent off in a wretched 1-0 defeat at the Emirates Stadium. Eight points adrift with just six games to play, it seemed Sir Alex Ferguson's prophecy that City would never finish above United in his lifetime, would once again ring true. It was a foregone conclusion wasn't it?

But City, far from being pumped with embalming fluid, took a giant swig of the elixir of Premier League life and proceeded to smash 12 goals, concede just one and amass nine points from wins over WBA, Norwich City and Wolves. United meanwhile suffered an unlikely 1-0 defeat at Wigan, seemed to get back on track thrashing Villa 4-0 before somehow squandering lead upon lead against Everton, as the Scousers snatched a dramatic 4-4 draw at The Swamp. The Last Rites, which had all but been delivered on Easter Sunday, were now null and void as City rejoiced in a five point and eight goal swing in their favour, with just 270 minutes of the season remaining. Sky Sports could not believe their luck as a fixture, which had appeared a dead rubber just three weeks earlier, was now a pivotal clash in a breath taking Premier League season.

United travelled to City for a Monday Night Football feast with hundreds of millions of TV viewers, not forgetting the 47,259 fans inside an emotion-charged Etihad Stadium, ready to witness the most critical Manchester derby of all time. What follows here are three contemporary match reports, penned in 2012, as I ventured tentatively into the world of football blogging and City ushered in a new age of success, coining the now familiar terrace mantra where City 'Fight 'Till The End'.

30TH APRIL 2012 - MANCHESTER CITY 1 MANCHESTER UNITED 0

HEAVEN & HELL

A Glaswegian pensioner edged closer to meeting his maker as sky blue heaven appeared on Manchester City's horizons at a turbo-charged Etihad Stadium.

Sir Alexander Chapman Ferguson will be hoping a derisive put down of the blue side of Manchester is not a self-fulfilling prophecy come the Premier League finale on 13 May.

He famously retorted 'not in my lifetime…' when asked if City – flush with Sheikh Mansour's riches – would ever finish above United.

Well we're just 180 minutes away from determining if City will ascend to Premier League paradise and Fergie goes in the opposite direction!

On the evidence of this titanic table-topping clash – billed as the most important Manchester derby of all time – and viewed by a global audience of 650 million people, Sir Alex should've started to put his affairs in order.

There was only ever going to be one winner after City emerged from an opening 20 minute spell where United had the upper hand with some incisive forward play.

With the world watching, City set about achieving what had seemed unthinkable just 22 days earlier – bridging the chasm of an eight point United lead forged on Easter Sunday.

City boss Roberto Mancini sent out an unchanged team overflowing with attacking intent to win the three points that would send the 'noisy neighbours' roaring back to the top slot.

By contrast Fergie had dumbfounded most pundits with his team selection, replacing the pace and youth of Valencia and Welbeck with the experience and solidity of Giggs and Park. Jones and Smalling were drafted in for Evans and Rafael as the reigning champions sought to shore up a defence that had leaked so badly against Everton's Dambusters. City were out to win whereas Fergie was trading United's traditional offence for a stalwart defence – a draw would suffice for the Reds.

Led by Captain Fantastic Vincent Kompany, the Blues denied a strangely subdued United a single effort on target, as City keeper Joe Hart must have thought the May Day Bank Holiday had been brought forward by a week.

Frenetic as it was, the game was lacking quality during the opening exchanges. The City faithful were in full swing on 'Wayne Watch' baiting United's main threat Rooney as he remonstrated with referee Andre Marriner at every opportunity.

Rooney – reviled by City fans – hardly endeared himself to the home support by feigning injury after an enthusiastic challenge by Kompany on the halfway line, resulting in yet another unwarranted yellow card. The friction and animosity between the pair traced back to the Belgian skipper's controversial sending off in City's valiant 3-2 FA Cup defeat in January. Rooney was instrumental in confronting ref Chris Foy and demanding a red card following Kompany's challenge on Nani. Little did we know that 'Kompany Karma' would strike in first half added time and spark an eruption in the Etihad. Silva swung a pacy corner kick into the six yard box, Kompany eluded his marker, Smalling, and powered a colossal header past a defenceless David De Gea in the United goal. Kompany careered away in triumph like a man possessed, forcing Fergie into a half time re-think.

City were deservedly edging the encounter, but with so much at stake few believed a solitary goal would settle matters. Mancini's men emerged steeling themselves for the inevitable United onslaught, but forever focused on delivering their own killer blow of a second goal. United huffed and puffed but the final through ball was missing. Fergie introduced Welbeck for Park while Mancini countered by swapping Tevez for De Jong. It looked like the Italian was preparing for a siege, but no – it was the signal to unleash Yaya Toure from his holding midfielder role. The Ivorian giant came close with two rampaging efforts, while the lacklustre Scholes and Carrick failed to provide ammunition to United's front men.

The second half fireworks were confined to the touchline, with a tetchy Ferguson hurling Glaswegian 'charm' at Mancini following an innocuous De Jong challenge on Welbeck. Forget the 'mind games' here was an animated and angry Sir Alex spewing bile and striding towards the equally fiery Mancini.

Ever humorous, a chorus of 'He's cracking up, he's cracking up, Fergie's cracking up…' echoed from the Colin Bell Stand as the almost comedic confrontation was quelled by the intervention of Fourth Official Mike Jones and City Assistant Manager David Platt.

United went for broke with Valencia and Young coming on, while City held firm with Richards and Milner helping repel the far from rampant Reds. Five minutes of 'Fergie Time' proved fruitless and City secured the double over United for the season, drew level on 83 points and opened up a healthy +8 goal difference advantage.

Mancini maintained – publicly at least – that United were still in pole position for the Premier League title, with City facing a difficult trip at high flying Newcastle on Sunday. If City can clip the Magpie's wings the Italian will surely be singing a different song. Barring United running up a cricket score against Swansea, City will be irresistible favourites.

6TH MAY – NEWCASTLE UNITED 0 MANCHESTER CITY 2

ONE FOR SORROW, TWO FOR JOY

So, it's one for sorrow, two for joy – and such wild unbridled joy – as Yaya Toure crafted an exquisite brace of goals to edge Manchester City tantalizingly close to their first Premier League title. Forget nursery rhymes and fairy tales, Roberto Mancini's all-conquering side is very much the real deal and just 90 minutes away from football utopia.

If five straight wins becomes 'six of the best' on Sunday, City will have staged the greatest comeback in Premier League history, after trailing Manchester United by eight points just four weeks ago.

City's 1-0 win in last Monday's much vaunted 'Title Decider' against United had failed to confirm the identity of the next champions. True, Vincent Kompany's bullet-like header had dropped the heaviest of hints, but victory over Alan Pardew's Magpies would put a genuine seal on City's credentials.

It was a case of déjà vu for MCFC Ambassador Mike Summerbee as he embraced the occasion. He had done so as a scorer in City's 4-3 win at St James' Park 44 years earlier – when he and the Class of 1968 had delivered the last title to the blue side of Manchester. His tears at Yaya's second and decisive goal just one minute from time, resonated with City's long-suffering support in the 52,000 capacity crowd and the millions watching on Sky TV.

The loyal City fans DO now have a 'dream in their hearts' and are no longer 'standing alone', as the Blue Moon rises and everybody, bar the United fans, wants to see sky blue and white ribbons on the Premier League trophy next Sunday.

With so much at stake the opening exchanges were bound to be tense as Newcastle, fresh from seven wins in their last eight games, sought to spring their Senegalese strike force of Cisse and Ba with long balls from the back.

City took time to settle but when they did it was gratifying to see that quick, crisp passing and movement was back in vogue with Messrs Silva, Nasri, Aguero and Tevez. The best chances of the half fell to the magnificent Barry whose 18 yard shot rebounded off the legs of Toon keeper Tim Krul, before a second attempt was cleared off the line by full back David Santon. Newcastle's closest cause for celebration stemmed from the lively Hatem Ben Arfa's rasping shot, expertly parried away by the ever alert Joe Hart in the City goal.

Five early yellow cards from referee Howard Webb illustrated the intensity of the affair and the match day officials were pleasingly efficient and uncontroversial – cue gasps of shock and amazement. As the stalemate held, the stress levels began to rise among the 3,200 travelling support. Who was going to break the deadlock?

The answer lay in the cultured right foot of Ivorian giant Yaya, after masterstroke substitutions and tactical revisions from Roberto Mancini. Nigel De Jong and Edin Dzeko replaced Samir Nasri and Carlos Tevez within 10 minutes of the second half and finally City had the set up to slice through the stubborn Newcastle defence.

Like a runaway juggernaut, Yaya began to batter the tiring Newcastle backline before a neat exchange with Aguero resulted in a curling shot low, beyond Krul's grasp in the 70th minute.

The impasse breached, City had belief surging through their play and it could – and should – have been 2-0 and 3-0 – as Aguero and Yaya contrived to miss chances they would ordinarily have buried. The usually clinical Aguero stroked the ball millimetres the wrong side of the post, when one-on-one with Krul. Moments later, Yaya surged into the Newcastle penalty area before inexplicably slipping over, but having the presence of mind to flick the ball back to Aguero whose shot deflected over the bar.

Would such profligacy come back to haunt City? Mancini was as animated as ever as the chances came and went. A Cisse header flashed past the post of Hart's goal before a slick move involving Aguero, De Jong and Gael Clichy ended with Toure deftly lobbing Krul from six yards out. With just a minute of the regulation 90 still showing, the 'Barcodes' had been scanned and City were leaving with three priceless points in their shopping bag. Mancini's men had shown their mettle where many had wondered if they would buckle under the weight of expectation.

At the final whistle the incessant booing and hostility of the Toon Army was replaced with gracious applause from the Geordie hordes, perhaps conscious they were hosting the champions-in-waiting. Another battle won on enemy territory and now for the final push against relegation-haunted QPR.

A returning Mark Hughes would love nothing more than flicking a proverbial 'V' sign at his ex-employers and de-rail history in the making. It would also enhance his status with the 'Dark Side' who he served so admirably as a player.

With a +8 goal difference advantage still intact, City know a win over a Rangers team boasting ex-City Academy favourites Nedum Onouha and Shaun Wright-Phillips, plus the shy and retiring Joey Barton, will hand them the PL crown.

13TH MAY - MANCHESTER CITY 3 QUEEN'S PARK RANGERS 2

NEVER IN DOUBT

With five minutes remaining of the most pulsating Premier League season in history, Manchester City were on course for the 'title' – but not the one they craved after 44 barren years. The title 'Typical City' was set to stick forever as football's perennial under achievers seemed hell bent on snatching defeat from the jaws of victory against an under siege, undermanned Queen's Park Rangers. As the seconds ticked by the sheer horror of what would be the greatest anti-climax - even by City's own extraordinarily bizarre standards –

had enveloped every man, woman and child sporting sky blue. Gut wrenching agony gripped the cursed City support, tears of anguish were already stinging reddened eyes as the Blue Moon prepared to plummet from its upward trajectory. QPR were hanging on to the most unlikely 2-1 lead and with it, their own Premier League survival. It wasn't supposed to be like this. It couldn't end this way…could it?

City were odds on favourites going into the match. As the proud possessors of the best home record in the league, unbeaten in 17 months, on the cusp of finally laying decades of demons to rest and wrenching the biggest prize in English football from their all-conquering neighbours, surely they weren't going to screw it up?

That they managed to swerve a catastrophe with virtually the last kick of the craziest ever PL campaign, can surely never be surpassed.

When Edin Dzeko levelled the score at 2-2 three minutes into added time it seemed academic. City had to win to edge past Manchester United and grab the glory on goal difference.

The Cup for 'Cock Ups' – once so eloquently articulated by City legend Francis Lee - was destined for the City trophy cabinet until the 94th minute when Sergio Aquero darted into the QPR box, took a Balotelli pass in his stride and shot City into a sky blue heaven of delirium and disbelief.

It was a goal of seismic proportions with a huge shockwave reverberating from the Etihad to the Stadium of Light.

Fergie, Rooney and Co were tentatively celebrating their own incredulous 'Great Escape' having seemingly retained their title against all the odds.

The day began in the almost universal belief that this was City's Day of Atonement - the mesmerizing myriad of twists and turns at the top of the table had finally run its course.

When Pablo Zabaleta put the Champions-Elect ahead in the 39th minute with his first goal of the season it all seemed so straight forward. The fact a Wayne Rooney goal had United leading Sunderland 1-0 was immaterial – all City had to do was win and sky blue ribbons would adorn the aesthetically challenged, but much coveted PL trophy.

Even the loss of birthday boy and powerhouse talisman Yaya Toure to a hamstring injury before half time was deemed an irrelevance as City dominated possession.

The party atmosphere juddered to a dramatic halt courtesy of a howler of a header from the usually accomplished Joleon Lescott.

An insipid glanced touch back towards Joe Hart fell horrifically short and into the path of Djibril Cisse. The QPR hit man buried his shot past the City keeper. QPR had offered all the threat of a blancmange and yet were now level. Spurred by the prospect of a Bolton win at Stoke, Rangers needed to avoid defeat to preserve their top flight status.

The fact Mark Hughes' side avoided the drop despite losing this encounter was hardly helped by the football delinquent known as Joey Barton. It wasn't enough that having been red carded for elbowing Carlos Tevez in the face, Barton then felled Aguero with a snide kick from behind and attempted to head butt City skipper Vincent Kompany. It was a sickening spectacle but strangely served to galvanise the West Londoners. As City launched wave upon wave of attacks they were exposed by a breakaway attack and Jamie Mackie plunged City into unutterable despair with a scoring header.

2-1 to QPR.

The unthinkable was now becoming a harrowing reality for the overwhelming majority of the record 48,000 Etihad capacity crowd.

Possession – and City had 81% – may rank as 9/10ths of the law but it was getting Mancini's men nowhere fast as they now laboured without sophistication, infected by the all-pervading panic being transmitted from the crushed home fans.

The introduction of Dzeko for Gareth Barry and six minutes later, Super/Mad Mario for Tevez, brought a sharper cutting edge up front and an aerial threat previously missing.

Sure enough it was the big Bosnian – effectively City's 4th choice striker – who breached QPR's stoical defence with a clean header from a David Silva corner in the 92nd minute.

Yes, the desperate City fans cheered, but it was an exultation tempered with resignation that it was just too little too late. United had already won 1-0 and were two points clear at the top.

At the other end of the table Bolton had been held 2-2 and a jubilant QPR bench and their supporters celebrated. Win, lose or draw they were staying up.

From the restart Rangers inexplicably hoofed the ball deep into City territory, rather like a rugby team seeking to get downfield and gain territorial advantage.

Of course that doesn't work with the round ball game and back came City, surging forward in search of their elusive Holy Grail.

Deep into the 94th minute, De Jong nudged a ball through to the irrepressible Aguero – all verve and electrifying vitality – just 30-yards out from Paddy Kenny's goal.

The Argentine pocket rocket – thigh muscles pumping like pistons – fired a quick give and go to a grounded Balotelli, powered into the penalty area, eluded a desperate attempt to bring him down and unleashed the goal of goals to send City into frenzied, untamed bedlam.

It was 'Typical City' no more and hello 'We'll Fight 'Till The End' with an earth shattering 'Aguerrrooo' thrown in until the end of time.

Incredible, unbelievable, beyond the wildest imaginings – Manchester City had snatched the title in dramatic fashion beyond compare.

As Martin Tyler said: "I swear you'll never see anything like this ever again. So watch it, drink it in…" and boy oh boy did the City fans gulp, guzzle and quaff the night away!

Now, nearly six years on, City have increased the Etihad's capacity by 7,000 to 55,000, with planning permission already obtained for a third tier on the North Stand, further boosting seating levels to 62,000+.

With average home attendances running at 54,000, the juvenile jibes about the so-called Emptihad, are like water off a duck's back to City fans.

Success breeds success and inevitably a club that has won two Premier League titles, two League Cups and an FA Cup in the past seven years is going to attract new fans on a global scale.

City are being supported by a wider and much younger demographic than ever before, a fan base who often need educating about the sentiments and the pain that lies behind those two words, 'Typical City'.

It's hardly their fault they probably weren't even born or were too young to witness the farcical goings on when the likes of Alan Ball, Phil Neal, Frank Clark and more latterly, Stuart Pearce, occupied the Manager's office at City.

Now in 2017, Pep Guardiola is likely to be the most successful manager in City's history, playing the most attractive football ever seen in English club football.

The club will undoubtedly attract a whole new generation of supporters – genuine fans who will hold City dear to their hearts – fans who won't melt away if, as and when adversity comes calling.

Hopefully they'll never have to endure the 'character-building' nights, borne of away defeats at Lincoln, Wycombe and York, but it need not devalue their future support.

Non-recyclable, single-use plastics are a hazard to the environment, a scourge on society and definitely not welcome in Manchester M11 3FF.

Conversely there's plenty of sincere and durable football fans who shouldn't be dissuaded from supporting the 'Best Team In The Land And All The World'.

The legacies of Mancini, Pellegrini and the future glories of Guardiola should see the ranks of the City faithful continue to swell like never before.

Their support will be built on access to live and televised City games and City's hugely impressive website, where they can see for themselves what Manchester City Football Club is all about.

It won't be based on anything as flimsy as a housewife from Cleethorpes who fancied Francis Lee – but if it's as enduring – it all bodes well.

19 - FOOTBALL FANZINES

PHILL GATENBY

TECHNOLOGY TODAY ENABLES football fans to communicate instantly with each other via various forums – social media, fan websites, fan TV stations, podcasts and blogs to interactive actions on mainstream sport TV stations, radio and other sports news media. Some fans have become minor celebrities by hosting post-match discussions from either outside the stadium the game was held at or from inside their own bedroom having watched the game on TV and posting it on Youtube. Every fan is capable of having an opinion and capable of having an outlet to say it.

Rewind back just over thirty years and fans being able to air opinions and discuss fan issues, it was year zero. There were pre and post-match radio phone in shows but they were strictly game related, as were letters in the Manchester Evening News Pink. Fan-centred issues were not anything the media wanted to pick up on – this was the mid 1980's when football fans were (after the miners) the Tories public enemy number two. There were a trio of incidents at the end of the 1984/85 season – one of which had the Government withdrawing all clubs from European competitions, the beginning of a campaign of "tough action" designed to curb hooliganism. On the same day as City fans celebrated promotion to the First Division on 11th May after the 5-1 win against Charlton Athletic, fifty-six fans died at Bradford City's Valley Parade and another fan was crushed to death when a wall collapsed at St Andrews after crowd disturbances at the Birmingham City v Leeds United game. Eighteen days later, thirty-nine fans died before the Liverpool v Juventus European Cup final in the Heysel Stadium, Brussels after crowd disturbances.

At the time football fans had few allies – celebrities certainly didn't fall all over themselves to declare their allegiance to their 'beloved' team (that all happened after the success of England at the 1990 World Cup). So in the absence of any kind of positive reporting of football fans or reporting of fan related issues, a small number of 'rank and file' fans started to produce fanzines. Inspired by the success of a couple of national fanzines, most notably When Saturday Comes, one by one each club began to be represented by an independently produced fanzine. The bigger clubs soon had two or more fanzines on offer, as the voice of fans began to get louder. You have to remember this was a period when Robert Maxwell wanted to merge Reading and Oxford United into the Thames Valley Royals, Ken Bates spoke of installing electric fences at Stamford Bridge and David Evans, the Luton Town chairman – and Thatcherite Tory MP – banned all away fans from Kenilworth Road.

Blue Print was City's first fanzine and I bought it outside Bloomfield Road in January 1988 as City faced Blackpool in the FA Cup - cover price: 40p. I read it excitedly on the train home and it was easy to understand the connection made of football fanzines labelled as being football's 'Punk movement' following on from a decade before when punks became frustrated that bands and the punk scene were largely being ignored in the local and national media and information was hard to come by, so fans put together their own photocopied fanzines and sold them outside gigs with the aim of promoting a positive image of local bands and bigger bands visiting the area. Football fans, sick and tired of the negative image portrayed by the media, used the fanzine movement to connect with likeminded souls – and the 'zine scene exploded over the next few years and eventually went mainstream, in the same way as punk did too, influencing how the media reacted to fan based issues and changing their format to include fan related issues rather than ignoring them.

Blue Print was the brain child of Mike Kelly and he was joined for issue 1 with fellow fans Frank Newton, Rob and Sue Dunford, and a few others including Dave Wallace – who soon set up his own King Of The Kippax 'zine which amazingly still exists today! After I had bought and read the 2nd and 3rd issues, I was influenced enough by the style and content to join up too and contacted Mike and I attended the next Blue Print meeting. From that point on I was a regular for the next six years, stood pre and post game outside the back of the North Stand and Kippax corner, selling Blue Print (for five years) and when that ended, my own 'zine This Charming Fan for two years – alongside fellow Blues selling at various times KOTK, Electric Blue (which became Bert Trautmann's Helmet), Main Stand View, Chips & Gravy, City Till I Cry, The Fightback, Are You Blue Or Are You Blind?, Singing The Blues and one or two I may have forgotten.

Blue Print was pretty much a ''leaning to the left'' publication, with the exception being Frank Newton. Frank, credited with starting the inflatable banana craze, saw his politics leaning to the right (we claimed that he wouldn't vote for Labour because of their association with the colour red, and voted Tory simply because they were the blues!). Monies raised from the sale of 'zines were invested into various projects and ideas. We sponsored Fletcher Moss Juniors FC, who had Blue Print emblazoned upon their shirts (the very team who decades later gave United Danny Welbeck and Marcus Rashford - there's gratitude for you!) and we gave away a flexi disc single entitled 'Blue Moon (the 5-1 remix)' produced by On-U-Sounds Adrian Sherwood that John Peel gave a spin one night on his Radio 1 show! We had made the biggest flag to be seen in an English ground that required about twelve or more fans to carry it through the turnstiles (often with a little kid rolled up inside to get in for free) and up the stairs to the back of the Kippax. Each time it was used, it would tear in places and cost around £100 to repair. When the Kippax re-opened as an all seated stand, we were prevented from bringing it in for the opening day as new ground regulations meant it needed a fire safety certificate, which it would not be able to get. The flag rotted away in Frank's cellar and ended up in a skip… At the 1991 derby, a few games from the end of the season, at Old Trafford, we paid for a small aircraft to take off from Barton Aerodrome with a banner trailing behind it declaring

'MCFC – The Pride Of Manchester' which circled the stadium three or four times during half time, much to the annoyance of the home fans! Further funds were spent on purchasing a gift for Alex Williams for his testimonial and a floral tribute taken to the Shankly Gates in the aftermath of the Hillsborough disaster.

One thing that set Blue Print apart from the other 'zines is that it was not controlled by one or two individuals, who, if they decided to pack it in, would mean the end of the 'zine. That's not a criticism of the other 'zines, far from it, but it meant that when Mike Kelly decided to move on to other things (he became manager of a local band), first Frank became editor and then Bill Borrows stepped into the chair. Writers came and went throughout the life of Blue Print, fans like Wilson 'Jocky' Pratt, Andy Webb and Mark Robison - as well as a young Blue with a keen and growing interest in the history of Manchester City – Gary James. Bill Borrows took the 'zine to another level in terms of not only content but also in production – this was Bill's first steps into what became a professional career in journalism seeing him write for Loaded, The Mirror, The Telegraph and producing TalkSport's online magazine as well as a host of other publications, along with writing a book on Alex 'Hurricane' Higgins. Sales of each issue saw 2,000 copies being printed and pretty much sold out before the next issue hit the streets. The issue that included the flexi single we had 4,000 copies printed and each one was sold quickly as the flexi single became a much sought after item.

Where today's bloggers and internet 'stars' have the advantage over the fanzines is obviously the issue of time. Online you can contact thousands of followers within seconds. Producing a fanzine involved writing the article, sending it in the post to the editor (or giving it to them at the next match) and waiting for the next issue to be produced, printed and delivered. Then you spend the next six or so games outside football grounds reaching out to fans wanting to buy it. That made content a little stale on a few occasions. By the time a fan is reading an article, it could have been written eight weeks ago and was now out of date or completely redundant. One edition of Blue Print was in the hands of the printers but thankfully hadn't been started when Mel Machin was sacked. An 'emergency meeting' was held that very night and we revamped the front page to reflect the manager leaving and were able to get a couple of pages of reaction in to it, replacing the same amount of pages that could be carried over to the next issue or dropped all together. A few days later the issue was on the streets being sold, with fans praising us for being on the case so quickly. Had the printer been quicker off the mark, it would have been at least two months before we had a chance to digest the sacking of Machin – by which time it would have been old news and also covered extensively in other rival fanzines too.

It wasn't always glamorous! Standing outside the ground for an hour and a half before a game and thirty minutes after, in all weathers and temperatures was never ideal. Even during the warmer days, I had to wear a big thick coat with deep pockets to carry all the coins given in exchange for a copy. Then there was the home game against Spurs in 1989 when myself and Frank were both 'nabbed' by the police at half time when selling in separate Kippax tunnels. We were escorted to a Portacabin, had our picture taken and ejected from the ground! Apparently Mr Swales had taken offence to one article that was critical of his tenure and he requested that anyone seen selling Blue Print inside the ground be thrown out! My written request to the infamous police chief, Sir James Anderton, requesting a copy of the pictures taken (complete with us holding up the ejection number – me wearing my Inspiral Carpets 'Cool As Fuck' T shirt) was sent without reply. On another occasion, City's souvenir shop owner, Eddie Phillips, approached me, asking me to stop selling the 'zine. I asked him who he was, which irked him even more, stating I knew exactly who he was (again, straight faced I denied it) and when I asked him if he had any authority to move me on (he knew he had no legal right to do so) he walked away grumbling to himself. Then there were intimidating moments between rival fanzines, when standing there selling the 'zine became an unpleasant hobby. Things came to a head when I was thumped in the face in one of the Kippax tunnels at half time by another fanzine seller, after a swoop on a bag of Blue

Prints that were placed in a carrier bag between my legs failed.

In the end, we would pay students a tenner a match to sell it as none of us could be bothered with the grief anymore. In the end even the students gave up, the verbal abuse being too much. As a result, things just fizzled out and after six years, Blue Print was no more. To be honest, it had run its course. Like a band that form and state "we will do two albums and call it a day!, Bill had his eyes on bigger things and a few of us were now bringing kids into the world and our priorities at this time were changing. I carried on solo with This Charming Fan for two years, with an obsession of using Smiths and Morrissey song titles for article headings, before calling it a day after six issues and a Kippax terrace tribute called Standing Ovation.

By this time, fanzines had very much influenced local media into involving supporter based issues – local radio stations regularly interviewed producers of fanzines of differing clubs and some were given regular columns in newspapers. Programmes such as BBC2's 'Standing Room Only' ran for three years. Presented by former Brookside actor Simon O' Brien and Shelley Webb, wife of the footballer Neil Webb, the weekly thirty minute show mixed topical football stories with fan related issues. Fanzines featured heavily in Steve Redhead's 1991 book "Football With Attitude". Redhead was the Director of Cultural Studies at Manchester Metropolitan University, and the book explored fan culture, the influence of fanzines and the crossover into the Madchester/rave scene of the time.

The growth and influence of fanzines went hand in hand with the birth and development of the Football Supporters Association. This was set up by individual fans who felt supporter issues were not being addressed by official supporters clubs, many of whom relied upon the goodwill of the club in supplying tickets to branches, sending players to branch meetings and of course having the social club at the stadium to use before and after games. Rocking the boat was not on too many supporters' club agendas. These supporter clubs were affiliated to the National Federation of Supporters Clubs and by the turn of the century, the football authorities decided they only wanted to talk to (and offer funding to) one group of fans, not two – pretty much forcing the FSA and the Nat Feds to merge, which they did (reluctantly at first) in 2002 - forming what we now know as the Football Supporters' Federation, who have campaigned tirelessly on issues such as safe standing, ticket pricing, representing fans at home and abroad in both club and national competitions as well as trying to stop Premier League games being played abroad. Many of those involved in the early days of the FSA/FSF were heavily involved in the fanzine movement on a club level before joining the FSF on a national level – as indeed I did, being elected onto the FSF National Council from 2002–2009 and leading the safe standing campaign, in attempting to have the government overturn its decision to ban standing in the top two tiers in football stadiums throughout England and Wales.

Do I envy today's technology and the ability of fans to communicate messages to others so quickly and frequently? I would be in denial if I said I did not. The thought of Blue Print being available to thousands of fans all around the globe at the click of a mouse or the uploading of a video would have been fantastic back in the late 1980's. However, I feel today's bloggers and YouTube 'stars' are also missing out on the personal touch. Sure they get 'likes' and so forth, but standing outside the back of the Kippax, meeting and talking with fellow Blues whilst selling the 'zine was something you couldn't beat (wet or freezing cold weather and abuse from rival fanzine sellers apart!) You got to recognize and know the regular buyers well over a six-year period and even after Blue Print was long gone, knowing nods or greetings as you passed by became a regular occurrence as the seasons wore on.

I also think fanzines had a 'quality control' system in place that is woefully needed in the world of the internet. To produce a fanzine you needed money and a lot more commitment. This, of course, was obtained through sales, which in turn paid for the fanzine to be printed. If a fanzine had a poor standard of content or a lack of commitment was prevalent, sales would be poor and in the short term, after a couple of issues, the fanzine would not re-appear. To my knowledge, no one produced a fanzine (regularly) at a loss or as an act of benevolence towards fellow fans. Bloggers and in particular the YouTube 'stars' have very little, if any, financial risk attached and therefore the quality of the product can be high or low, or purposely controversial (to get 'hits') or simply of (unintentional) comedic value for the same result – see United's 'Mr Flying Pig HD' or Arsenal Fans TV as a prime example, 'you know what I'm saying Blud?'. From City fanzines alone, as mentioned, Bill Borrows has had a twenty-five year career in journalism and is still writing strong. Highly acclaimed books on Manchester City have been published during the past decade by Dave Wallace, Dante Friend and myself ('Teenage Kicks' in 2013) so it is fair to say that from fanzines, there was talent among the writers – will today's bloggers be able to follow in the same footsteps in years to come? Only time will tell.

Fanzines became an essential part of football culture – at a time when fans were under represented and ignored. Fanzines organised, informed and empowered fans to make a their voices heard and in doing so they created the platform that fans now have throughout the media and within the game through the likes of the Football Supporters' Federation. It was a time when fans didn't matter – look at the crumbling wrecks of stadiums we were penned into each week. Club chairmen, directors and those officials charged with running the game on a national level didn't think our wellbeing or our opinions mattered. But from 1988 to 1994, Blue Print and the other City fanzines mattered to fans and the fact Blue Print is still fondly remembered thirty years later only increases my pride in being part of that football fan revolution.

20 - SAFE STANDING

PHILL GATENBY

IN 1990 WHEN THE Government announced (after recommendations from the Taylor Report) that all ninety-two clubs in the top four tiers of football in England and Wales (later changed to just the top two tiers) had to convert terracing into seated stands by the end of the 93/94 season, I felt back then that it was an unnecessary action to take. Yes, make terraces safer and definitely remove the hideous fences and pens but terracing itself was not unsafe and was not the reason why ninety-six fans were crushed to death at Hillsborough. I said this at the time in the fanzine Blue Print and I said it again in my Kippax terrace tribute "Standing Ovation". The problem was, Hillsborough was so fresh in everybody's minds that daring to voice objections to the recommendations of The Taylor Report would invoke a backlash from a number of corners. I felt then (and still do even more today) that the government – who unsuccessfully tried to implement an ID scheme on football fans - used the inquiry to gain control over football fans.

In October 1999 I was on holiday in the Algarve, Portugal, in the resort of Praia de Rocha. I asked the hotel manager about the possibility of watching a local team play and he informed me that Portimonense Sporting Clube played in the Second Division and it was just a short walk to the all seated stadium, in the town of Portimao. So off I went one afternoon to find the stadium and have a look around. There was a door open leading right into the Main Stand – the only covered part of the ground. The first thing I noticed was there were no seats in any part of the ground, just large concrete steps with lines dividing the space where a fan should sit and a number to notify each fan where their 'seat' was. I saw a groundsman and he confirmed that only under the roof of the Main Stand did fans sit down, elsewhere they stood up. And that was the beginning of a ten year 'crusade', campaigning to allow fans to be able to have the choice in how they watch a game of football. It led me all over Europe talking to club officials, fans and football authorities, taking two trips to Germany, as well as going into the heart of the UK government and understanding how undemocratic our democracy really is.

Of course, at that time, plans were in place for City to move into the vacant Commonwealth Games stadium in readiness for the 2003/04 season. If UEFA passed for what was in place as seating in the stadium in Portimao, then could City use the same design in the City Of Manchester Stadium? I was reading a piece in The Independent one day asking the question as to why fans could stand up in a stadium in the third tier but when the club moved into the Championship, the stadium had to be converted to all-seater. I contacted the journalist and said I was going to ask UEFA and the FA if the 'seating' in Portimao could be used in the new stadium in Manchester. The journalist called me back as he had then done a little investigating with the question I posed and informed me that as of 2001 such 'seating' will be outlawed. A seat – from 2001 – will consist of being 'a set measurement off the step and made from non-inflammable material'. The campaign was over before it had even begun.

Then, just two days later, the journalist called me back with good news. A friend of his had returned from Germany and was raving about a stadium where fans were housed in convertible standing/seated areas. The campaign was officially on and after lots of thinking about a name with a great acronym, 'SAFE' – Standing Areas For Eastlands - was launched. The simple acronym defining what the campaign was about, safety of fans first and foremost and not (as we repeatedly had to state) seeking a return of the terraces of yesteryear. The Independent ran a short piece about the campaign with an email address to contact me if interested, which about forty fans from all over the country did. The use of the internet and emails was new to me – from previously producing fanzines and selling them in all weathers, to being able to contact or be contacted by fans throughout the country and leaving notices on message boards was what made the campaign explode from the original forty odd fans that became hundreds in a matter of weeks. I was able to send newsletters as and when information came to me. At this time not too many City fans had shown an interest, despite the aim of the campaign being to have a standing area in our new shiny stadium. I did, however, attract the attention from the more politically astute fans at Manchester United. The Independent Manchester United Supporters Association (IMUSA) got in touch and between us we held a meeting in the Woolpack pub, next to the River Mersey and the pyramid in Stockport. Along with IMUSA, there were a couple of representatives from the Football Supporters' Association (FSA), Leeds United supporters club, Everton supporters club and a journalist. Plans were made to spread the word and to contact Kate Hoey MP, who was the Minister for Sport, under the Department of Culture, Media and Sport (DCMS) where her boss was Chris Smith MP.

Kate Hoey replied to the question posed to her, 'Could German style convertible standing/seated areas be built into stadiums in England & Wales?' The answer, she stated, was a clear 'no' as she had been informed that such areas were decrepit and being phased out as new stadiums throughout Germany were being built in preparation for the bid to host the World Cup in 2006. Indeed Hoey went further in adding that the previous Minister for Sport, Tony Banks MP, had stated that in no way could there be standing areas in English grounds because England was seeking to host the World Cup in 2006 and could not do so if grounds were not 100% seated! I knew SV Hamburg's stadium was being redeveloped, so emailed a supporters organisation there, to ask about the redevelopment and if it would include a standing area. The reply was that for home fans there is a new convertible seated/standing area behind one goal and a further section for away fans in an opposite corner. He also confirmed that similar areas were being incorporated into other stadiums being developed for the World Cup bid too. So Hoey was correct in stating that many of the German terraces were decrepit and being phased out. What she had not been informed was they were being retained using a modern and safer way to enable fans to stand up – that allowed for the stadium to convert to a seated arena when required to do so for UEFA and FIFA competitions. The double irony of Germany not only winning the World Cup 2006 bid but hosting the games where nine of the ten stadiums used had convertible standing/seated areas (only in Berlin was it a 100% seating) was delicious and something Tony Banks had not seen coming!

So I wrote back to Hoey, informing her that the information she received was incorrect. She responded with an invite to come down to her office to discuss this further. I travelled to London with Mark Longden, an official from IMUSA, to the DCMS offices on the edge of Trafalgar Square. Here we showed her pictures taken from the internet of Hamburg's standing area in their newly rebuilt stadium as well as information regarding other stadiums in Germany. She was very interested in the information given to her and duly passed it on to her ill-informed advisors at the Football Licensing Authority (FLA) – the public funded body charged with overseeing the all seated regulation and new stadium designs. We informed Hoey that we intended to go to Germany on a fact finding mission and visit three stadiums and would report back to her. Myself, Mark and Kevin Miles, from the FSA, flew to Germany and were met by Stuart Dykes, an Englishman living in Germany, fully fluent in German and a Schalke 04 fan representative who acted as a translator. We visited Schalke's new stadium which was under construction and were shown an example of how the convertible seated/standing would work. Here, they would actually attach seating to the concrete when needed, replacing them with barriers for standing in what was a replica of a traditional style terrace though the barriers were more frequent than on old terraces. At Hamburg, the seats folded up and were placed under the stand when used for standing. Finally at Werder Bremen, they had the rail seating where the seat was folded up against the barrier which ran the length of the area, every two rows. For using the seats, the seat was unlocked and pushed down, as seen in many bus stops. Of the three different versions, we preferred the Bremen model and reported this back to Hoey. She in turn, asked the FLA to go and inspect the German stadiums and they refused to go! They said they didn't need to go as they wouldn't approve of any design to be installed into stadiums in England & Wales! Hoey put her foot down and instructed them to attend.

I had also been contacted by broadcaster Adrian Goldberg, from BBC1's Watchdog who was interested in reporting the issue on the consumer affairs programme. He interviewed both myself and Mark Longden outside Maine Road before a derby game (they initially wanted me to wear a City scarf and Mark a United scarf to identify which club we supported… Mark understandably wasn't too keen on the idea). Of course, whenever a camera appears, other fans are attracted to it like a moth to a flame – including the one and only Paul Nolan whose anti-BBC rant when we were being filmed nearly scuppered the whole interview! Goldberg then flew to Hamburg to witness the convertible seating/standing system and interview an official at the club. The icing on the cake for the film was an interview with Kate Hoey who (appearing without her boss's knowledge, and we all being sworn to secrecy that she was appearing) stated that the issue of standing at football stadiums should be looked at. This blew the whole campaign wide open and took it three levels higher. The back pages of every paper the next day covered the story – many condemning Hoey for demanding standing be brought back. The Hillsborough Families Group (HFG) attacked Hoey for the same reason and her timing (a week before Christmas). Hoey stood firm and said at no point had she called for standing to be returned but that in the light of new technology, the Government had a duty to look at any new evidence and act accordingly. It was the beginning of the end of her time at DCMS.

So the FLA went to Hamburg and saw for themselves the system in place. They were instructed to report back to Hoey but her boss, Chris Smith, had other ideas and demanded they report directly to him. I was in London on the day the report was due out, being filmed in a debate on the issue for the Discovery Channel. The evening before I was in a hotel near to Euston Station when

Hoey called me, asking for a fax number. She was furious that Smith had received the report from the FLA and had issued a statement stating that as a result of the report, the conclusion was that the convertible seating/standing system was not suitable for stadiums in England & Wales. Hoey faxed me the report and she also knew I was going live on TalkSport in the morning but around the same time the statement would be released so I couldn't talk about it as if I had read it – she did suggest I should simply ask "who issued the statement". In the morning, I was talking on air over the phone with presenter Alan Brazil, who favoured safe standing. He informed me that the government had dismissed the new technology and I asked him who had prepared the statement – and he took the bait. "I don't know", he replied, adding "but I do not think it was Kate Hoey, she seems to have been pushed aside".

Once I had finished with the Discovery Channel, I raced across London to DCMS office and together, myself and Kate Hoey, wrote a press release from SAFE condemning her boss's decision to dismiss the Hamburg design and demanded the issue be looked at further (she said she liked my style and I should have a job in politics writing statements for MP's!) Hoey gave the hand written statement to her PA, who typed it up and handed it back to me. I was then instructed to use an internet café across the square, to send the press release out to various media outlets – sending it from a DCMS fax machine would have been a little too risky! All the way home on the train, my phone didn't stop ringing with the national newspapers wanting an interview and more details.

Around this time, I was also trying to contact City to see if they would support the campaign – to no avail as the then Chief Operating Officer Chris Bird refused to meet me five times. My final letter stated I would contact local media and inform them the club refused to meet with me. That worked and we were invited in! Bird simply stated his hands were tied and until the government changed their stance there was nothing the club could do. I begged to disagree, highlighting Manchester's history in trade unionism and the suffragettes, arguing that you can't sit there and wait for the government to change policies but you have to challenge the government in order to do so. Bird replied that it wasn't for City to take that fight to the government. I had a banner made declaring 'Standing – A Safe Choice' and took it to a home game and placed it behind the corner flag in the family stand. Within half a minute stewards were taking it down and I had to retrieve it. However, the club had fallen into my trap. I had secretly hoped they would refuse to display the banner – and I went straight to the Manchester Evening News who happily reported the issue. So instead of 30,000 people inside Maine Road seeing the banner, every reader of the MEN got to see it, with the issue gaining a wider audience. The club responded to the MEN stating that a football ground wasn't the place for political statements.

City fans on the whole were positive towards the campaign as I toured the supporters clubs seeking support but were very slow in actively becoming involved. It was a similar scene across the country. A good deal of fans were not that interested as "it doesn't affect us" because their club wasn't being targeted by the FLA for persistent standing. Some Blues took delight in the fact that United fans were being hammered by Trafford Borough Council with threats of stand closures and bans on fans. As soon as one club would be targeted, all of a sudden their fans were keen to join the campaign. Fans in England are very parochial at times when they should be joining forces to protest. I also got a little stick from City fans for working closely with IMUSA – "How are your red friends?" I would get asked frequently. I was told that IMUSA were using me to hide behind, fronting their fight against Trafford Council. The truth was I was using IMUSA more than they were using me. As mentioned, IMUSA were very politically astute and I learnt a lot from them in using the media to get the message across and how to get the campaign up and running and the do's and don'ts over various aspects of the campaign. I was accused of "sleeping with the reds" and can confess now that I did indeed share a double bed in a hotel with Mark Longden in Germany. He kept me up all night snoring!

In 2002, The Football Supporters Association merged with the National Federation of Supporters Clubs – individual fans joining with supporters groups. At the first AGM, at Highbury, The Football Supporters' Federation (FSF) was born and I was elected onto the National Council (a seat I held for eight years) with the portfolio for leading a national campaign challenging the Government's regulation on all seated stadiums. SAFE became "Standing Areas For England". Progress was slow – on the whole those in authority simply refused to budge but one by one little chips would appear that we could move a little nearer to our goal. Once, in the Portcullis building opposite Whitehall, Kate Hoey (by now no longer Minister for Sport, she was replaced by Sheffield MP Richard Caborn, who began every letter or conversation with "I went to Hillsborough the morning after the disaster…" and shut down the debate) organised a conference, in which she invited a stadium designer to outline how a standing area could be built into a new stadium at not much extra cost than building an all seated stadium. A representative from Everton was there and he indicated that Everton would be interested in hearing more about it, as their fans had expressed such an area in discussions about a possible new stadium in Kirkby. The meeting was supposed to be private but Sky Sports News were there and they ran with the "Everton want safe standing in their new stadium" headline. Again, like with Hoey back on Watchdog, Everton didn't state they wanted safe standing but that they were open to the idea and would like more information. Once again the issue became back page news with the FLA and the Hillsborough Families Group (especially with it being Everton) coming out to condemn Everton. It appeared no one actually wanted a debate and the quicker the topic was silenced the better. The FSF, myself included, did meet with the Hillsborough Families Group and although we had to agree to disagree, the one thing we gave them full credit for is the fact HFG wanted standing banned in every sports stadium in the country. At least they were consistent.

Then there were the lies, damn lies and statistics. Fans were encouraged to write to their MP for the issue to be raised in Parliament. The standard reply that each fan received, included the 'fact' that since Arsenal's North Bank went all seated, female fans had increased by 30%. I contacted DCMS using the Freedom of Information act, asking "30% of what original figure and where did the information come from?" After the time limit for a response passed with no reply, I contacted them again to be told they needed another twenty-eight days to respond (which was not an admission that did or did not have the information required). Just before the twenty-eight days passed, I received a letter informing me that they did not have the evidence requested and could not identify the original source. I wrote again suggesting that in the absence of any proof of the statistic they are using, could they therefore please stop using it!

The Premier League were at it too – in readiness for their annual fans survey, the FSF asked the Premier League to include the direct question "Would you like to see safe standing areas introduced into stadiums?" Instead, the Premier League asked "Do you feel safe inside a football stadium" – and then used the obviously high returning vote that said "yes the vast majority of fans felt safe in their stadiums" to report that fans did not want to have safe standing areas – implying the notion that seated areas were safer than standing areas. We had to go back to the Taylor Report to show where Taylor himself had stated that "standing up was not intrinsically unsafe" but he did state that "seating does more to achieve those (safety) objectives than any other single measure". Sadly Taylor died in 1997, it would have been interesting had he been alive and able to see and comment on the new technology not available in 1989, that the FSF believed enhanced crowd safety. It was a good number of years before the government finally admitted publicly to the FSF that standing was 'not unsafe'.

We did get excited once. When a new Parliament is in session, MP's can bring an Early Day Motion (EDM) to the House. EDMs are used to put on record the views of individual MPs or to draw attention to specific events or campaigns. Topics covered by EDM's vary widely and are submitted for debate in the House of Commons for which no day has been fixed. As there is no specific time allocated to EDMs very few are debated. However, many attract a great deal of public interest and media coverage. So we had fans contacting their MP asking them to sign in support of the EDM on safe standing. Many did. Each day, time is set aside for three topics to be discussed but there is no time limit set to enable all three EDM's to be debated. Safe Standing was the second of the three topics, the first being about Cornish pasties only being allowed to be called so if they were made within the Cornwall boundary and using specific ingredients. Word had clearly got out that the standing issue was not to be debated, so the Right Honourable Gentlemen talking about Cornish pasties did just that. Talk and talk. Even when other MP's wanting to discuss the other two topics, stating that the MP in question had gone "off topic" he was allowed to continue with his subject until time was called on the whole session and safe standing and the third EDM were no more, lost forever as an EDM that never was. And they call it democracy and wonder why voters become apathetic? I was very disillusioned with the campaign for a few weeks after that. It really felt like I was banging my head against a brick wall saying the same things over and over and getting nowhere fast. For every door that was opened very slightly, three more were shut firmly.

Occasionally clubs would come out privately to the FSF in support of the campaign but more were being open about it, usually lower league teams such as Wycombe Wanderers – who already had terracing but if they gained promotion into the Championship would be forced to convert to seating. One Championship club that was vocal in support of the campaign was Norwich City. But like the other clubs before them – and those to follow – once the FLA "had a word with them", they went silent as the Football League would issue their regular statement stating their support for the current legislation.

To prepare for a large publication produced by the FSF in support of the campaign in 2007 I went back to Germany and took in three games from a Friday night to the Sunday afternoon, at Schalke 04, Werder Bremen and Borussia Dortmund. I gained a press pass for each stadium and was able to take pictures with standing areas empty, filling up and full. I was able to chat with fans and officials from all three home clubs. The report was published, it made the news again, for a day or two (with TalkSport once again never getting beyond the 'Hillsborough' issue) and the football authorities and the FLA did what they did each time – just ignored it. "Ignore it and it goes away" must be their motto.

I stood down from the National Council of the FSF in 2010 for two reasons. I was battle weary after ten years of fighting the same arguments over and over. Younger, fresher blood was needed to carry the campaign on to the next level. I was also in the process of moving to America, which I did in September 2011 and where I remain now, first in Boston, Massachusetts and currently in Tampa Bay, Florida since early 2015. I have kept in touch closely with the FSF and one of the biggest breakthroughs for the campaign was Glasgow Celtic receiving permission to install rail seating at Park Head in 2016. Scottish clubs were never part of the all seated rule – as long as the Scottish FA 'voluntarily' complied that clubs in the SPL had to be in all seated stadiums. However, since Scottish devolution, this enabled the clubs in Scotland to challenge the ruling made by the UK Government and Celtic did successfully. In 2017, West Bromwich Albion became the first Premier League club to come out and publicly declare an interest in safe standing and offered the Hawthorns up to be used as a trial. Meanwhile, in the lower leagues, Shrewsbury Town were given permission to convert a seated stand into one with rail seating. The club launched a crowd funding campaign, needing £70,000 to make the change, a target easily met and now for the first time a ground in England and Wales can legally build and use a safe standing area. It has been a long, hard battle for the past seventeen years but I still stand (if you pardon the pun) by every action taken and words said over the campaign and just hope that it won't be too long before a Premier League club can be granted permission to house a safe standing area as seen in German stadiums week in and week out. And once we get that approved, then we go after the ban on drinking alcohol in view of the pitch... there's still a campaign left inside me!

21- MIDDLETON BLUES

BY KEOGH

IDDLETON, TO THOSE OF US who live there, is classed as being in Manchester, after all who really wants to be part of Rochdale?

I believe Middleton had its own Council until it had the unenviable opportunity of being placed under either Oldham or Rochdale by the Local Government Act of 1972. For whatever reason Rochdale won the right and since then Middleton has been classed as being under the Borough of Rochdale but we are still in Greater Manchester.

Middleton has a few main areas, Langley, Boarshaw, Hollin and Alkrington being amongst them. Langley is the most famous or infamous depending on your view. There is a joke about the people from Langley; someone at a charity event in a pub once said that the people from Langley were the salt of the earth, which was nice until someone else shouted out, "yes they should be kept in a cellar".

I am concentrating on the Blues from Langley as that is where I lived from the age of 3 until I was 24 and it is here I met and became friends with the lads who like me are Blues and will be forever, except for the odd exception. One lad I will not name who was a City fan once changed to become a United fan and then a few months later changed back to following City. I remember getting in his taxi and he was sat with a United top on. I had known this lad for years and in astonishment I asked what he was doing. This was around 1994 and he said he could not take it any longer and wanted to follow a club that would win something. I was amazed and told him that no one would take his stance on football seriously anymore. I like to think he did it to hopefully jinx United as his support for City was doing us no good but then he changed back. Again I got in his taxi to see him wearing a City shirt and I just laughed whilst he tried to explain but to no avail.

I am a proper Manc as I was born in St Mary's hospital in 1970 and I also lived in Ardwick from birth until we moved to Langley when I was about three. I am very proud of that fact and was a little upset that my wife chose Oldham General Hospital ahead of Crumpsall to give birth to our two children but it was not my decision. My two are still Blues though.

So who are the lads that I will concentrate on? Well I have mentioned this chapter to them but I am not sure I can or should give full names but I will use either the nickname they have or their first name to 'protect' them.

This is a list of some of those who I have had the pleasure of travelling with, firstly to Maine Road, then the Etihad as well as all over the UK and Europe:

Fudge, Greg, Jay, Gary, Yip, Army, Stu, JT, Tony, Tom, Colin, Bungy, Bryan, Yosser, Cliff, Ainsey, Sharpy, Mike, Shaggy, Chris, Tony, Tommo, Andy S, Squadge, Pat, Dek, Joey, Dean, Derek, the Kingy's, Drew, Jaffa, Greeny, Ryan, Harry, Dink, Porter, Tink, Slowe, Burnsey, Rick, Chris, Scotty, Matt, Alex and Sam.

I have missed loads out as the list would get way too long and I apologise to those I have overlooked.

Middleton has a really good regular City following. I know of three official supporters clubs in the area, the Langley Branch, the Woodside Branch and the Alkrington Branch. These three clubs must have close to 250 members between them and yet myself and the lads listed above are not members of any of these branches. For any given home game travel is organised by the above clubs for their members. Other travel is also organised by several private groups. The biggest private group is that which I am a part of which travels from the Albion pub where 70 or more go to most home games.

Home games are good but the best for me are the away games, this is where the fun starts. I have said on many occasions that as soon as a group from Middleton set off on a journey they change. It is as if a switch is either turned on which makes people act, what

I can only call differently.

Alcohol has a big part to play as Middleton people like a drink. I remember reading once that Middleton per capita drank the third most amount of alcohol in Britain. Not bad (or not good) for a town the size of Middleton.

I met the first group of lads I have been to matches with during my school days at St Marys Primary and Cardinal Langley High or whilst hanging about on the streets of Langley and finally through boozing in the same pubs. I can break this group down firstly to four; they are Fudge, Jay, Greg and Army who are in the same age bracket as me. The other part of the group now includes Tony, Colin, Bungy, Bryan, Gary, Yip, Stu and JT.

I was asked to detail some stories of the Middleton Blues and this is difficult when you think of all that has happened on our many trips to watch City. I remember a few from the mid 1980's like the time when Fudge was running on the platform at Liverpool Lime Street station after a night match at Everton to try and get a seat for the journey home. He slipped on the wet surface and almost slid under the train, but managed to grab the step onto the train to prevent his full body going under. I laughed my head off at that. Some games later he got his own back when I jumped off a coach slowing down on Aytoun Street after visiting Villa Park. Instead of running with the flow, or momentum I tried to stop. My feet stopped but my top half did otherwise. I fell flat on my face in front of 40 other disembarking Blues.

The day before the Full Members Cup Final at Wembley versus Chelsea we played United at Old Trafford. Imagine that happening these days, two games in two days; no frigging chance. Fudge and me had tickets but they were in the Stretford End. We went to the game with a lad nicknamed Wavo who was a United fan but once in the ground it was obvious that we were not welcome. We asked a steward what the chances of getting moved were. He escorted us to the City end but to get there we had to walk down the side of the United Road stand. It was great for some young lads to walk round and give the rags some flak and when we got to the City end to be applauded with chant 'Blues are here, Blues are there'. In reality we were bottling it and wanted the safety of our end.

The next day we went to Wembley by car driven by one of my cousin's husbands, Barry. Over 25,000 City turned up for that game and in among them were my mates Greg and Jay. Funny how you bump into mates in such big crowds.

City were drawn away to Blackpool in the FA Cup in January 1988 and a lad we knew at the time worked as a printer and the tickets for this game were just so easy to reproduce. So to make some money we had a few printed off. We sold these no problem on the train and the surrounding area around the ground. All of us had pockets full of loose change and made a few quid to pay for the day. Nowadays, with individual seats, this would not be possible and neither would we do it. Hillsborough had not happened so any thoughts of causing an incident were not given.

Going to West Brom in the early 90's Greg was thrown out of the ground for being too drunk, the lads thought he had been arrested so went to the nearest police station to see if he was there. There was no sign but due to the detour and the delay they had to get a later train. When they got back to Middleton, there is Greg sat having a nice pint. Seems he was simply thrown out so went home. No mobile phones in those days.

We went to Luton away in a midweek cup game when our minibus was stopped by a police car at some traffic lights. We were all sat there waiting when someone noticed we no longer had a driver. He had scarpered as it turned out he was serving a three-year driving ban. The police were that slow coming to the driver's window another lad dived into the seat and fortunately a fight had broken out further up the road so they left us. We never knew why we had been stopped or how the driver got home as we never saw him again.

Fudge parking the car we used to get to Maine Road and being asked for money to 'mind your car, mister'. He only had loose change, about £3. The lad took the money looked at it and called Fudge a tight bastard and then threw the money away. He then shouts 'you will not have a car when you get back'. Fudge looked at him and shrugged and said, "Not arsed, not my car........."

and we walked off.

Spurs away under Pellegrini, we had lost the game 4–1. Jay and me left on about the 80th minute and walked into a pub that was called, if my memory is right, The No.1. It was a big white painted pub with a cockerel sign on the outside. Inside the pub were a load of Spurs fans who must have watched the match there and one lad sat on his own. This was a mate of ours called Jaffa. He had tried to get into the ground using a kid's ticket but at the age of 48 he was pushing his luck. The final whistle goes and this pub starts belting out the Chas 'n' Dave songs. So to spoil the party we start singing and dancing along. The locals were not too happy as we took their fun, but as we told them 'we never win at home and we never win away', they left us to it.

In Krakow for Army's stag do, City were set to play Swansea away. Before our game United were playing Leicester so as the 10 of us that were there settled in a pub it slowly starts filling up with a few groups of wearing red shirts. As they come in we ask them where they are from, 4 groups in total. One of the groups was from Southampton, two were from Ireland and one from the midlands. One of our lot as loud and proud as you like simply shouts "rags are like rats, you are never more than 5 yards from one!" We left that pub and found another which we made our own for the Swansea match.

Fudge and I went to Paris to see City play PSG and he wanted to do some sight-seeing especially the Eiffel Tower. I am scared of heights so did not fancy it but he persuaded me to go as we had hours to kill, I would rather have found a pub but off we went. It was agreed if my bottle went I would go only half way up but that was never going to happen as I knew I would have the piss taken out of me forever. Like I said I am scared off heights, we got to the top and my stomach went. Luckily there is a toilet on the top so I can tell everyone I have literally had a shit at the top of Paris.

A few other tales from other Middleton Blues include the time Kingy, Drew, Jaffa, Greeny, Kiddo and Ryan were travelling back from West Brom by train. They had to switch trains in Wolverhampton and due to having a wait decided to go into a local pub. As they were heading to one such place they were warned by the police not to go into a pub near the station as it was a Wolves pub. Drew popped his head in and saw it was empty so the 6 of them ignored the advice and entered and bought a drink. In the space of 30 minutes the pub filled up with a load of Wolves lads. Soon the 6 sat at their table were surrounded by some of the Wolves lads. Obviously they were not known faces. One bends over to Drew and asks him in his yam yam accent who they were and what they were doing in the pub. By now the 6 were what can only be described as shitting themselves and getting ready for a punch or two. However Drew is Scottish so he simply replied in his broad Glaswegian accent that him and his 5 mates were from Glasgow and were in Wolverhampton to see some university mates. The others nodded and the Wolves lad simply acknowledged the comment and turned away. The 6 drank up and left pretty sharpish.

Drew tells a tale about the away match to Stoke when we won 5-2 but were still relegated to the then Division 3. He did not have a ticket so climbed a tree to try and watch what he could of the game. Those who have been to the Britannia Stadium will know that the two corners near the away end were open in those days. Drew climbed the tree where another lad was also doing the same. They got talking and the lad said he had a ticket but liked the view from the tree and so sold the ticket to Drew so he quickly got down the tree and legged it in to watch the game.

Going back to the Paris match; that was one of the games where you still had to pick up tickets from City staff on European trips. Why, I do not know, it wastes everyone's time especially when the collection point is miles from anywhere. It does not work either, one of our group got into the Real Madrid semi-final using his passport when it was ordered for a work mate, different name and details. Fans will find a way into a game but the club should not make it harder than it already is now that City are a big draw, the loyalty points system I agree with but enabling the purchase of platinum points has created a worse system.

I could keep on with stories like the above and they do give a flavour of what we are about in Middleton when watching City.

We love the football but we love the social aspect of following City as it goes hand in hand, also over the years we probably enjoyed the social side a bit more than the football as we have seen City when they were not as good as they are nowadays.

8 of us used to get a taxi to Maine Road driven by a great bloke called Pete Noi. He was, and still is, a character but now he has retired he does not drive a mini bus to the games but goes with us all to home games and many away. Back in those days though Pete would pick us up at about 2.45pm and somehow we would make it with a minute or two to spare to Maine Road, those were the days when matches kicked off at 3pm. Sometimes we would be told by Pete where he was dropping us off, no questions asked, places like the Denmark and then we would walk the rest of the way. He would tell us to be there for our lift home and not to worry as he knew everyone in there so we could have a beer and be safe. Moss Side was a lively place in the late 80's and early 90's.

The best trip I have ever had with these lads was the 1999 Gillingham game and I have no doubt that a lot of City fans will say similar things about that game. On occasions like that you remember who you were with and as you get older and time passes it becomes the stuff of legend.

My second child was born on the 4th May 1999 so he arrived at a time when we saw some light after years of darkness. It was the 19th May that City beat Wigan to book a place at Wembley to play Gillingham and the lads decided that it would be a weekend away in London. With my new-born and a two year old daughter I managed to muster the funds to go down on the day of the game and come back the next day, so it was one night for me in the big smoke. I travelled down with Greg and Rick.

Some of the others also went down on the Saturday; this group was Jay, Fudge, Army, Gary and Yip. One of these had booked the accommodation, a 'lovely' place in Sussex Gardens for the price of £20 per person per night.

I remember on the Saturday at about 5pm I was sitting in my house (kick off was on the Sunday) when the landline rang and it was Fudge who sounded a bit worried. They were in a pub near the hotel and he was ringing to say he had lost all of the match tickets for the 5 of them who had travelled by train that afternoon. He rang to ask me if I could call the City ticket office to try and sort something out. What exactly he expected me to sort out and how he expected me to sort it I will never know. The ticket office was shut, the game was a sell out and as for records of purchases, imagine the bad ticket office we have now and times that by 10.

About an hour later the phone rings again and it is Fudge, he has found the tickets. Turns out when they arrived at Euston they headed into some cafe for some grub. For whatever reason Fudge had taken the envelope holding the tickets out and placed them on their table, but when they left the cafe he completely forgot about the tickets. They traced their movements back and when they reached the cafe, there on the waitress's trolley that she used to collect dirty plates were the tickets. Fudge lived to breathe another day.

When they arrived at the digs it soon became apparent that it was what we would call a 'shithole', a basic place with no frills other than beds and running water. What more do lads out on the piss and only visiting for the football want? Nowadays it seems some want a bit more.

That first night the 5 of them set off for a few drinks around town and when they decided to come back they realised no one had brought a key. Seems forgetting things was becoming a running theme. So they knocked on the door but got no answer. Gary saw a light on in a downstairs room so walked over to knock on the window to see if anyone there could help. As he got closer there was a gap in the curtain and there in full flow was the owner's son with his girlfriend going ten to the dozen. Gary shouts the others over and soon ten eyes are getting a show. The son must have heard the immature giggles as he should have been manning reception and not his girlfriend, he knew what the eyes required. The window was opened in a flash and a key chucked out.

The next day Greg, Rick and myself showed up at the digs very early and none of the 5 were yet out of bed. We checked in and dropped our bags in our triple room and went to find the others. They were split in a double room and a triple. In the triple room were Army, Fudge and Jay, as we headed into the room I could see three beds but only two actual bodies. Jay was missing; I asked where he was when suddenly from the floor he popped his head up. During the night the slats on the bed had broken and he had ended up on the floor, yet the frame remained intact. Army said the crash was loud followed by Jay shouting 'kin hell, this place is a shithole'.

We set off from the digs at about 10am, first to get some breakfast and then to have a few drinks before the game began. No City fan needed telling what a big game this was so the nerves were there but we also wanted to have a good time.

I cannot remember which way we headed exactly, obviously towards Wembley but we were never going to go straight to the ground as experience tells us that the pubs around the grounds are always packed, full of plastic pots, constantly watched and harassed by either the police or stewards. That is not for us, we like to do our own thing.

We headed towards Wembley by tube and chose to dive off every now and then and look for the nearest pub outside the station we had disembarked from. In those days City and Millwall had what can only be called a fractured relationship. We did not like them and they do not like anyone, to be fair I think most City fans were indifferent to Millwall until they turned up at Maine Road mob handed for the game we beat them 3-0 in that season.

The first pub we walked in happened to be a pub with a big Millwall flag on the wall and we thought 'here we go' but to our surprise the locals were all very welcoming and the price of a pint was £1.70, who in London is going to give that a miss? We stayed there for over 2 hours and had a mingle.

We got outside Wembley after a few more stops and drinks at around 2.30pm; we were fortunate that out of the eight, seven of us had tickets in the same row. We were on the side facing the 39 steps. Rick had a ticket behind the goal. As touched on earlier, what has always surprised me at football matches is that no matter the numbers or the size of a crowd, as soon as I walk in a stadium I always bump into a Blue from Middleton. This time it was a mate called Jamie who I had not seen for a couple of years in Middleton never mind anywhere else. We had a chat and a laugh at the river of piss in the toilets which was ruining everyone's new Wembley trip trainers. Every time I go to Wembley I ensure that I have a new outfit, this usually means new trainers, jeans and a top. In those days this was a treat as it was rare for us to get to Wembley; apart from 1999 I had only been to Wembley once to see City in the Full Members Cup Final in 1986. I do not do replica shirts which is another thing about Middleton, not many wear replica shirts for the actual match.

I remember after the actual match talking to a Gillingham fan and he said he had never witnessed fans like City's. He said the Gillingham end was packed out from about 2.15pm as they waited for the kick off, yet the City end was no more than a quarter full. He said at about 2.55pm he heard what he described as a rumbling and then a roar of Blue Moon as our end filled up. He obviously exaggerated but he is right, since that conversation I have noticed that we do turn up late, look now at the queues at the Etihad. The club constantly asks fans to get there earlier but it is not our way.

We all know the result of the match and how it was a nerve racking and at times soul destroying game followed by euphoria but my main memories of the match are that immediately sat behind me was a man and woman who had with them a baby that was no more than a few months old. The baby slept all through the match, the penalties and the party afterwards.

My other memory is when the second Gillingham goal went in a few of us wanted to leave and just float off to a pub. Fudge was on the end seat of the row we were in and simply refused to let any of us past him to get out. He kept saying we stay to the end on the basis that it had been years since we had been to Wembley and also the fact the lads deserved it for the season's efforts. I am grateful for his refusal to let us pass him as I saw one of the greatest things I have ever seen in football, never mind City. He lived on it for a while but we will let him have that one.

After the game we ended up in the Bear pub and stayed there

for a couple of hours, again bumping into loads of City fans we knew. Eventually we headed to Soho along with a few hundred City fans who had done the same, in one side street a game of football broke out and a few local pub/club owners were nervous but it was all in good spirits.

Around midnight loads had gathered at Trafalgar Square to celebrate, I remember a lone Arsenal fan turned up with a big carrier bag of cans and was singing along with us simply because he hated United.

Rick climbed one of the Lions and instead of climbing down decided to jump, he regretted that as soon as he hit the floor. The soles of his feet were sore for a few days afterwards. On the Friday another lad called Greeny had done the same but had badly twisted his ankle. Drew, the Kingy's and Jaffa had pushed him to the match on the Sunday in a Morrison's shopping trolley as he could not walk.

From there we set off for some late night food and for some unknown reason we ended up in a Chinese restaurant. As we were walking in, and by this time we were the worse for wear, Jay thought it would be funny to grab some food from a customer's plate as a taster. This bloke was with a lady friend and was not amused as he shouted "get your maulers out of my grub". It was not a great moment as we in effect all told him to shut up and sit back down. By now we were getting noticed by other customers but also the waiting on staff. Why we went there I do not know but as beers all round were ordered we proceeded to debate why we had come into a restaurant when all we needed was a bite to eat. A row broke out between us all and we were asked to leave as the beer arrived. A few tried to drink the pints but with no great success as we were ushered out.

A few more stops in bars and a burger joint happened before we were ready for home, where 'home' actually was, was anyone's guess. We thought it was a good idea to try and hire a few cycle rickshaws to get us back to our digs but that was not going to happen as we tried to barter with the cyclists, one told us in no uncertain terms to fuck off as he misunderstood us, our request was to go to Sussex Gardens hotel and not actually Sussex the County

Taxis were sorted eventually and we headed back. Rick, Greg and myself were one of the first back and our room window was directly above the front entrance, this was too good a chance. We filled the waste paper bin with water and waited for a victim. It was Fudge, as he staggered out of the taxi towards the door the bucket of water hit him, we could not have asked for a better shot. As we were rolling around laughing in our room it was not long before there was a banging on the door. Greg, for whatever reason, opened the door and in burst Fudge with a fire extinguisher and he proceeded to open it up all over me and Rick whilst Greg hid behind the door.

It was an eventful trip and one that we will always remember.

Recently we have come into some good fortune at City with our new owners but with that has come what I think is a new kind of stress, that associated with following a top team. I found following City before the takeover very easy going most of the time as I think I went for the social side of it a bit more. I was as annoyed and upset as the next fan when we were relegated more than once but there was a bigger sense of togetherness I believe amongst the fans. That is not to say we do not still have it now but I have sensed that when things are not going well the fans can turn quicker than in the past.

I found the most stressful time was the run up to the first title win. It all came to a head for me at the Arsenal game when Balotelli was sent off.

When Mario Balotelli was sent off I was sat somewhere near the back of the away end. I went running down the aisle to shout my disapproval at Mario and the ref, in fact anyone. As I ran down I bumped into a steward on the aisle who had his back to me. I then was at the front of the stand near the wall onto the pitch shouting when another steward made a grab for me. We pushed each other once when I was then grabbed by another 3 or 4 stewards and dragged out of the stand and taken to a holding cell behind the stand. Here I was arrested and handcuffed to a police officer who was from Liverpool. He was an Everton fan and we had a good chat about football in general. As I was under arrest he should not have let me use my mobile phone but fair play to him he let me use it whilst I rang my wife who did not believe I had been arrested until the officer confirmed I had been (she was not amused) and I also rang the lads I had come down to London with to tell them I would be making my own way back home.

I was put into a van along with 3 other lads, one City and two Arsenal, I was put into a little cell of my own in the back of the van whilst those three were all sat together. I was in a joking mood as I did not see any real severity in the whole situation and was expecting to get released without charge.

Whilst being processed before interview I had to give them my personal belongings. I had sold some tickets that day and had about £600 on me plus the ticket I had used to get into the ground was a disabled ticket. The police were asking me which limb was missing and also if I was some sort of tout. My response was along the lines of being in the big smoke meant I needed lots of money.

It was at this point one officer coming out of one of the rooms in the station said he knew my accent, turned out he was from Heywood, a town next to Middleton. He got me a brew and a packet of biscuits.

I was held in a cell for about 2 hours before being interviewed and it was here that I made a big mistake. I wanted out so instead of waiting for the duty solicitor I was interviewed on my own. In my defence I was a bit drunk, the game kicked off at 4pm that day and I had been drinking since about 8am. I more or less under interview admitted to killing JFK, I was taking it all as a bit of a joke as nothing serious had happened. I thought it was going to be a quick telling off and then I would be on my way home.

I was let out of the station at about 9pm. I now had to either find a way to get back to Manchester or stay overnight in London .Luckily I knew some lads who were staying over so I rang them and they agreed to let me bunk down in their hotel. I ended up sleeping on the floor whilst they snored their heads off all night.

A few weeks later I was asked to go down to Highbury police station to be formally charged with two charges of common assault. This was a shock and not one I was expecting. In total I had to go back to London three times and it cost me a fortune. I was very surprised that I was charged with common assault. I only pleaded guilty on the advice of my solicitor as in his view it was quicker and easier, for him it was no doubt! I wish I had fought it as, although a criminal record is not the worst thing that could have happened, it was certainly not what I wanted. I felt that due to the cost, distance and hassle it caused, everything was against me.

One part that was a little amusing was due to now having a criminal record I had to get a visa to visit America to go to Florida. Whilst being interviewed at the US Embassy I was asked if my criminal record was caused through alcohol. I replied that all offences at football matches are usually caused through alcohol. They were not amused and sent me for a medical at a Harley Street doctors at the cost of £250. Here I was given the most thorough medical I have ever received. Cough and drop, chest x-rays and blood tests for every kind of illness.

Due to the Arsenal match it was decided that it was best for me not to attend the Newcastle game which we won 2-0. I have never forgotten the hurt and gutted feeling I felt as even though I celebrated the goals I was not there.

The above are a few stories of Middleton Blues and in between all of that one thing is for sure, Middleton will always have a Blue family that sticks together.

22 - MOONCHESTER JUST FOR ONE DAY

PHILL GATENBY

I EMIGRATED TO THE US in 2011, missing out on the FA Cup win and subsequent trophies in the process. TV coverage of the Premier League is excellent and I rarely miss a game, either at home, at work or a bar.

In 2014, City announced a pre-season North American tour, including a game against Liverpool at Yankee Stadium in New York on 31st July. I was living in Boston at the time which is roughly the same distance from Manchester to London. I booked a cheap Megabus round trip, leaving Boston at 7am, arriving around noon in the Big Apple and returning at 12.30am the following morning and straight into work for 8am!

I had bought my match ticket through the NY Blues supporters club and was set to meet up with everyone at the famous Mad Hatter pub on 3rd Avenue. On walking in, I recognise one face immediately and was greeted with a warm smile which was a pleasant and welcoming surprise. This Blue in particular I had known since the early 80's and her alter-ego is also known to many thousands of City fans (although they wouldn't recognize her if they saw her in person) as Moonbeam, one half of the club's intergalactic mascots. To keep her anonymous, I shall refer to her as 'Debbie'. I got myself a drink and joined her where she was sat and we had a bit of a catch up chat as it had been a few years since we had last met. After a while I asked her if she was attending the games working or just for pleasure. Debbie began to tell me that she was indeed working, having contacted the club to let them know she was travelling to watch the games. I asked her if Moonchester was over too and she replied that he couldn't afford the trip so she was her on her own. Then she asked me a question that needed no time to reply 'yes!' 'Would you like to be Moonchester for the day?'

Debbie made a quick phone call to a club official, giving my name and I was confirmed as Moonchester! I was given instructions by Debbie – the first one being 'don't tell anyone, the club aren't keen that people know who we are, it kind of de-mystifies the experience for fans'. I was also informed that we don't speak, just thumbs up or clap or other forms of hand signals to communicate. We are space aliens after all! We would have a 'minder' each who would follow slightly behind us. This is for two reasons. Firstly the view point out of the head isn't that great so you can't see if a young fan is stood patiently behind or beside you waiting for a greeting/photograph. Secondly, if any idiots decide to take the piss they can intervene and tell them to clear off or get the help of a steward to remove them. The 'minders' were City fans who volunteered their time to support the mascots in their duties.

We had to be at the ground 3 hours before kick-off. I had just finished my fifth pint when it was time to leave the Mad Hatter and get the subway to Yankee Stadium in the Bronx. Right before we left I made a final trip to the toilet – where I contacted my daughters (aged twenty-two and twenty at the time, who had grown up going to Junior Blues and supporters club meetings and meeting Moonchester and Moonbeam many times) informing them that their dad, aged 51, was going to be Moonchester! Oh, I also posted it on Facebook. Oh yeah, and on the BlueMoon forum too. You see, I can keep a secret…

Off the pair of us went on the subway and we were soon at the stadium and in the player's entrance receiving our passes. We were met by a club official and taken to a small room where the costumes were. The Liverpool mascot and 'minder' were in there too. The Liverpool mascot was a paid employee of the club and had his entire trip paid for by the club and was given a car to get to each game. In contrast Debbie had to finance her own travel both getting to the States as well as accommodation too. I made sure I paid a last visit to the toilet before getting the costume on and very soon I was all ready to go! The stretchy outfit was able to circumnavigate my beer belly and when I breathed in, I didn't look too bad!

My dream of being on the pitch and greeting Yaya and co onto the field was shattered when we were told we could only walk around the circular concourse due to the majority of the seats not being pitch side but elevated above the baseball field, but undeterred we set off in one direction and the Liverpool mascot the other. Immediately I was struck on how hot it was in the costume (this was New York in July!) and especially inside the head. I thought of Frank Sidebottom and wondered how the hell he lasted night after night with his papermache head on. I was surprised by how many adults approached us, against kids and soon I had many attractive twenty/thirty something women putting their arms around me, posing for pictures. We met the Liverpool mascot half way round and had a "friendly stand-off" before the three of us posed together. By the time we had gone around the concourse once, it was an hour and time for a break, get the head off, go for a pee (no mean feat in that outfit!) and drink two bottles of water – and start again for another lap!

There were a few fans wearing other English team shirts, most notably Chelsea, whilst at one point a young lad in his early twenties and wearing a United shirt approached me. I pointed at his shirt, wagged my finger in a 'no no' manner and then waved him away – to a roar of laughter from all around. I posed with a couple of kids but I was looking at this lad, clearly a little humiliated by his experience and I imagined the club receiving an email saying how the club mascot ruined his day etc, so once I had finished with the kids for the photo shot, I pointed to the United fan, gave him a thumbs up and beckoned him over. He clearly was pleased now rather than upset and although I gave the thumbs up for the picture with him, in my mind I was saying 'fuck off you rag twat!'

We had made it safely back to the changing room again and had to get changed out of the costume fairly quickly so we didn't miss the start of the game. I wanted to stay in the costume for the duration of the game, going around the stands. I was on a roll and in a role! I knew this was my one and only chance and was very much enjoying it. It was my moment of City fame, albeit anonymous City fame, but it was fantastic being the mascot representing City at such a big game (even though it was a friendly). But those two laps of the concourse pre-game was the gig. And within minutes we were both walking on the concourse in our regular clothes as our regular selves, walking past all those fit women who for the last two hours had been putting their arms around me and posing for pictures. Now I was back to being the 51 year-old balding and beer bellied but beaming man I was when I'd entered the stadium but I was beaming with pride.

I was once Moonchester. And no one could ever take that away from me!

23- OVER LAND AND SEA

WHAT FOOTBALL FANS HAVE demonstrated for years is their passion and unwavering support for their team. We see fans of non-league teams turning up in their hundreds and thousands on cold nights to cheer their teams on. We have fans criss-crossing the country after finishing work or throwing a sickie to make sure they get to the game. Nowadays it is even better for City fans as for the last few years we have been in the Champions League and have been playing against some of the best teams in Europe. Planning trips to play at Barcelona, Real Madrid or in Moscow was only a pipe dream not many years ago as we set off in the coaches and trains to York, Bury and Swindon.

Fortunately getting to most European venues is not too expensive and pretty straightforward except for one or two that can be a bit of a ball ache like the time we played in the Faroes which was very difficult to get to. However if you think we in the UK have it bad, what about the fans of CSKA Moscow when they played at Khabarovsk - it is a 16,600 km round trip, 16 hours flying time with a seven hour time difference - or nine days of driving and a temperature of minus twenty-two degrees when you got there. I thought someone was winding me up when they told me those statistics but apparently it is true, well I tell you now, no matter how much I love and support my club there is no way I would be putting on my Ushanka (Russian hat) and setting off in a Lada for that fixture. One saving grace is the cans of lager would never get warm! It would be bad enough for a player to make the trip, never mind the supporters. In all honesty I doubt if many did make the trip and can you imagine watching the game in those temperatures? I bet the person selling the vodka did a roaring trade but that's what supporting your football team is about, you have to take the rough with the smooth. But let's hope they never get in the Champions League and if they do City don't play them.

Having said that I am sure there would be plenty of Blues who relish the chance to go and visit another new and, dare I say it, interesting place.

Alan wrote about his epic trip to Vienna to watch City in the European Cup Winners' Cup Final but that seems like a piece of piss compared with what our Russian friends have to contend with, even with all the pampering the players get nowadays, that trip would be enough to test the patience of any seasoned traveller never mind a footballer. Many fans treat the European trips as a holiday and plan accordingly and depending where we play will take the family with them. As we are now regulars in the competition (didn't think I would be saying that a few years ago) many fans will pick and choose which away trip to go on, as it can work out a bit of a dear do if you go to every game plus it can be difficult getting time off work so some fans will opt out of going to a ground they have already been to in favour of somewhere new. At one time we could only dream of getting to the Final of the competition but one day in the not too distant future I am sure we will have as good a chance as anyone else. The European trips make a change from the Premier League fixtures which I believe is the hardest domestic competition anywhere in Europe and possibly in the world to win, and for the next few seasons there will be five or six teams who have a realistic chance of winning it. It hardly seems credible that since the Premiership was formed only six teams have won it (see if you can name them without Google) and that teams like Liverpool and Spurs have never won it and another team which used to have a proud history, Leeds United, have never had a sniff of winning it and are now midway in the EFL Championship (Old Division 2).

When I worked at Prestwich Hospital there was a male nurse there called Brian who was from Devon and for some strange reason he was a Leeds United fan. There are many reasons why people support a club from a different area from where they were born and usually it is because the team they are supporting is successful. I don't know the reason why he started supporting Leeds (no doubt he has told me many times) but give Brian his due he went all over the place to watch them and for many trips he went on his own. He has now moved back down to Devon and he is still going strong getting to many games home and away each season. Well if I'm honest, Leeds have been shit for many years but their fans have stood by them and that's what happens when you support a football team. Directors, managers and players all come and go and usually leave a lot richer than when they first arrived but the supporters are like the bunny in the Duracell advert, they keep on going and going.

Recently City played Feyenoord of Holland in the Championship League group stage, the first leg was in Holland and City won 4-0. For the return tie in Manchester, City had already qualified for the next stage of the competition and Feyenoord had no chance of qualifying as they had lost all of their games and were bottom of the group. If you were viewing the fixture through non-footballing eyes you would think it was a meaningless game and not many fans would shell out a lot of their hard earned money for a 'pointless match' on a cold and wet November evening. But that is the difference between football fans and non-football fans; no game is pointless and no match is meaningless if your team is playing, you want to go and watch them. While the crowd was a little lower than normal, there were still well over 40,000 at the Etihad and Feynoord brought over 4,500 to watch the game. Besides the game, they came to enjoy themselves and, boy, do those lads like to party. The night before the game they had pre-booked a nightclub in Manchester and hundreds of their supporters were bopping the night away into the early hours. After breakfast on the morning of the game they gathered again, this time in Shambles Square, and had another great day partying and drinking. The Manchester Police managed the fans brilliantly with no evidence of the heavy handedness or brutality fans routinely have to suffer on some European trips. When it was time to leave for the match they formed up like an invading army and with the police at the front of them they marched towards the ground in good spirits and in good voice and they carried on singing at the top of their voices. It didn't matter to them that they couldn't qualify, they came for a good time and they certainly had one.

Now I have a soft spot for Feyenoord, as do plenty of other City fans, as we have formed a bit of a special relationship with their supporters over the last couple of decades. It all started about 20 years ago, when a group of Manchester City fans who were living and working in Amsterdam formed an unofficial supporters club; they used to meet up to watch the games, have a few drinks and even produced a regular newsletter. A lad called Angelo, a fanatical Feynoord supporter, had watched City play on his trips to Manchester and went to a couple of meetings where he met my brother Bob who lived and worked in Amsterdam at the time.

One time when Angelo was coming over to watch City I picked him and his mates up from the airport and took them to their hotel and over the weekend had a few drinks and went to the match with them. City were playing Gillingham so the Dutch lads could hardly be accused of glory hunting could they? After the game, on the way to the pub, we saw a group of Gillingham fans and one of the lads said he was very surprised that the Gillingham fans were not attacked as that would be the norm back in Holland. I explained that Gillingham didn't exactly have a reputation for football violence and no-one would attack them as they were ordinary fans just minding their own business, I could see the lads were genuinely shocked. It just goes to show how times have moved on in the UK from the 60's, 70's and 80's.

That was the start of a great friendship between the two sets of supporters. From the beginning when Angelo and Michel first came, many others also came over including Patrick and Denis to name just a couple and they have all stayed at my house and Patrick and Michel even stopped over at mine for the game in November. They are all friendly with dozens and dozens of other City fans with many Blues going over to Holland to meet up with them and watch the Feyenoord games.

I have been over a few times and their hospitality is second to none and the atmosphere the fans create at the games, whether home or away, is incredible. My eldest lad, Steven, went over once and stayed with Denis. The game they went to see was the big derby – Feyenoord v Ajax – and he said while the atmosphere when City play United is always brilliant the atmosphere on that day was on another level. Over the years there has been some serious violence carried out by both sets of supporters and it became so bad that when they now play each other, away fans are not allowed to travel to support their team. The 2016-2017 season saw Feyenoord win the league for the first time in donkey's years and we were all chuffed for them and the internet was kept busy with all the messages of support finding their way over the North Sea.

My mate Lee has a restaurant in Whitefield called 'one eighty eight' and City and Feyenoord fans met there for lunch and a few beers together before heading off into Manchester. After this trip no doubt more friendships were made and it won't be long before both sets of fans meet up again. My mate Angelo couldn't make it over as he had work commitments he could not get out of and he told me on the phone that he was pig sick he couldn't make it.

Most football fans from time to time have gone to a match which was pretty pointless, whether that be a pre-season friendly or a cup game where the manager has played a weaken team or to an away game at the end of the season where the result is meaningless but saying that, the trip is usually only a couple of hundred miles at most so it is not a massive inconvenience or a big hassle as you would be there in a couple of hours. Now if there is one meaningless game in the Champions League it was our last group game against Shakhtar Donetsk recently. Whatever the result, it didn't matter who won or who scored the most goals as it would make absolutely no difference as both teams had qualified with City finishing top and Shakhtar finishing 2nd and whatever happened on the day wouldn't change a thing. With this in mind I thought I would ask my mate Sean if he was going. Sean follows City everywhere and I think he has only missed one competitive match home and away in about 30 years and that was because City fans were banned from watching a game in Russia. I thought he might have decided to give the game a miss and save a few bob - I should have known better; the saying 'do bears shit in the woods' springs to mind. So in his own words this is what he had to say when I asked him.

When the draw for the Champions League was made, the game in Kharkhiv was the stand-out game for me and a few other Blues I know, regardless of whether the game had any bearing on our qualification or not, I would be there! The reason for that is, it's relatively cheap to do the 4,000 mile round trip (the official day trip is £299), it's the hardest destination in our group to get to and it is being played in their temporary ground which is 200 miles from their home city which is considered extremely dangerous to visit due to the ongoing conflict in the Ukraine. So part of the attraction is seeing City play in a stadium where they may never play again in our life time. The flying time is around four hours and the whole trip will mean a full twenty-four hours on the move. The temperature out there will be a cool minus six degrees centigrade but the pitches are heated so providing we don't get heavy snowfall, the game should go ahead as planned. I suspect around two hundred to three hundred Blues will be going, all the usual faces will be there for the same reason I am and everyone will have plenty of layers of clothing on. When you get to my age, the wrong side of fifty, it is thermals all the way and of course I will be wearing a good quality hat. Spending money is not an issue, on previous visits to Kiev with City twenty quid will easily cover general expenses for food, drink etc. It is not a rip off like other places in Europe. Obviously you need to have your wits about you (we were jumped on in a subway in Moscow before the CSKA game and they stole our flag) but incidents like that will never put me off going to games whether home or away.

I like to think we are ambassadors for both City and the City of Manchester and I know it gives me and other Blues a lot of personal satisfaction to do what we do and represent our club and country in the best possible way. Quite often on these trips the match can be incidental; it is all about the trip and a new adventure. For some it is visiting a new country or city, meeting up and chatting with the home fans (the friendly ones that is) and seeing and experiencing the culture and exploring the city and to do a bit of sight-seeing as time permits. All in all it is a fantastic hobby which we are very privileged and fortunate to do.

FOOTNOTE

For decades Shakhtar Donetsk has been one of Eastern Europe's most successful football clubs. The team won Ukraine's premier league five years running and the stadium hosted the England national team in the Euro 2012 Championships but for the last few years the club's fifty-thousand plus seated stadium has lain empty because the fighting in the eastern Ukraine with Russian separatists has made it too dangerous to play there and the airport has been reduced to rubble in the bombings. The ground, which was only built in 2009 and cost 550 million dollars to build, has also been hit by shelling, no-one knows if the team will ever play there again or in fact whether the stadium will join the airport and be reduced to rubble. As the conflict escalated the Donbass Arena has served as a depot and distribution point for supplies and humanitarian aid for the people who are suffering in the area.

In May 2014 the then captain of Donetsk, Darijo Sarna, was told he had to leave quickly, and he told reporters everything was left in his house and his shirts are still hanging up in his wardrobe. He believed the war would be over quickly and they would be able to return in six months. Years later there is still no sign of returning. As a Mancunian living only 4 hours flying time away I just can't believe something like that is happening in this day and age, as if you lived there it would be hard to get your head round it, plus there is little or no reporting in the UK about what is happening in their city. Let's hope the situation gets sorted sooner rather than later and no more lives are lost.

24- ENGLAND

DURING THE 1970S Manchester City supplied the England team with many great players including Franny Lee, Mike Summerbee and Colin Bell and before England played in the World Cup in Mexico City fans started singing:

> *Pardoe, Pardoe,*
> *He's off to Mexico*
> *With Bell and Lee*
> *And Summerbee*
> *Pardoe, Pardoe, Pardoe…*

In reference to our great full back Glyn Pardoe. The little fact that Mike Summerbee and Glyn Pardoe didn't even go to the World Cup in Mexico didn't stop fans singing the song for many years. Well at least it rhymed, good job he wasn't called Smith or he wouldn't have had a song about him. While we are on about Glyn, I will tell you about his other claim to fame besides having a song made about him about going to a place he never went to, he was the youngest ever player who turned out for City's first team at the age of just 15 years and 314 days, it is a record that stands to this day and I for one can never see it being broken, as the rules today state no one under the age of sixteen can play in the English leagues. For the statisticians among us, his debut was against Birmingham City. He started as a centre forward but converted to a fullback. While at the club he won the League Championship, FA Cup, League Cup and European Cup Winners' Cup. Unfortunately Glyn suffered a serious injury in 1970 while playing for City against the rags at Old Trafford. George Best was late in a tackle and Glyn was so badly injured that it took about two years for him to recover from his injury. What made the situation even more shocking was the fact that the ref wasn't going to stop the game or even award a free kick until the City players gathered round the ref to make him aware of how serious the situation was. When he eventually stopped the game and after consulting with the linesman he booked Best but for some strange reason didn't send him off, even though the horror tackle did certainly warrant an early bath. Yellow and Red cards were not around in the English leagues at that time although the yellow and red card system was first introduced in the Mexico World Cup in 1970. It wasn't until 1976 when English fans were first treated to the sight of the refs waving the different coloured cards about. Here's another one for the stats brigade; the first player to be shown a red card was Blackburn Rovers winger Dave Wagstaff and George Best was the second. I bet you will all sleep better tonight knowing that little piece of history… you might even thank me one day if you ever get on a quiz show on telly and you get asked that question or if it comes up in a pub quiz somewhere.

After Glyn retired from football he went on to join the coaching staff at Maine Road where for many years he had a successful career coaching the youth team. Glyn's grandson Tommy Doyle is training at City's youth academy. Tommy's other grandfather was City's ex-captain the late, great Mike Doyle. Fuck me, Tommy is going to be one hard bastard when he is older if he turns out anything like his grandparents.

In 2016 young Tommy was skipper of City's under-15 youth team and they went on to win the national title and Tommy picked up the Player of the Tournament award. All City fans are waiting for the day he makes it to the first team, and you never know he could even be a future Manchester City captain.

Oh I do get a bit distracted don't I? Now where was I? I was on about England and City - don't worry I'm back on track. In the 1970's City had some fabulous players that played for England and no-one was more respected than Colin Bell whose career was cut short after a serious injury playing the rags (a bit of a pattern emerging here I think!).

While serving in the Royal Navy whilst on HMS Achilles, I had a stroke of luck when the ship visited Cardiff on a goodwill visit, as at the same time England were playing Wales. Many of the ship's crew including myself were given tickets for the game and after a few drinks we went to the stadium and watched a cracking game and lo and behold Colin scored for England. For my first England game at Wembley we played Luxemburg and if my memory serves me correct England won 5-0. I also went to Wembley for a World Cup Qualifier, England against Italy in 1977. As Peter Barnes was in the national team, I travelled down to Wembley on my own but soon met up with some lads I knew from Maine Road and I also met up with my old mate Rattler from the Royal Navy. After a few beers in the Royal George pub, which was near Euston train station, it was time to get the tube to Wembley. No matter how many times I have travelled on London's underground system I always find it very confusing to find my way about, more so when I've had a few drinks, (which I usually have to be fair) but we eventually made it to Wembley and England won 2-0.

Ron Greenwood was the manager at the time and he had only been in charge of England for a couple of months as he had taken over from Don Revie, who was sacked as England manager for gross misconduct. What had happened was while the England team was on a tour of South America, Don Revie was in Finland and supposed to be watching one of our World Cup Qualifier opponents but it was later discovered by the media that he was in fact in discussion with officials from the United Arab Emirates where he was secretly trying to do a deal to manage a team in the Middle East. He received a ten year ban from the FA which was eventually overturned. Now there is more than one version of those events as it was also reported that in fact he wasn't sacked but that he had resigned and the reason he wanted to work in the Middle East was that he was going to be outed as a match-fixer. The Daily Mirror was later sued by Revie as they were one of the first papers that brought the scandal into the public domain. He did not pursue his legal action though and I don't think any further action was taken over the match-fixing allegations. Sweeping brushes and carpets spring to mind.

How someone of Don Revie's stature could become embroiled

in such a scandal was beyond me. He had a great career as a footballer and whilst playing for Manchester City in 1955 he became the first Manchester City player to win the Player of the Year award and followed it up by helping us win the F.A. Cup at the end of the next season. Then he embarked on a glittering managerial career with Leeds United where he won two League titles, an FA Cup, a League Cup and two Inter-Cities Fairs Cup (precursor to the UEFA Cup) before taking over the England job. So much was expected of the England team whilst he was the manager but it was another false dawn. Whatever the rights or wrongs of what Revie did or did not do, once again it was the paying public and the ordinary football fan who were let down and even though that was back in the 1970's nothing much has changed as the FA has once again been dragged through the mud over the way it has mishandled complaints from some England female players.

The England football team have always had a great following and fans have followed the national team all over the globe and many fans who support teams from the lower leagues take great pride in following the national team and on their travels their flags can be seen proudly flying outside pubs, railway stations and at the grounds.

Unfortunately in the 1980's and 1990's England fans had a terrible reputation abroad and quite often there were major problems at many places where the National team were playing. Often though it wasn't the England fans that were the cause of the problems and at many places it was local thugs and even local police that instigated the violence. I remember once watching on TV when England played in Denmark and trouble broke out in the ground – the camera zoomed in on England fans being attacked by the Danish supporters and one fan in particular was getting battered by two large blokes. It later turned out that the 'fans' attacking the England supporters were in fact plain clothes police.

Many times police use water cannons and tear gas to disperse the fans but if it is used indiscriminately and without warning innocent fans, women and children are caught up in the resulting mayhem. Many supporters including City fans have come back from trips abroad with horror stories of how they were treated on their travels.

About ten years ago I went to Holland with a load of other City fans to watch England play and both the Dutch fans and the police were excellent and treated the English fans brilliantly and in return there was no trouble from the England supporters which goes back to an earlier comment, if you treat fans like animals they will behave like them but on the flip side if you don't they won't – in other words treat people how you yourself would like to be treated and usually there won't be a problem.

In 2018 the World Cup is going to be played in Russia and many City fans are going over to follow the National team as at least four City players will be in the English squad; Kyle Walker, John Stones, Raheem Sterling and Fabian Delph. Russian fans have always had a bad reputation for violence against visiting supporters and many fans have come back from trips to Russia recalling how they were subjected to unprovoked random attacks and some fans were very badly injured.

In the 2016 Euros, played in France, there was some of the worst football violence seen in Europe for a very long time and Russian 'fans' seemed to be in the thick of it. Several England fans were seriously injured in Marseille after violent clashes with rival fans both before and after the opening game against Russia, a number of other fans also ended up in hospital after a day and night of violence and chaos in the French city. Marseille emergency services said thirty-one people were in hospital following the disorder including England fans who had been kicked unconscious. The British Ambassador Julian King tweeted that 'a number of Brits were in hospital overnight' and before the game there were also running battles between England and Russian fans in the old port area and trouble also flared in the Stade Velodrome after the match. The trouble in the ground started when a couple of hundred Russian fans, many dressed in black and wearing balaclavas, broke through the line of stewards and indiscriminately started attacking the England supporters. Observers at the time referred to the

Russians as 'like an organised paramilitary group' and a leading Russian football official, Igor Levedev, said Russian fans involved in the violence in Marseille should be praised for defending the honour of their country. He also said 'I don't see anything wrong in the fans fighting' and wrote on Twitter 'well done lads keep it up'. He also went onto say that in nine out of ten cases football fans go to a game to fight and that is normal. 'The lads defended the honour of their country and did not let the English fans desecrate our mother land.' How accurate these reports are, are anyone's guess but I cannot remember him denying them at the time. Now these comments are not made by some lackey but someone who sits on the Executive Committee of the Russian Football Union and was an MP for the Liberal Democratic Party and Deputy Chairman of the Russian parliament.

While many England fans were arrested and charged for various offences, prosecutors said one hundred and fifty extremely well trained Russian hooligans had avoided arrest. The head of Britain's Euro 2016 policing operation had said the Russians in Marseille were wearing gum shields, martial art gloves and were carrying knives; other people reported many Russians also wearing balaclavas and were carrying metal bars.

Assistant Chief Constable Mark Roberts told reporters that while a small minority of England fans were out to cause trouble at the match there were hundreds of Russian trouble makers in Marseille at the time. The trouble is when violence on such a scale breaks out as mentioned before many innocent people get caught up as the violence is indiscriminate and when the police intervene with water cannons and tear gas it affects everyone in a wide area and even England centre forward Jamie Vardy's wife was caught up in the trouble in Marseille when tear gas was fired near to a restaurant she was in.

I just think 'thank fuck I'm not going to Russia for the World Cup' because if government ministers are backing the hooligans and observers are saying they are well trained I can see something serious happening out there.

Getting back to the football though, it has been a long time since City have had four players representing England at the same time and I hope all the England fans, as well as the City fans that will be going to Russia, stay safe and avoid any confrontation and violence. Russia has so much to offer and Moscow is a lovely place to visit, so whilst doing the tourist bit visiting fans don't want to be on tenterhooks worrying whether they are going to be attacked or not. Over the years many innocent fans who have been watching their local or National team have been wrongly arrested and many police don't discriminate between an active participant or a bystander being in the wrong place at the wrong time. If you are in an area where disorder breaks out, you will automatically be on the police radar and if you get arrested god help you because there will be little sympathy from the prosecution or the government back in the UK as the 'no smoke without fire' syndrome will kick in.

Now what chance have England got in doing well? On past performances I would say they don't have much of a chance, we have decent players but the manager does not inspire me with a great deal of confidence. We struggle at times against all manner of teams and we never seem to have a plan B. Even though Italy did not qualify and they won't be going on the plane to Russia there are some quality teams going which I believe will give England too much to deal with.

Germany, Brazil, Spain and France have got to be among the early favourites but you never know, if the manager plays all the Manchester City players at the same time we might have the best chance in years to do well. At most tournaments there is usually a team that surpasses all expectations and goes on and does well, and it could be England's turn to spring a surprise and it won't be before time if we do. Let's hope the 'Spirit of 66' kicks in again and the manager and players makes the country proud of the national team again.

Raheem Sterling, Fabien Delph, John Stones and Kyle Walker… it's a pity none of the above rhyme with Russia otherwise we could have the makings of a world cup song on our hands, sod it I will leave the singing and song writing to Chas & Dave.

25 - FAVOURITE PLAYERS

ALL FANS HAVE THEIR favourite player or ex-player. Over the years while I was Chairman of the Prestwich & Whitefield Supporters Club I came into contact with many players and ex-players and loads of times I have been asked out of all of the ones I have met, who is my favourite. I haven't got one I have got loads and for different reasons, so in no particular order here are some of my favourite players with a quick explanation.

GIO KINKLAZDE

The first time I met Gio was just after he joined City and it was down at the Platt Lane Training Complex. It was raining cats and dogs but he didn't go indoors until he had signed autographs and had his photo taken with all the fans who wanted one. Then after he left City about seventy of us went over to Amsterdam to visit him and he came and joined us in a backstreet pub near Amsterdam train station for a party and a bit of a knees-up.

KIT SYMONS

He was fantastic in dealing with fans and attended many supporters' meetings and charity events. After one event he gave my sons a lift home in his sports car and they were buzzing for weeks after that. Our family have also been to his house for our tea and we also went to his wedding in Portsmouth so I have to admit to being a bit biased.

TOMMY BOOTH

He was the first-ever guest at our supporters branch and be has been to loads since. He will help out supporters in any way he can, nothing is too much trouble for him plus he is a local lad from a big City supporting family.

IAN BRIGHTWELL

He got me some passes for the players' lounge at Maine Road and also away at Swindon. Well that's a good enough reason for him to be one of my favourites isn't it? Plus I was in the Stretford End paddock at the swamp when he "wellied it" into the back of the net and we went on to draw which was no mean feat for us back then. I also had a drinking contest with him once to see who could drink a pint the fastest – I came a miserable second.

ANDY DIBBLE

He was our first branch President and he enjoyed a drink with us, plus he phoned our house up once and wound Cath up as he pretended to be a journalist. Cath was not amused…

CHRIS GREENACRE

He was our second branch President and I also went to his wedding and we still send and receive Christmas cards from his mum.

NEIL MCNAB

A great bloke who ended up at my house for a drink after he had been to one of our supporters' events. Unfortunately Neil suffered a stroke late in 2017 and was for a time in intensive care. I will use this opportunity to wish him all the best from all football fans and hope for a speedy and full recovery.

UWE ROSLER

Another fan favourite who had plenty of time for the supporters and he named one son Colin after Colin Bell and the other son Tony after Tony Book. Colin has recently been playing very well in City's youth Academy. When Uwe attended one of our supporters' events we introduced him to Guinness and he quite enjoyed it.

Then there are the likes of Tony Book, Andy Morrison, Joe Corrigan, Paul Lake, Mark Lillis, Gerry Gow (RIP) Gary Owen

Bleeding hell there are loads and I haven't finished yet, please bear with me while I get a brew as I am doing sober November and this is thirsty work and as I can't have a beer I need something to wet my whistle.

Right I'm back now, that's better, I've had me brew! You will have gathered by now this isn't a list of the best players or indeed the fans' favourites but players I have met and thought they were decent people because I can assure you, I have met many players and ex-players who are full of shit and won't give you the time of day, okay let me carry on with me list…

MICK McCARTHY

Well I've have to mention Mick, one because he is hard as nails and also when he was the Ireland manager he came to a few charity events we organised and he also sent me a few signed shirts to auction for the charities.

DAVID BALL

He is now at Rotherham after doing well at Fleetwood. He was at the youth academy and because he was a local lad from Whitefield the branch sponsored his football boots.

TREVOR SINCLAIR

Brought up on the Hillock Estate in Whitefield, he's a great TV pundit but dropped a clanger recently, I'll leave it at that.

TONY TOWERS

Managed the Church Inn public house in Whitefield, well that's a good enough reason to stick him on my list is it not? It was a belting Joey Holts pub till it got knocked down to make way for a

Morrison's supermarket.

COLIN BELL

Well nothing I can add to what you already know about Colin except that for years he was co-owner of the Bell and Waldron restaurant on Elms Square in Whitefield.

Have you noticed yet there is a pretty big connection with Whitefield, must be something good about the place.

JOHN FOSTER

A belting lad from Blackley who had a great future until he suffered a bad injury, and was never the same after that. A genuinely nice person who had loads of time for City fans and would always attend supporters events. It is such a shame he didn't fulfil his potential

Hope you are still reading and haven't got bored yet of my ramblings of my favourite players? Please bear with me as I've nearly finished.

LEE CROOKS

Never met him but after finishing playing football he went and joined the RAF Regiment and saw active service. Respect

NICKY WEAVER

For his heroics at Wembley in 1999 and for once stopping in his Mercedes on Claremont Road to see if I wanted a lift. Yes I was walking up towards Wilmslow Road to meet my mates when Nicky pulled up - quality bloke.

PAUL WALSH

Along with Andy Dibble, Paul was the first 1st team player to attend our supporters meeting. Whilst working as a pundit for Sky in London he flew up to Manchester to attend a supporters event we held to honour the career of the great City servant Tony Book .

SHAUN GOATER

Found it hard when he first joined City but soon became a cult hero who scored some cracking goals for us .He is so popular in his native Bermuda they have named June 21st "Shaun Goater Day" after he was awarded freedom of the island .What an honour plus City fans will never forget a goal he scored against United when Gary Neville 'fed the goat' .I Met Shaun at a City charity event one year and he was absolutely brilliant with the fans .

PETER BARNES

A great player and his dad used to play for City as well. Everyone remembers Dennis Tueart's overhead kick at Wembley to beat Newcastle in the 1976 League cup final against Newcastle but Peter also scored that day and he was also awarded the PFA Young Player of the Year Award that season.

Ok that's all folks I bet you are all gutted that I am writing no more about my favourites but it is time for my bed. Now, those of you who read all on my list will probably have said by now, 'why has he included that dickhead' or 'why has he not included so and so' or 'that prick is a wanker what's he doing on the list?' We all have different opinions and that is the great thing about being a football fan, we can agree to disagree and no harm is done unless you disagree with a Russian fan then you will probably get your head kicked in.

Goodnight for now.

MANCHESTER CITY FOOTBALL CLUB

QUICK HISTORY

Founded 1880 in Gorton as St Mark's then changed to West
Gorton before shortening the name to Gorton then changed to
Ardwick 1887

Named Manchester City 1894

GROUNDS

Hyde Road	1887-1923
Maine Road	1923-2003
Etihad.	2003-Present day

*Between 1880 and 1923 we also had short spells at Clowes Street/
Thomas Street. Kirkmanshulme Cricket Club, Queens Road, Pink Bank
Lane and the Bulls Head Hotel.*

10 HIGHEST ATTENDANCES AT MAINE ROAD

1924 v Cardiff City	76.166 FA Cup
1926. v Huddersfield Town	74.799 FA Cup
1928 v Stoke City	73.688 FA Cup
1934. v Stoke City	84. 569 FA Cup
1935 v Arsenal	74.491 FA Cup
1937 v Arsenal	74.918 Div 1
1938 v Bury	71.937 FA Cup
1955 v United	74.918 Div 1
1956 v Everton	76,126 FA Cup

*The Attendance against Stoke in 1934 was a record for a domestic game.
It was only broken in 2017 by Spurs but they had the advantage of
borrowing Wembley*

CLUB HONOURS

League Champions: 1937, 1968, 2012, 2014

Division 1 (second tier) winners 2002

Division 2 winners (original) 1899, 1903, 1910, 1928, 1947, 1966.

Division 2 (third tier) Play off winners: 1998–1999

FA Cup Winners: 1904, 1934, 1956, 1969, 2011.

FA. Cup Finalists: 1926, 1933, 1955, 1981, 2013.

League Cup Winners: 1970, 1976, 2014, 2016.

League Cup Beaten Finalists 1974.

Full Members Cup Beaten Finalists: 1986

European Cup Winners' Cup: 1970

Charity Shield Winners: 1937, 1968, 1973, 2012.

Charity Shield Runner's Up: 1934, 1956, 1969, 1974, 2011, 2013

FA Youth Cup Winners: 1986, 2008

FA Youth Cup Runners Up: 1979, 1980, 1989, 2006, 2015, 2016, 2017

Thanks to Ric from Blue Moon & Gary James for help with some statistics and dates. For an in-depth look at Manchester City's History read

Manchester- The City Years by Gary James

EPILOGUE

OVER THE YEARS there have been some great and not so great times following City. Many thanks to all who have contributed to the book and put into context the passion of ordinary City fans and their experiences over the years. I hope you agree the stories written have been very original, barmy, brilliant and entertaining.

Can you imagine anyone in this day and age hitchhiking to Europe then climbing over a wall to get into the stadium where a European final was about to take place and kipping there for two nights? Or how about turning up and joining the players in a drink just hours before a game? And fair play to Eric from Holland who became a City fan and has had a forty plus year old love affair with City just because he was sent a Junior Blues scarf. Some cracking stuff from the ladies that sent in their stories. As it has been pointed out hooliganism hasn't been eradicated but it is not as bad as when a young Sean went to Old Trafford for his first game only to witness a pitch invasion and all that followed. Frank McGhee, who was Daily Mirror sports editor at the time, said in the strongest possible terms that the hooligans were a cancer that needed cutting out of the game and advocated that the Stretford End be shut for a season.

What I hope readers have not failed to notice is the character and spirit of the writers and how as fans their support never wavered through the lean times of the club and now as well as all the other City fans who never faltered are now reaping the rewards by watching some brilliant football at a well-run football club. It is great news that more women and families are now going to watch football whether it's at the Etihad or at other grounds round the country.

It has been a joy, a pleasure, and a privilege being involved with all concerned in producing this book, as I have had a few laughs getting it all together and I am very pleased with everyone's efforts.

I hope each and every person who has read the book has enjoyed the journey we have taken you on. The fans involved are simply ordinary people who have written their memoirs with so much enthusiasm and they have told their stories without airs or graces – and that has been a real plus for me.

When I started planning this book I did not have a clue who would be involved or what stories they would be writing, so I was very apprehensive until the stories started coming in and each person involved should be proud of the part they played in getting the book to the bookshelves.

We have spent a lot of time editing the book and checking the grammar, spelling and making sure that dates and places and venues match, if anything has slipped through the net please let us know. Many thanks for taking the time to read it

Finally, I would really appreciate your opinion of the book and would be grateful if you could leave a review on www.amazon. co.uk

If there is any part of the book you would like to discuss with me please email: don-price@live.co.uk or Empire Publications – enquiries@empire-uk.com